
MARKETING ETHICS

Cases and Readings

MARKETING ETHICS

Cases and Readings

Patrick E. Murphy

University of Notre Dame

Gene R. Laczniak

Marquette University

Upper Saddle River, NJ 07458

Library of Congress Cataloging-in-Publication Data

Marketing ethics : cases and readings / Patrick E. Murphy, Gene R. Laczniak, editors.—1st ed.

    p. cm.

Includes bibliographical references and index.

ISBN 0-13-133088-8

1. Marketing. 2. Business ethics. I. Murphy, Patrick E. II. Laczniak, Eugene R.

HF5415. M219 2006

174′.—dc22

                                                  2004028876

VP/Editorial Director: Jeff Shelstad
Project Manager: Ashley Santora
Editorial Assistant: Rebecca Lembo
Marketing Manager: Michelle O'Brien
Marketing Assistant: Joanna Sabella
Managing Editor: John Roberts
Production Editor: Suzanne Grappi
Manufacturing Buyer: Michelle Klein
Production Manager, Manufacturing: Arnold Vila
Cover Design Manager: Jayne Conte
Cover Design: Bruce Kenselaar
Composition/Full-Service Project Management: GGS Book Services,
   Atlantic Highlands
Printer/Binder: Courier

Credits and acknowledgments borrowed from other sources and reproduced, with permission, in this textbook appear on appropriate page within text.

Pearson Education LTD.
Pearson Education Singapore, Pte. Ltd
Pearson Education, Canada, Ltd
Pearson Education–Japan

Pearson Education Australia PTY, Limited
Pearson Education North Asia Ltd
Pearson Educación de Mexico, S.A. de C.V.
Pearson Education Malaysia, Pte. Ltd

10 9 8 7 6 5 4 3 2
ISBN: 0-13-133088-8

Dedicated to our predecessors who cared deeply
about marketing ethics

Raymond F. Keyes
Boston College

T. R. Martin
Marquette University

Clarence C. Walton
The American College

J. Howard Westing
University of Wisconsin—Madison

On whose foundation we build

CONTENTS

PREFACE

The overriding purpose of putting together this book of cases and readings is to foster ethical and socially responsible behavior in marketing. When trust in business is at an all-time low, it is time for academics, students, and business leaders to take action. We see this project as contributing to this activity by recognizing the higher-order obligations of marketing and by providing a forum to discuss critical issues and incidents that raise questions about ethics in marketing.

We see this book as being flexible enough to serve many purposes. For example, it could be one of two or three featured books in a "marketing ethics" or "marketing and society" class. Or it could easily be used as a supplementary text, helping to cover ethical issues, in almost any marketing course. This anthology includes enough variety that it will allow instructors to select and combine readings, short cases and/or long cases, as befits their class needs and preferred pedagogical approach.

We view this book as attempting to accomplish several specific objectives. First, we want to raise the ethical awareness and recognition of students and managers. A writer in a famous business ethics article observed, "Real moral dilemmas are ambiguous, and many of us hike right through them, unaware that they exist." At a minimum, heightened awareness and recognition of ethical issues in marketing is essential. Second, we identify key ethical concepts and in so doing contribute to "ethical knowledge" (see Chapter 1). Third, we hope that the students and managers who use this book will improve their ethical judgment—that is, their moral reasoning skills and their ethical decision making. Finally, we desire to stimulate a willingness to undertake ethical leadership on the part of our readers. Enhancing the capacity to play an essential role in doing business ethically is our aspiration for the next generation of marketing managers and business leaders.

We believe that the goal of business organizations is not purely bottom-line driven but also the use of a healthy bottom line to enhance the economic benefits of society. Without diminishing the latest theoretical knowledge in the study of marketing, we believe marketing practice is self-actualized only when marketing strategy and tactics are tempered with a concern for ethics—integrity, fairness, and justice in the marketplace.

This book is divided into four chapters, and a few words about each are warranted. Some students and marketing practitioners think that cases and situations in ethics can be discussed without a theoretical context. They believe their opinion is as good as the next person's. We disagree strongly. Hence, Chapter 1 contains material on ethical theory and moral reasoning. The cases in Chapters 3 and 4 can best be analyzed using the concepts introduced in the first chapter. We would particularly draw your attention to Exhibit 1-3, which shows the recently adopted statement of ethical norms and values for marketers, promulgated by the American Marketing Association. It is our hope that these ethical perspectives will be used extensively by marketing students and executives.

Chapter 2 contains articles from the business press that examine a range of ethical issues in marketing. Among the topics that these selections cover are respect for consumers, buzz marketing, vulnerable consumers, dangerous products, socially controversial products, bribery and gift giving, power in the retail channel, and trust in marketing. We pose questions at the end of each reading but presume that classroom discussion of ethical issues will range far beyond them.

Chapters 3 and 4 present nine and six cases, respectively. Each case deals with one or more ethical situations that marketing practitioners may face. The first case in Chapter 3, "Toy Wars," is included for illustrative purposes. It is one of the "classic" cases in marketing ethics. We analyze the case using one decision-making approach as well as answer the questions posed in the case. We have also asked the "protagonist" from the case to reflect on his interaction with the client almost 20 years ago and present the "rest of the story." The subsequent cases are intended for student analysis. Some deal with well-known companies such as Starbucks, Abercrombie & Fitch, and Athlete's Foot. However, most are from less well-known companies or are "disguised" cases where the names of the company and/or participants have been changed. Chapter 3 presents shorter cases that allow for discussion in a more compressed time period. The cases in Chapter 4 are more complex and would almost certainly require a full class period devoted to their discussion and analysis. Two cases in each of the chapters focus on ethical issues in an international setting.

It is our hope that these readings and cases will stimulate meaningful and enlightening discussion about ethics in marketing. While this text will not reduce the number of ethical challenges that marketing managers will face, it should make each reader better prepared to cope with and respond to such dilemmas. We have great admiration for the many highly ethical and hardworking marketing managers throughout the world whose reputation is tarnished by the unethical actions of a minority of their peers. We are optimistic that the next generation of marketing executives will be even better prepared to take the "high road" in their professional lives.

In closing, we adapt the advice of one of our favorite writers and storytellers, Garrison Keillor, by encouraging our marketing students to always do good work, to be well, and ever seek to maintain personal integrity since it is a prized and irreplaceable possession.

ACKNOWLEDGMENTS

Editing any volume requires that appropriate material is available. We were fortunate that we could secure the needed readings and cases from several sources. In the first chapter, we draw on our own work that is published in a new text, *Ethical Marketing*. The second chapter includes readings from leading business publications such as *Fast Company, Financial Times, Forbes, Sales and Marketing Management*, and the *Wall Street Journal*. One of the selections was written by a colleague, Kirk Davidson, as a feature in *Marketing News*. We thank these publications for permitting us to reprint articles that first appeared in their pages.

We particularly want to recognize the authors of the cases that appear in Chapters 3 and 4. Several of our marketing and ethics colleagues have contributed cases that we hope will make for stimulating discussion. They are Peggy Cunningham, the late Raymond Keyes, Ron Nahser, Manuel Velaquez, and John Weber. Several of our former students have also authored cases that appear in this book. They are John Bargetto, Meg Connolly, Lori Lepp Corbett, Anu Davgun, Catherine Hart, Amanda Hilger, Lance Kidder, and Trevor Prouty. To all our case authors, we offer a hearty thank-you.

The process of assembling this material, editing some of it, and putting it in a usable format was a challenge. Two individuals at the University of Notre Dame assisted in this endeavor. Jami Kirk, a marketing student, did extensive editing on several of the cases and also assisted in securing permission to reprint the business press material. Deb Coch, administrative assistant for the Institute for Ethical Business Worldwide, ably typed, reformatted, assembled this material and put it into final form. We are indebted to Jami and Deb for their fine work.

At Prentice Hall, our first editor was Wendy Craven, who encouraged us to undertake this project. After she moved to another position within the company, Katie Stevens was also supportive in both substantive and financial ways. Finally, Ashley Santora and Rebecca Lembo helped us in the final stages of the project. To all at Prentice Hall, thanks a lot.

Despite the efforts of these individuals, errors still will occur. We take full responsibility for them (as we should for an ethics book!).

Patrick E. Murphy
Gene R. Laczniak

ABOUT THE EDITORS

Patrick E. Murphy is the C. R. Smith Co-director of the Institute for Ethical Business Worldwide and professor of marketing in the Mendoza College of Business at the University of Notre Dame. He served as chair of the Department of Marketing for 10 years. During 1993–1994, he was a Fulbright Scholar at University College Cork in Ireland. Previously, he was a faculty member and Marketing department chair at Marquette University. He specializes in business and marketing ethics. His work has appeared in leading journals, and his most recent book (with G. Laczniak, N. Bowie, and T. Klein) is *Ethical Marketing* (Prentice Hall, 2005). He was named in 1997 as one of the top researchers in marketing for sustained contribution to the field. He served as editor of the *Journal of Public Policy & Marketing* and is now section editor for marketing at *Business Ethics Quarterly* and on five editorial review boards. Currently, he is an invited fellow of the Ethics Resource Center (Washington, D.C.) and is an academic adviser of the Business Roundtable Institute for Corporate Ethics. He holds a BBA from Notre Dame, an MBA from Bradley, and a PhD from Houston.

Gene R. Laczniak is the Wayne and Kathleen Sanders Professor of Marketing in the Straz College of Business Administration at Marquette University. He is a former chair of the Department of Marketing there with 10 years of service. From 1998 to 2002, he was the associate vice president/provost for academic affairs at the university. He has been a visiting professor or visiting fellow at the University of Western Australia (Perth) on several occasions. His research focuses on the influence of marketing strategy on society, especially on questions of ethics. He has published numerous articles and papers and has previously coauthored three books with P. E. Murphy, including *Ethical Marketing Decisions: The Higher Road*. He was a member of the editorial review board of the *Journal of Marketing* for 15 years and currently serves on four other editorial review boards. His bachelor's degree is from Marquette University, and he holds an MBA and PhD from the University of Wisconsin—Madison.

MARKETING ETHICS

Cases and Readings

CHAPTER

1

Ethical Reasoning and Marketing Decisions

Patrick E. Murphy, Gene R. Laczniak, Norman E. Bowie, and Thomas A. Klein

---

Scenario 1

Buzz marketing is a relatively new marketing technique. Its objective is to seek out trendsetters in each community and subtly push them into talking up the brand to their friends and admirers. These people are hired to generate favorable word of mouth. This approach builds on the well-known "opinion leader" concept and the influential nature that some individuals hold over their reference group. With teenagers, companies strive to seek out individuals who are "cool." Buzz marketing is catching on with many marketers, particularly those selling sneakers, jeans, cars, and certain packaged goods. This technique is a special favorite of cigarette and liquor manufacturers for which advertising is restricted.[1]

Buzz marketing is different from other forms of marketing in that the consumer usually does not know that the product endorser is being paid (in money, free goods, or some other item) by the company to promote its product. The marketers "plant" the product in areas of high traffic and use these salespersons to create a "buzz" about the product. While some consumers think these are spontaneous encounters, most situations are carefully orchestrated by the marketers.

An example is Ford's introduction of the Focus. Rather than spend a lot of money on 30-second commercials, Ford recruited several opinion leaders in a few markets and gave them each a Focus to drive for six months. The responsibility of these individuals was to hand out Focus trinkets and talk up the car to anyone who expressed interest in it but not to tell them that Ford had given them the car to drive. Is this an ethical technique? Why or why not?

Scenario 2

Recent commercials in the United States for Swiss-based Roche Group's weight-loss drug Xenical appear to break new ground. Xenical is an oral prescription designed to help considerably overweight people shed pounds by blocking about one-third of the fat in food from being digested.

Under Food and Drug Administration (FDA) rules, a full-length commercial touting a product by name for specific medical conditions must include a sometimes lengthy list of unpleasant side effects. Roche, however, got around that requirement by advertising Xenical not with one full-length commercial but with two shorter ones separated by unrelated commercial time.

The first Xenical ad describes the condition—unhealthy weight gain—the drug is designed to treat and shows an image of a cuddly baby morphing into a heavyset woman. But it doesn't name the drug. The second ad uses the same images and music and mentions the drug by name but says nothing about losing weight. This ad states, "Your doctor cared about your health then: He cares about it now. Ask about Xenical." When taken together, the two commercials are 45 seconds long, or longer than many full-length spots. But side effects never are mentioned.[2] Is this advertising ethical?

VIEWS OF MARKETING ETHICS

The opening section of this book examines several different views toward marketing ethics. We begin with the personal or individual view. Then we turn our attention to the organizational view. Since most ethical issues arise in a business setting, this view is particularly important to understand. The third view is a societal one. A number of concerns, such as *fairness* in the marketing system and protection of the physical environment, fall under this view. The final view is a "stakeholder" one. It is essential to introduce, define, and illustrate the stakeholder view at the outset.

A Personal View of Marketing Ethics

Some marketing managers contend that they are relatively exempt from ethical dilemmas or that moral pressures do not generally affect them. In reality, most studies confirm that between 65 and 75 percent of all managers do indeed face major ethical dilemmas at some point in their careers. An *ethical dilemma* is defined, for our purposes, as a situation where it is not clear what choice morality requires. The situation may involve the trade-off between one's personal moral values and the quest for increased organizational or personal profit. However, it may not involve such a trade-off, as in the decision to cut the labor force to increase shareholder wealth. In other words, marketing managers sometimes feel compelled to do things that they feel ought not be done. Based on the reports of practicing managers, most marketing executives are *not* exempt from dealing with ethical concerns. Our view is that most marketers do face ethical dilemmas but that they may not recognize them. Judging from the questions being raised about the propriety of marketing practices, many decisions clearly have significant consequences.

An Organizational View: Corporate versus Individual Ethics—Is There a Difference?

The ethics of the organization and the values held by the individual manager may not be the same. The issue is this: When does a person follow individual values, and when does a person follow corporate values? When these values are not compatible, a conflict may arise between organizational pressure that impels a particular action and what the individual believes ought or ought not be done. The typical conflict in such cases involves a manager or employee who holds a higher standard of behavior than that expected by the organization. In such situations, the manager may be pushed toward an action that reflects ignoring or lowering personal standards in order to achieve some organizational goal. These dilemmas produce "moral stress" in the manager because the core values of the organization, as embodied in the corporate culture, seem to imply a choice different from that which would be selected by the manager based on personal values. Another real issue occurs when the boss orders you to do something that violates organizational values as well as your own values. One way organizations have addressed this issue is to explicitly develop a "values statement" for the firm. For example, Hanna Andersson (the maker of high-quality children's clothes) lists three major values: respect, integrity, and responsibility.[3] They guide this firm when it is faced with ethical quandaries.

Corporations with an organizational climate that causes managers to act contrary to their individual values need to understand the *costs* of unethical behavior articulated in this chapter. Sometimes managers who choose to follow organizational pressures rather than their own conscience rationalize their decisions by maintaining that they are simply *agents* of the corporation. In other words, as company agent, the manager assumes the duty to do exactly what the organization most desires—often translated to mean maximizing return on investment, sales, or some other managerial objective.

The weaknesses of assuming that managers are merely organizational agents who need to override their personal values are several, including the following:

1. Managers can never totally abdicate their personal responsibility in making certain business decisions. The defense of being an agent of the corporation sounds suspiciously like the defense given by certain war criminals that they were only following orders. (Companies frequently prosecute rule breakers to make an example of them even if the manager's intention was to help the firm.)

2. It is quite possible that the manager does not *fully* understand what is in the best interest of the organization. Short-term profits, even if advocated by the manager's immediate supervisor, may not be the most important consideration for the organization.

3. The manager has an irrevocable responsibility to parties other than his or her organization. This understanding moves us to the *stakeholder concept* (explained later), which explicitly identifies various publics to which organizations have duties and obligations.

While the trade-off involving appropriate personal values and questionable organizational values suggested previously is most typical, other situations are also found. We can envision instances where organizational values should trump personal ones, such as when the employee has a character flaw or does not subscribe to legitimate corporate expectations. One other circumstance involves organizational values that are more rigorous than personal values. Here the manager may not appreciate the reasoning behind certain policies (along the lines described in item 2 in the previous list) and, for personal or organizational gain, is inclined to violate them. To avoid values misalignment, senior management must bring clarifying ethical standards into employee selection, orientation and training, and advancement or dismissal decisions.

Still another situation generating ethical anxiety is when an employee's ethical standards are overly *scrupulous,* leading to actions—or omissions—that unnecessarily disadvantage the employer. For example, concerns about lavish customer entertainment may prompt an inexperienced sales representative to avoid even modest lunch or dinner expenditures and thus neglect the kind of social interaction on which sound customer relationships may be built or reinforced. If the goal is to establish a workable set of ethical norms for an organization and its marketing personnel, management policies and programs must strive for agreement between what individuals and companies view as acceptable and unacceptable. Openness in communications is necessary for this goal to be attainable.

An Industry View

Industries vary greatly in the approach they take to ethical issues. Some industry sectors have out of necessity developed detailed strategies to address ethical problems peculiar to their sector, such as the promotion of responsible drinking by the brewing industry. Other industries are highly regulated by government, such as the chemical industry. And still others, like private waste haulers and construction trades, have a reputation for being somewhat tough minded in the way they operate. The point is that the amount of ethical guidance an individual manager receives from "industry norms" is highly idiosyncratic. Nevertheless, whatever norms are operant should be learned and integrated into the manager's ethical decision-making calculus. Companies and their marketing managers can take some *cues* from the industry, but as we advocate in this chapter, each firm must make a conscious attempt to set and maintain high ethical standards.

A Societal View

From the vantage point of society in which our economic system is nested and provisioned through marketing activities, the role of marketing ethics can be seen as critical to both social order and justice.[4] *Trust* is an essential ingredient of a fair and efficient marketing system.[5] Market participants—buyers and sellers of goods and services—should have faith that transactions in which they take part are characterized by openness or transparency, that is, that they are not being deceived by untruthful claims or unknowingly exposed to risks associated with unsafe products. They also need to have faith that they are being treated fairly; they are not being discriminated against because of circumstances that are regarded as inappropriate bases for differential pricing, quality, or service levels. Absent these characteristics, market transactions lead to distortions in the level of welfare generated by the market. When such faith is not present, buyers or sellers are subject to exploitation, extra costs of inspection are incurred, and, when damages are experienced, injured parties undertake efforts to resolve disputes, adding additional costs. In other words, lack of disclosure, unfair treatment, and unexpected risks lead to inefficiencies in the form of injuries and dispute settlement that would be avoided if transactions occurred in a more open and ethical manner. For example, the emerging economies of eastern and central Europe are struggling with how to attain a political-economic system that fosters these characteristics.[6]

Societies also have an interest in marketing systems in the more profound sense that their sustainability and prosperity depend on the conservation of resources that are not directly involved in buying and selling. Economic activity depends on the availability of natural resources—air, water, and land. The depletion or pollution of these resources places the long-term survival of communities and nations at risk. When people recognize the prospect of such risks, they seek ways to ensure survival through means that replace or intervene in markets—laws and administrative procedures that prohibit or limit pollution or depletion or that tax or penalize marketers to compensate for the *social costs* associated with these events. Economists refer to these effects of marketing as *externalities,* or unpriced outcomes that are not accounted for among the costs and benefits that constitute the conditions of market transactions. A societal perspective on marketing ethics requires marketers to avoid, wherever possible, actions that expose societies to disorder and to the prospect of inadequate resources and to respect those laws and regulations formulated to ensure order and sustainability for all citizens and future generations.[7]

A Stakeholder View

A perspective that now must be considered, because marketing is usually undertaken in the context of an organization, is the *stakeholder concept*:

A stakeholder in an organization is . . . any group or individual who can affect or is affected by the achievement of the organization's objectives.[8]

For example, typical corporate stakeholders include customers, stockholders, suppliers, employees, host communities or countries (where the company has operations), and various other parties. To this list might be added other individuals and groups that may affect the company's success, even though they may not be usually affected by the company's activities, such as regulatory agencies and the media. The stakeholder concept is useful in ethical analysis because it provides a framework for weighing obligations and gauging the impact of decisions on all relevant groups, not just the firm and its managers.

At times it is helpful to distinguish among the *primary, indirect,* and *secondary stakeholders.* Primary stakeholders have a formal, official, or contractual relationship with the firm; indirect stakeholders have an ongoing or abiding interest in the firm but no direct transactional contact; all others are classified as secondary stakeholders. Primary stakeholders are the owners, suppliers, employees, and customers of the organization. Citizens who may be affected by pollution are a good example of an indirect stakeholder. Secondary stakeholders encompass public interest groups, the media, consumer advocates, and local community organizations that have occasional interest in the various corporate activities. For example, the amount of paper and plastic packaging generated by fast-food chains is a concern of local environmental groups, while the media may be more interested in the firm's treatment of its minority employees. Exhibit 1-1 illustrates the three types of stakeholders for Amazon.com.

Although primary stakeholders have a direct relationship with the firm, they should not always receive the greatest weight by a manager determining which particular strategic option to choose. For instance, an action that may be in the best interest of stockholders and customers—building a distribution center on recreational parkland—may be villainized by the media (a stakeholder group) to the local community (another stakeholder group), generating overall public opinion (a third stakeholder) against the project. Organizations that subscribe to the stakeholder concept largely try to see that its primary stakeholders attain their objectives while at the same time keeping other stakeholders satisfied. One management expert characterizes the goal of

EXHIBIT 1-1 Stakeholder Analysis for Amazon.com

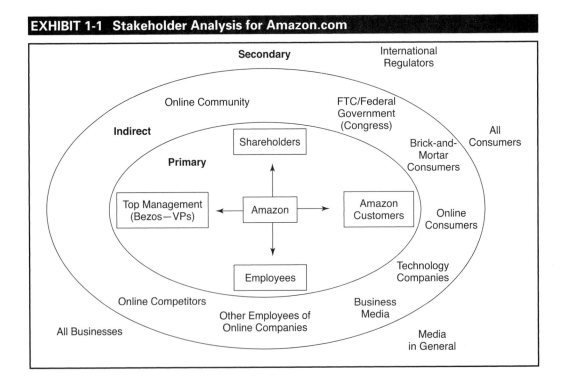

stakeholder analysis as creating the classic "win-win" situation for all stakeholders.[9] In other words, the task of marketing management is to seek solutions that will ideally achieve the goals of all stakeholders. Failing that, management must at least select options that generally optimize net stakeholder benefits.

One example of an organization that has apparently internalized this approach is Johnson & Johnson (J&J). Its corporate "credo," an embodiment of the stakeholder concept, in both English and Arabic, is shown in Exhibit 1-2. This document recognizes responsibilities to consumers, employees, communities, and stockholders (top line of each paragraph). The credo was first introduced in 1945. In the 1970s, former J&J Chairman James Burke held a series of meetings with the firm's 1,200 top managers; they were encouraged to challenge the credo. What emerged from those meetings was agreement that the document functioned as originally intended; it was slightly reworded but substantially unchanged from when the credo was originally published. The company has now reprinted the credo into 36 languages for non-English-speaking employees.[10]

Most important, the credo still influences how J&J conducts its operations. In recent years, the company has surveyed all 100,000 employees in its 20 companies about how well the company meets its responsibilities to its four principal stakeholders. The survey questions employees from all 51 countries where J&J operates about every line in the credo. The tabulation and reporting of results is confidential. (Department and division managers receive only information pertaining to their units and composite numbers for the entire firm.) A J&J employee recently told one of the authors that a low score for a unit causes substantial discussion about how it might improve.

Does J&J's credo work? Top management feels strongly that it does. The credo is often mentioned as an important contributing factor in the company's exemplary handling of the Tylenol product recall 20 years ago when that product was subject to tampering. It appears that the firm's commitment to its credo makes ethical business practice a high priority.

Increasingly, more and more organizations are accepting the stakeholder concept. They are beginning to develop procedures for linking stakeholder concerns to the strategies they conceive. In order to implement a stakeholder management approach, organizations need to do several things, including the following:

- Identify the company's stakeholders
- Determine which ones are primary, indirect, and secondary as well as exactly what stakes each group holds in the organization
- Establish what responsibilities (economic, ethical, legal, or philanthropic) the organization has to each stakeholder group
- Identify any conflicts between stakeholder criteria
- Decide how the organization can best respond strategically to the opportunities and threats inherent in stakeholder claims, especially where conflicts are likely to require creative compromises

Again, the rights and interests of various stakeholders are important, as they are the objects (some may say moral subjects) to which the different ethical theories or

EXHIBIT 1-2

Our Credo

مبَادئُنا

We believe our first responsibility is to the doctors, nurses and patients, to mothers and fathers and all others who use our products and services. In meeting their needs everything we do must be of high quality. We must constantly strive to reduce our costs in order to maintain reasonable prices. Customers' orders must be serviced promptly and accurately. Our suppliers and distributors must have an opportunity to make a fair profit.

We are responsible to our employees, the men and women who work with us throughout the world. Everyone must be considered as an individual. We must respect their dignity and recognize their merit. They must have a sense of security in their jobs. Compensation must be fair and adequate, and working conditions clean, orderly and safe. We must be mindful of ways to help our employees fulfill their family responsibilities. Employees must feel free to make suggestions and complaints. There must be equal opportunity for employment, development and advancement for those qualified. We must provide competent management, and their actions must be just and ethical.

We are responsible to the communities in which we live and work and to the world community as well. We must be good citizens - support good works and charities and bear our fair share of taxes. We must encourage civic improvements and better health and education. We must maintain in good order the property we are privileged to use, protecting the environment and natural resources.

Our final responsibility is to our stockholders. Business must make a sound profit. We must experiment with new ideas. Research must be carried on, innovative programs developed and mistakes paid for. New equipment must be purchased, new facilities provided and new products launched. Reserves must be created to provide for adverse times. When we operate according to these principles, the stockholders should realize a fair return.

إننا نؤمن بأن مسؤوليتنا الأولى هي أمام الأطباء والممرضات والمرضى، وأمام الأمهات والآباء وغيرهم من أولئك الذين يستعملون منتجاتنا ويستفيدون من خدماتنا. فمن أجل تلبية احتياجاتهم يجب أن يكون كل ما نقوم به في مستوى عالٍ رفيع. علينا أن نعمل دائماً على تخفيض تكاليفنا للمحافظة على أسعار معقولة وكذلك يجب أن تلبى طلبات الزبائن بسرعة ودقة، وأن يكون لموزعينا ومورّدينا فرصة للربح.

ننا مسؤولون تجاه موظفينا، أولئك الرجال والنساء الذين يعملون معنا في جميع أنحاء العالم. يجب النظر لكل منهم على نه إنسان علينا احترام كرامته وتقدير فضائله. يجب أن يشعر موظفونا بالأمان في أعمالهم. كذلك يجب أن تكون الأجور عادلة وكافية، وظروف العمل نظيفة، مرتبة وآمنة. كذلك يجب ن يشعر الموظفون بأن لهم الحرية في تقديم الإقتراحات والشكاوى، ويجب أن تكون أمامهم فرص متساوية للتوظيف والتطور والتقدم للمؤهلين منهم. علينا أن نوفر إدارة تتمتع بالكفاءة وتتّسم تصرفاتها بالعدالة والخلق.

ننا مسؤولون أما المجتمعات التي نعيش ونعمل فيها وأمام لمجتمع الدولي. كذلك علينا أن نكون مواطنون صالحين ـ علينا ن نؤيد الأعمال الصالحة والخيّرة وأن نتحمل نصيباً عادلا من لضرائب. يجب أن نشجع أيضاً تحسين الظروف المدنية الصحية والتعليمية. ويتوجب علينا أيضاً المحافظة على البناء لذي كُرّمنا باستعماله ، وحماية البيئة والمصادر الطبيعية.

مّا مسؤوليتنا الأخيرة فهي لحاملي أسهمنا. يجب أن نحقق رباحاً مناسبة، وعلينا القيام بتجربة الأفكار الجديدة. يجب واصلة الأبحاث ، وتطوير البرامج المبتكرة والمحاسبة على لأخطاء. يجب شراء معدات جديدة، وتوفير التسهيلات الحديثة، تقديم منتجات جديدة وعلينا إيجاد إحتياطيات تحسباً أوقات الشدة. عندما نعمل وفقاً لهذه المبادىء فلابد لحاملي سهمنا من تحقيق مردود جيد.

جونسون و جونسون (مصر) ش.م.م.

Johnson & Johnson (Egypt) S.A.E.

Source: Johnson & Johnson, New Brunswick, New Jersey

frameworks are applied. Since a large part of ethics is *deciding what is properly owed to whom,* identifying stakeholders and their claims is analogous to establishing the interests in a legal case. Consider the example of a public relations firm asked to represent a foreign country seeking economic development as a client. Suppose the country has acceptable diplomatic relations with the United States but is also accused of violating human rights. The stakeholders include the employees of the public relations agency, the U.S. government, the client country's government, the stockholders of the public relations firm, other customers, the media, and the citizenry of both the United States and the nation being considered as a client. Each group might very well view the ethical stakes involved in this controversy from a different perspective. Agency employees are concerned with their right to earn a living; the U.S. government may be preoccupied with maintaining cordial relations with the developing country; stockholders are motivated by the prospect of a client signing a lucrative, long-term contract; and the media may be energized by the news value associated with the apparent hypocrisy of helping a government most U.S. citizens find abhorrent—which may also complicate the agency's ability to service its less controversial clients. Meanwhile, the prospective client nation's citizens may be torn between the value of anticipated improvements in their economy and dismay that such improvements may imply foreign approval of their country's human rights record. The complexity of stakeholder analysis is apparent from this example.

PRINCIPLES FOR ETHICAL DECISION MAKING

What standards do marketers use to grapple with questions that have ethical implications? Several shorthand decision rules are often used by businesspeople. We offer two types of simple "rules of thumb" for marketers. The first is the ABCs of marketing ethics, and the second is a list of maxims.

ABCs of Marketing Ethics

One easy way to examine the major thrust of marketing ethics is to think of a series of words/phrases that begin with A, B, and C. This is a shorthand and relatively straightforward approach to simplifying marketing ethics. However, we must caution you that behind each of these relatively basic ideas is a complex set of issues. The three As are "applied," "above the law," and "aspirational." The three Bs are "beneficial," "beyond the bottom line," and "breaking new ground." The three Cs are "compliance," "consequences," and "contributions."[11]

Applied   Marketing ethics is an applied morality, like legal, engineering, and medical ethics. Each of these professional fields draw rules from moral philosophy or religious traditions and applies them to the problems specific to the relevant area. For example, we apply these standards to dilemmas faced by marketing managers, salespeople, advertising executives, and retail managers throughout this book.

Above the Law   Ethical questions are those that exist somewhere above the legal minimum. Unfortunately, some companies view ethics as synonymous with legal requirements. We view the law as the floor. As a response to the scandals that occurred several years ago, the floor was raised by the passage of the Sarbanes Oxley Act in the United States during 2002. As an illustration, one might think of a famous dance of the baby-boom generation, the limbo. The purpose of this dance was to continue to dance under a stick and get progressively closer to the floor. The challenge was "how low can you go?" This, unfortunately, also describes marketers who try to do the moral minimum.

Aspirational　Marketing ethics at its best should be aspirational. Both junior and senior marketing executives should aspire to do better from an ethical standpoint. This approach is covered within the virtue ethics and moral development models examined later in this chapter. For a number of years, one of Levi Strauss & Company's ethics publications was called its "Aspiration Statement," which signaled to the world that Levi aspired to a high level of ethics, even though they did not always attain it.

Beneficial　This point means that good ethics is beneficial to the firm. The one caveat is that it is beneficial in the "long run." There are good theoretical reasons for believing that practicing good ethical behavior is beneficial to the firm. We admit, however, that the empirical evidence is mixed with respect to whether good behavior usually results in increased profitability. We do know that a systematic lack of transparency with customers, stockholders, and the public is financially disastrous. Immoral behavior can ruin a company (e.g., Arthur Andersen and Enron).

Beyond the Bottom Line　Marketing managers must think beyond just the financial impact of their decisions. They should understand the environmental and safety implications of their products, whether toys or automobiles. In fact, Royal Dutch Shell now regularly provides information on what they call a "triple bottom line," including economic, environmental, and social performance. The latest report can be found online.[12]

Breaking New Ground　The most ethical firms think "outside the box" and employ moral imagination in dealing with intractable ethical concerns.[13] In particular, problems for which the most obvious alternative solutions all involve harm to multiple stakeholders call for creative thinking to devise a solution that either minimizes such harm or, ideally, produces results that permit the parties in conflict to gain. For example, pollution control efforts sometimes generate cost reductions (e.g., less waste) with economic value.

Compliance　At minimum, marketing managers must comply with the policies and rules of their companies as well as those of their nation's legal system. In fact, most corporate codes of ethics are written as compliance documents by spelling out prohibitions and approved responses to ethical situations known from company experience. In research we have done with large companies, about half report taking a compliance approach to ethical issues facing their firm.[14]

Consequences　Virtually all marketing managers worry about the consequences of their actions. In fact, one set of ethical theories uses the yardstick of whether good or bad consequences will result in deciding whether a decision is ethical or unethical. For instance, a decision to move a manufacturing plant to a lower-cost-of-labor country will likely mean good consequences for the company in terms of lower costs of production. What negative consequences for the company can you think of arising from this decision?

Contributions   Most marketing managers and other top managers of companies do *not* look at their position or corporation as just being in the business of making money. They often speak in much more enlightened terms, such as improving convenience for consumers or offering more product choice. Thus, marketing contributes to a more productive economy and a happier society. Whether this vision is always fulfilled is debatable, but businessmen and -women often see themselves as contributing to society and not just in a narrow microeconomic sense.

Maxims for Ethical Marketing

Several maxims that might aid a marketer facing an ethical dilemma are the following:

The golden rule: Act in a way that you would hope others would act toward *you.*

The professional ethic: Take only actions that would be viewed as proper by an objective panel of your professional colleagues. (The new American Marketing Association Ethical Norms and Values for Professional Marketers presented in Exhibit 1-3 is an example of a professional code.)

The TV/newspaper test: A manager should always ask, "Would I feel comfortable explaining this action on TV or in the front page of the local newspaper to the general public?" (This test is sometimes referred to as the *Wall Street Journal* or *Financial Times* test.)

When in doubt, don't: If a manager feels uneasy about a decision, there is probably reason to question it. We advise our students that if the decision does not seem right in the head, heart, or gut, then the decision should be postponed. The individual should probably seek guidance from a trusted person before proceeding with the decision.

Slippery slope: This maxim suggests that companies must be careful not to engage in debatable practices that may serve as a precedent for undertaking other, even more questionable strategies later. For example, there could be good reason for a sales manager to push sales "up the channel" toward the end of a fiscal quarter so that a hardworking group of sales reps achieve their bonuses. However, such tactics may lead to an increasing acceptance by management that it is okay to be "fast and loose" with inventory figures (i.e., the slippery slope). (Although this maxim does occur in marketing, we see the recent scandals that plagued several firms in the accounting profession as classic illustrations of the slippery slope.)

Kid/mother/founder on your shoulder: Would a naive child, your mother, or the company founder be comfortable with the ethical decision being made? Could you explain it to them in commonsense terms they would understand?

Never knowingly do harm: This implies that a manager would not consciously make or sell a product not deemed to be safe. Certain observers call this the "silver rule" because it does not hold marketers to as high a standard as the golden rule does. (What marketers might be guilty of not following this guideline?)

Some thumbnail rules are difficult to apply in specific situations. The application of different rules of thumb to the same situation may sometimes lead to quite different solutions. For example, if salespeople pad their meal expense accounts 15 percent because

EXHIBIT 1-3 American Marketing Association

Ethical Norms and Values for Marketers

Preamble

The American Marketing Association commits itself to promoting the highest standard of professional ethical norms and values for its members. Norms are established standards of conduct expected and maintained by society and/or professional organizations. Values represent the collective conception of what people find desirable, important and morally proper. Values serve as the criteria for evaluating the actions of others. Marketing practitioners must recognize that they serve not only their enterprises but also act as stewards of society in creating, facilitating and executing the efficient and effective transactions that are part of the greater economy. In this role, marketers should embrace the highest ethical *norms* of practicing professionals as well as the ethical *values* implied by their responsibility toward stakeholders (e.g., customers, employees, investors, channel members, regulators, and the host community).

General Norms

1. Marketers must first do no harm. This means doing work for which they are appropriately trained or experienced so they can actively add value to their organizations and customers. It also means adhering to all applicable laws and regulations, as well as embodying high ethical standards in the choices they make.
2. Marketers must foster trust in the marketing system. This means that the products and services offered are safe in addition to being fit for their intended use. It requires that marketing communications about goods and services are not intentionally deceptive or misleading. It suggests building relationships that provide for the equitable adjustment and/or redress of customer grievances. It implies striving for good faith and fair dealing so as to contribute toward the efficacy of the exchange process.
3. Marketers should embrace, communicate and practice the fundamental ethical values that will improve consumer confidence in the integrity of the marketing exchange system. These basic values are intentionally aspirational and include: Honesty, Responsibility, Fairness, Respect, Openness and Citizenship.

Ethical Values

Honesty—this means being truthful and forthright in our dealings with customers and stakeholders.
*   We will tell the truth in all situations and at all times.
*   We will offer products of value that do what we claim in our communications.
*   We will stand behind our brands if they fail to deliver their claimed benefits.
*   We will honor our explicit and implicit commitments and promises.

Responsibility—this involves accepting the consequences of our marketing decisions and strategies.
*   We will make strenuous efforts to serve the needs of our customers.
*   We will avoid using coercion with all stakeholders.

EXHIBIT 1-3   American Marketing Association (*Continued*)

- We will acknowledge the social obligations to stakeholders that come with increased marketing and economic power.
- We will recognize our special commitments to economically vulnerable segments of the market such as children, the elderly and others who may be substantially disadvantaged.

Fairness—this has to do with justly trying to balance the needs of the buyer with the interest of the seller.

- We will clearly represent our products in selling, advertising and other forms of communication; this includes the avoidance of false, misleading and deceptive promotion.
- We will reject manipulations and sales tactics that destroy customer trust.
- We will not engage in price fixing, predatory pricing, price gouging or "bait and switch" tactics.
- We will not knowingly participate in material conflicts of interest.

Respect—this addresses the basic human dignity of all stakeholders.

- We will value individual differences even as we avoid customer stereotyping or demographic (e.g., gender, race, sexual orientation) exploitation in our promotions.
- We will listen to the needs of our customers and make all reasonable efforts to monitor and improve their satisfaction on an on-going basis.
- We will make a special effort to understand suppliers, middlemen and distributors from other cultures.
- We will appropriately acknowledge the contributions of others, such as consultants, employees and co-workers, to our marketing endeavors.

Openness—this focuses on creating transparency in our marketing operations.

- We will strive to communicate clearly with all our constituencies.
- We will accept constructive criticism from our customers and other stakeholders.
- We will disclose significant product or service risks, component substitutions or other foreseeable eventualities affecting the customer or their perception of the purchase decision.
- We will fully disclose list prices, terms of financing as well as available price deals and adjustments.

Citizenship—this involves a strategic focus on fulfilling the economic, legal, philanthropic and societal responsibilities that serve stakeholders.

- We will strive to protect the natural environment in the execution of marketing campaigns.
- We will give back to the community through volunteerism and charitable donation.
- We will work to contribute to the overall betterment of marketing and its reputation.
- We will encourage supply chain members to ensure that trade is fair for all participants, including producers in developing countries.

Conclusion

Finally, we recognize that every industry sector and marketing sub-discipline (e.g., marketing research, e-commerce, direct selling, advertising, etc.) has its own specific ethical issues that require policies and commentary. An array of such codes can be linked to via the AMA website. We encourage all such groups to develop and/or refine their industry and discipline-specific codes of ethics in order to supplement these general norms and values.

Source: AMA Ethics Committee (O.C. Ferrell, chair; M. Etzel, G. Findley, G. Laczniak, L. Lee, and P. Murphy, members) (2004). Adopted by AMA Board.

customary gratuities (i.e., tips) are not technically reimbursable in the absence of a receipt, the "professional ethic" rule might indicate the practice is okay despite its variance from the letter of company policy. Why? Because this is the only mechanism to recover a legitimate cost. In contrast, the "when in doubt, don't" rule questions whether padding expense accounts is ever acceptable. (Of course, the company that has such a rule might be viewed as guilty of placing their employees in a "no-win" situation, one that could be avoided if a specific provision for tips were included in its expense reimbursement policy.)

Despite such ambiguity, these short maxims can have considerable value. One wonders whether the product manager who permitted the controversial ad (Scenario 2) to continue to be advertised could feel comfortable explaining those actions to the general public on television (i.e., pass the TV test). Similarly, the "professional ethic" rule can be extremely useful for those subspecialties in business that have a code of professional conduct that covers certain recurring situations. For example, various groups of professional marketing researchers have developed detailed codes of ethics that cover situations commonly encountered by their peer group. Included, for instance, in many marketing research codes of ethics would be stipulations that respondent confidentiality should be protected when promised, that data not confirming the hypothesized findings of the researcher are not suppressed, that the limitations of the statistical methods used are identified in the research report, and so forth.

Whenever such rules are used, the consensus regarding what constitutes proper ethical behavior in a decision-making situation tends to diminish as the level of analysis proceeds from the abstract to the specific. Stated another way, it is easy to get a group of managers to agree *in general* that a practice is improper; however, casting that practice in a very specific set of circumstances usually reduces consensus. For example, most managers would agree with the proposition that business has the obligation to provide consumers with facts relevant to the informed purchase of a product or a service. However, let's test this proposition in a specific situation:

> A manufacturer sells a cleaning concentrate with instructions calling for mixing one part of the concentrate with four parts of water; this product has been sold in this manner for 25 years. Now assume that an issue of *Consumer Reports* indicates, based on several test applications, that the product is just as effective when mixed with one part concentrate to eight parts water. Thus, consumers need use only half as much concentrate. Does the company have an ethical responsibility to inform customers of this fact?

Most managers will agree that business has the obligation to provide consumers with facts relevant to an informed purchase. But does such an informed purchase include full disclosure of this *new information,* especially if further product testing in different cleaning situations might produce different results?

THE IMPORTANCE OF ETHICAL THEORY

In order to better structure ethical questions, managers should enhance their ability to reason ethically. What is meant by *ethical reasoning*? It is the process of systematically analyzing an ethical issue and applying to it one or more ethical standards. This process will generally consist of three steps:

1. *Definition of ethical problem*:   The first step necessitates determining whether a marketing decision has ethical implications. This requires an assessment of the nature and consequences of the action. This step frames a marketing question as an ethical problem. For example (recalling Scenario 2), is it acceptable to highlight medical benefits and minimize side effects in an advertising campaign?

2. *Selection of an ethical standard*:   Various theories of recommended moral behavior exist. While most theories will lead managers to the same solution given similar circumstances, different standards sometimes lead to divergent solutions. The existence of competing moral theories is one reason why well-intentioned managers disagree about what is ethically *proper*. (One goal of this chapter is to elaborate on the major ethical theories.)

3. *Application of the ethical standard*:   Once an ethical standard is chosen, it still must be applied to a specific situation. For example, a standard can be applied to a particular ethical dilemma, and the subsequent determination of an ethical choice is the completion of the ethical reasoning process.

If marketing managers do not follow this or a similar procedure, ethical discussions too easily degenerate into a clash of personal opinion or preference. For the most part, ethical reasoning ability is grounded in a knowledge of ethical theory. If managers understand ethical theory, they can apply specific principles or rules to guide decision making. Those principles can then be unpacked and examined in order to determine the appropriate choices emanating from an ethical problem. For example, a manager considering marketing a soft drink banned in the United States because of health questions raised by the FDA might consider the following:

1. Sending the product to the foreign market where it can be legally sold
2. Waiting for additional research information that might further validate or invalidate the danger of the substance
3. Exporting the product with a warning label
4. Dumping the product as waste
5. Disposing of the product to a wholesaler at a severely discounted price and letting that independent business firm make its own determination as to what to do with the controversial product

Each of these options raises ethical questions.

How should a marketing manager go about deciding what to do? How does one go about reasoning to an ethical solution? The answer to these questions lies partly in understanding different ethical theories. This response is not without its challenges. As noted earlier, the difficulty in choosing among various theories is that different ethical theories may lead to different conclusions. However, this realization should not be sufficient to dismiss the study of ethical reasoning as a fruitless exercise. Ethical issues regularly stem from "tough cases." Few people maintain that ethics is an easily understood subject. The existence of ethical dilemmas, where different approaches lead to different solutions, should not be a cause of cynicism. Some ambiguity is inherent in grappling with tough ethical problems, whether in marketing or in other realms. The fact that differing principles sometimes generate different decisions opens up more options than may have been considered initially. A more optimistic view is that managers should take some satisfaction from knowing that the application of various ethical theories to a particular situation will most often lead to consensus. At minimum, ethical theories will usually not generate unethical solutions. Finally, for those who may be skeptical about the values of ethical theory in marketing, we offer this statement by the classic philosopher Cicero in resolving a conflict between a grain trader and the famine-starved citizens of Rhodes in favor of the latter:

To everyone who proposes to have a good career, moral philosophy is indispensable. (**De Officiis,** *44 B.C.*)

TWO PSEUDO-"ETHICAL" APPROACHES

Many observers of marketing ethics invoke either relativism (situational ethics) or egoism as rationales for discussion. We do not consider them to be comprehensive theories (hence the quotation marks around "ethical"), but they do need to be examined before moving on.

Cultural and Ethical/Moral Relativism

The most prevalent form of this approach is *cultural relativism*. It is a *descriptive* claim that ethical practices differ among cultures—that, as a matter of fact, what is considered right in one culture may be considered wrong in another. Many believe that one should adjust his or her ethical thinking depending on the culture in which the firm is operating.[15] The long-standing phrase "When in Rome, do as the Romans do" captures the essence of this idea. One cannot determine what one ought to do mainly from the fact that some people permit it.

Moral relativism is a stronger claim that advocates what is *really* right or wrong is what the culture says is right or wrong. Relativism, then, presents a challenge to marketing executives, especially in the global marketplace. Managers must adjust to a certain extent to the tastes and needs of diverse consumers. In addition, defenders of ethical relativism argue that there is no better, more valid basis for making ethical judgments because any other conclusion assumes some absolute set of norms that would not be sensitive to situational factors. Nonetheless, managers who act solely on the basis of ethical relativism run both legal and reputational risks, especially in an era of worldwide communications. For marketing managers, relativism would guide them to engage in bribery if that were the norm in a certain country. However, for U.S.-based firms, bribery is effectively prohibited by the Foreign Corrupt Practices Act.

Several traps brought on by relativist thinking should be avoided. The first trap is that we should be careful not to hold ethics to too high a standard of proof. If we start with the assumption that ethical judgment must be proven as absolutely certain and beyond doubt, then ethics assuredly will fail to meet this standard. The second trap involves confusing the fact that there is wide disagreement about values with the conclusion that no agreement is possible. The fact of disagreement provides no reason for concluding that all these diverse opinions are equally valid. A third trap involves confusing values such as respect, tolerance, and impartiality with relativism. Respect for other people is a fundamental ethical value. Part of what it means to respect someone is to listen to his or her opinions and to show tolerance for opinions that differ from our own. But tolerating diverse opinions and values is not the same as ethical relativism.[16]

Managerial or Organizational Egoism

Egoism is a philosophy asserting that individuals act exclusively in their own self-interest. Consequences are judged only as they affect "me." The late twentieth century saw manifestations of egoism in phrases such as the "me generation" or "looking out for number 1." Thus, *egoism* holds that executives should take those steps that most efficiently advance the self-interest of themselves or their divisions or firms. An example of individual egoism might be the product manager who postpones making needed improvements to a mature product because she knows already that she will be promoted in the next year to a new division and she is interested only in next quarter's financial performance. An example of organizational egoism would be a firm that was ordered to install pollution abatement equipment because of illegal discharges and that delays doing so until the deadline date so that interest earned from cash on hand can be maximized. An obvious problem with such a philosophy arises when pursuing organizational goals conflicts with their impact on other stakeholders. Often managerial egoism is used in conjunction with a legalistic approach—the adage that the fiduciary duties of management boil down to "obey the law" and, beyond that, to the view that "the business of business is to maximize profits." Presumably, other required controls over unacceptable behavior will be provided by the invisible mechanisms of the marketplace, competition, reactions by customers, and so forth.

Several problems arise with managerial egoism. First, some moral philosophers do not see egoism as a philosophy at all. Why? An egoist has problems "universalizing" egoism as a guiding philosophy for others because if the egoist advocated that everybody act in their own self-interest, that prescription itself would *not* be in the self-interest of the egoist. A second problem is that some see egoism as being incompatible with the human tendency to be concerned for others in addition to oneself. Finally, there are obvious potential conflicts between individual and organizational egoism. However, philosophical semantics aside, managerial egoism does not stand up to scrutiny for other reasons.

Many questionable marketing practices seem to illustrate the egoistic approach. For example, until recently, public accounting firms were enthusiastic about developing codes of ethics, driven by the belief that these would allow them to continue to bid on audit and consulting contracts despite past scandals. It is also clear that the marketplace does not always provide a fair and level playing field for business organizations and consumers. Furthermore, early growth in the dot-com industry was often characterized by "bending the rules" and "get rich quick" mentalities, ignoring investor and larger industry interests. Responsibilities are owed to stakeholder groups other than shareholders, and these groups may not hold a primary interest in seeing the maximization of short-term return on investment. Insofar as the long-term goals of the managerial egoist are often limited to economic considerations, the long-term interests of the organization are not necessarily best served using this approach.[17] A disastrous example of taking the egoistic short-term view is Enron.

Having addressed the "pretender theories" of relativism and egoism, we now briefly present four general categories of ethical theory—utilitarianism (i.e., consequence-based theories), duty-based approaches (i.e., deontological theories), contract-based perspectives, and virtue-based ethics.

COMPREHENSIVE ETHICAL THEORIES

Unless a manager operates in a completely intuitive manner (and some do), the ability to reason about ethical questions requires some familiarity with the principal theoretical frameworks that have come to dominate the field of moral philosophy. The previously mentioned four major categories of ethical theories are now presented along with a discussion of how they relate to marketing decisions.

Consequence-Based Theories

Consequence-oriented theories are sometimes called *teleological,* from the Greek word *telos,* meaning "end" or "purpose." That is, a marketing decision is judged as ethical or unethical depending on the *outcome.* Hence, if the foreseeable consequences of a decision are positive, then the decision is ethical. The major category of theory that falls within the consequences approach is utilitarianism.

Utilitarianism

Probably the most widely understood and commonly applied ethical theory is *utilitarianism.* In an organizational context, utilitarianism basically states that a decision concerning marketing conduct is proper if and only if that decision produces the *greatest good for the greatest number* of individuals. "Good" is usually defined as the *net benefits* that accrue to those parties affected by the choice. Thus, most utilitarians hold the position that moral choices must be evaluated by calculating the net benefits of each available alternative action. Importantly, *all* the stakeholders affected by the decision should be given their just consideration. As mentioned previously, teleological theories deal with outcomes or end goals. The often-stated declaration that "the end justifies the means" is one classic expression of utilitarian thinking.

Several formulations of utilitarianism exist. Their differences harken back to the original writers on the topic, the nineteenth-century philosophers Jeremy Bentham and John Stuart Mill.[18]

One major school of thought, *act utilitarianism,* focuses on the *action* that has been taken, analyzing it along the lines of whether the selected action produces more good than bad consequences. For example, a pharmaceutical company may operate by the principle that it will release any FDA-approved drug with some side effects as long as it helps more persons combat a particular disease than the number troubled by a minor side effect. For another example, Scenario 2 discusses a new drug product dealing with weight gain advertised using two short commercials, one part that introduces the product and a second part that touted its benefits. However, the side effects are not discussed. If the benefits are sufficiently great and the problems with the side effects sufficiently limited, then the action of the pharmaceutical in Scenario 2 is justified on act utilitarian grounds.

A second formulation, *rule utilitarianism,* looks at whether the option or choice conforms to a *rule* that attempts to maximize the overall utility. Some have criticized act utilitarianism on the grounds that it often gives the wrong ethical answer when evaluating individual actions. To use an example from banking, suppose a banker is considering whether it is right to foreclose on the mortgage of a widow and her children. To consider that action in isolation, it is fairly easy to show on act utilitarian grounds that foreclosure would cause more pain than not foreclosing. However, suppose we had a rule that said that banks should not foreclose whenever the action of foreclosing would cause more harm than foreclosing. If that rule were adopted, then banks would be reluctant to lend money. Thus, the rule permitting foreclosure on widows is better for society than a rule that forbids such disclosure. Rule utilitarians, then, focus on the rules for acting rather than on individual actions themselves. For a rule utilitarian, a rule is morally correct when it provides more social good than any alternative rule. For act utilitarians, rules are just rules of thumb. For rule utilitarians, rules are determinate of right and wrong.

Business executives commonly embrace such consequentialist approaches to ethical problems because they are so compatible with traditional business thinking. Why? Just as this results-based theory seeks to maximize happiness, or *the good,* business executives often hope to maximize profit, return on investment, or share price. If a businessperson draws the broader conclusion that the greatest good is equivalent to the highest profitability and this situation produces the most benefits for society, it is easy to see how these two systems, both oriented to optimum results, are philosophically compatible.

Consequence-Oriented Philosophy and Marketing Management

A strong appeal of the utilitarian approach is its *cost-benefit* character. Marketing managers regularly weigh the pros and cons of alternative economic and managerial actions. This approach to solving business problems is a staple of most MBA programs and therefore is ingrained in the psyche of many managers. Business executives appreciate the fact that most utilitarians recognize that not everyone will benefit from a particular action. Hence, the emphasis in utilitarianism is on the *net* utility of the set of outcomes resulting from a decision being considered. Marketing managers, of course, also realize that their business decisions must often be placed in the context of a "win-lose" situation. That is, the consequences of a business action are seldom singular; rather, they are multiple and may "cut both ways." For instance, in mature markets, the only way to *gain* market share is for at least one competitor to lose share. Or the only approach to increasing long-term shareholder value is to sacrifice near-term profits (and perhaps management bonuses) in favor of future product or market development expenditures.

Another reason marketing managers are so accepting of utilitarian thinking lies in its flexibility in response to differing situations. Utilitarianism accommodates complex circumstances more easily than other, more absolute, philosophical approaches. The factors considered in a utilitarian framework can be conveniently varied from the short term to the long term or from financial to nonfinancial criteria. While conflicting stakeholder claims *can* be recognized, managers typically weigh business owner or stockholder goals associated with corporate profitability as more important than the goals of other groups such as employees or the community. Do you think this weighting is proper?

For example, in a situation involving the distribution manager of the supermarket chain sending lower-quality cuts of meat and vegetables to lower-profitability stores in disadvantaged neighborhoods, one can see how this approach *might* be defended. The manager rationalizes that as long as the meats and vegetables are above some minimally acceptable quality level, it is in the best financial interest of the supermarket chain to take whatever action it can to enhance overall operations. With respect to units located in the least affluent areas of the city, economic advantage is maximized by systematically discriminating against these less profitable units. Alternatively, management may also calculate (quite reasonably) that the marginal value of the inner-city store can be maintained only by offsetting the impact of higher insurance and security costs and lower sales volume per square foot with other cost-cutting measures. This reasoning may also be combined with recognizing the need to provide higher quality to customers in more affluent areas that may also present the greatest threat from competitors. When compared to the alternative of closing an otherwise unprofitable store (with the external costs of unemployment and less service to that neighborhood), the current practice *may* be the most ethical in a utilitarian sense.

Limitations of Utilitarianism

Consequentialist approaches to ethical reasoning are obviously not without their problems. Perhaps the most evident concern, which applies to almost any formulation of utilitarianism, is the question of who decides what "the greatest good" is. Indeed, usually many opinions exist as to what constitutes the nature of the actual benefits of a particular action. When this is the case, *who* is it that decides which perception of what "good" shall prevail? Is it the chief executive officer, the vice president of marketing, the product managers, or a panel of customers? Second, it appears that utilitarianism is a philosophy where ends sometimes may justify otherwise unacceptable means. That is, just because the outcome of a particular action produces a "net good" for a corporation or, for that matter, the whole of society, should that necessitate a penalty or expense for some parties? Should any product be permitted in the market if it causes a significant and lasting health problem for a minority of users? Those who practice most forms of utilitarianism recognize that one *cannot* cause great harm to certain others in order to achieve a desirable or noble end. This seems to be the point that animal rights activists stress in advocating a ban on the use of animals in safety testing such products as cosmetics. In fact, one of the greatest ethical precepts (mentioned earlier) is *never knowingly do harm*. But the definition of what constitutes "a harm" or a significant harm is subject to debate.

Third, those marketing managers who adopt a primarily economic interpretation of utilitarianism must answer whether such an approach is compatible with the concept of justice. The transformation of utilitarian theory into economic utilitarianism is somewhat understandable in the sense that a business organization is primarily an *economic* enterprise. But just because an action is economically beneficial, does this mean it is just and proper? For instance, because the market demands sexually explicit Internet pornographic material—and pornography is profitable to most of the parties involved in its production and consumption—is it ethical to market such material? Even though a particular action has produced the greatest economic good for the greatest number, that still does not *prove* that the action is just and proper when both production and consumption are seen to victimize some participants and, arguably, the consumers as well in other than economic terms.

In short, the utilitarian principle to act in a way that results in a greatest good for the greatest number is a popular method of ethical reasoning used by many marketing managers that also presents problems in some circumstances.

Duty-Based Theories

A second category of ethical theories are classified by philosophers as *deontological*, the term coming from the Greek word *deon*, "duty." This impressive-sounding word basically indicates that actions are best judged as "good," standing alone and without regard to consequences. Thus, the inherent rightness of an act is *not* decided by analyzing and choosing the act that produces the best consequences, but rather according to the premise that certain actions are "correct" in and of themselves because they stem from fundamental obligations. Intentions or motivations, then, determine whether a marketing decision is ethical or unethical.

Perhaps the most famous duty-based theory was developed by the Prussian philosopher Immanuel Kant.[19] Kant contended that moral laws took the form of categorical imperatives—principles that defined behavior appropriate in all situations and that should be followed by all persons as a matter of duty. Kant proposed three formulations of the categorical imperative as follows:

1. Act only on maxims that you can will to be universal laws of nature. (universality)
2. Always treat the humanity in a person as an end and never as a means merely. (never treat people as means to an end)
3. So act as if you were a member of an ideal kingdom of ends in which you were both subject and sovereign at the same time. (moral community)

The first formulation argues that there are universal moral standards. For example, could any society universalize customer shoplifting? The answer is no. Similarly, bribery of government officials by marketers is unethical following the first formulation. The second formulation is concerned with treatment of all stakeholders as persons. The application of this principle in marketing is to never treat customers as means, manipulating their behavior to attain company goals. One of the controversial areas of marketing that might violate this formulation is sex-appeal advertising. Exhibit 1-4 reports on a variation of this issue in a European context. The third formulation views any marketing organization as a moral community. Managers, then, should respect the humanity of all workers in the firm, and employees should try to achieve common goals and shared ends.[20] In a larger sense, a market, including suppliers, competitors, and customers, constitutes a relevant moral community.

For business, duty-based approaches to ethics have important implications. This theory suggests, among other things, that cost-benefit analysis is inappropriate to the evaluation of some situations. Why? Decisions that produce good corporate outcomes

EXHIBIT 1-4   The 'Porno-Chic' Advertising Controversy*

France, known for its liberal positions toward nude advertising, has taken the initiative to lead the European protest against indecent and offensive marketing campaigns. The "phenomenon" at the center of the controversy has been termed "porno-chic." For a time, porno-chic was the marketing basis for several European fashion gurus. A far cry from conservative US marketing standards, the objection of the French (and many other European nations) to porno-chic comes not from its use of nudity. "Nude women in advertising don't pose any problem," says a female official in the Employment Ministry. "It's the violence and degradation that offends people."[1]

So what exactly is porno-chic? Porno-chic is a "naked woman, caressing herself into a state of ecstasy" posted over hundreds of Paris bus shelters. Porno-chic is "women who are bruised, bullied, even consorting with animals."[2] Recently ordered out of Italian advertising was an ad for Cuban beer that featured: "a sultry model kneeling in black bikini with a bottle of Tinama beer between her legs." The tagline: "Have yourself a Cuban."[3]

It is not only the French who have found these types of ads to be degrading and humiliating to women, but also Italy, Germany, and even the European Union have discussed the implementation of more rigid advertising guidelines in both print and television. Although ad agencies cannot be forced to comply with new rulings, most are expected to withdraw press and poster ads if asked to do so. Governments have urged citizens to take action and voice their objection to messages that are "degrading and humiliating" to women. In doing so, authorities maintain that it is not nudity in and of itself ("Bare breasts are used to promote everything from pullovers to Parmesan cheese in continental Europe.") that is under attack, "it is the use of nudity" that is being questioned.[4]

With a market seemingly overrun by attractive naked women, European marketers have been forced to look beyond what has traditionally been considered "bold and sexy." In doing so, they have ignited a moral controversy.

The French government released a report condemning a new breed of ads that were perceived as degrading and humiliating to women. Finally, France's Truth in Advertising Bureau issued new standards on what is acceptable when the human body is portrayed as a means to sell products. These regulations come as a result of a governmental report issued in July.

* Prepared by Diana Laquinta under the supervision of Professor Patrick E. Murphy.
[1]Stephen Baker and Christina White, "Why 'Porno Chic' Is Riling the French," *Business Week*, July 30, 2001, 47.
[2]Ibid.
[3]Alessandra Galloni, "Clapdown on 'Porno-Chic' Ads Is Pushed by French Authorities," *Wall Street Journal*, October 25, 2001, B4.
[4]Ibid.

but significantly hurt other stakeholders in the process are not morally acceptable using this line of reasoning. If marketers have a special obligation to vulnerable consumers, such as the elderly, children, or the less educated who are unable to resist advertising appeals that more sophisticated consumers receive with skepticism, those advertising appeals violate that obligation. In addition, it suggests that the goal of seeking the maximum *net* consequences of an action may include intermediate steps that could be judged as morally inappropriate. Why is this so? Because *means* as well as *ends* should be subjected to moral evaluation. Thus, an implication of duty-based theories is that sometimes business executives must take actions that do *not* produce the best economic consequences. To do otherwise could be morally wrong. That is, some actions might violate the basic duty to treat everyone fairly. For example, reflection indicates that the customers of the low-income stores where the poorest cuts of meat and vegetables are sent have been used merely as a *means* to obtain a satisfactory economic *end.* For Roche in Scenario 2, certain overweight consumers have been unjustly discriminated against to the benefit of others. A similar judgment might be applied to the use of fear appeals in promoting certain financial service products. Finally, buzz marketing (Scenario 1) is likely unethical from a duty-based perspective because the intention is to mislead consumers.

Like utilitarianism, duty-based theories are controversial in part because there are many different deontological theories. Various moral philosophers have compiled different lists of basic obligations or duties. While the lists overlap, they are not identical. Second, duty-based theories represent the antithesis of modern relativism (i.e., the notion that moral decisions can be made only in the context of particular situations). Hence, they are viewed by some as not being well suited to our complex, multicultural, and global marketplace because they emphasize the development of *universal* rules. The very nature of such absolute approaches includes certain problems that are inherent in the development of categorical imperatives. Among them are the following:

1. ***There are always contingencies that seem to complicate real-world situations***:   For example, suppose that a sales organization has an absolute rule against the practice of providing gifts to customers. Suppose further that it enters a new international market where gift giving is a common and expected practice. Now also consider the prospect that success in this market will determine whether the firm can survive. Should the universal rule be violated or changed to accommodate these contingencies? Other examples also might be explored. What about the prospect of dire consequences if one tells the truth? Are duties to customers or employees conditioned by their comparative vulnerability?

2. ***Universals also do not take into account the ethical character of the formulator of the universal principle***:   That is, if the morality of the person formulating the principle is flawed, it is possible that the principle itself will be deficient. For example, one might take issue with the universal maxims formulated by egoistic managers who see business as merely a game, the sole purpose of which is the accumulation of personal wealth.

3. ***There may not be a mechanism for resolving conflicts among two absolute moral duties***:   Managers clearly have a fiduciary responsibility to their shareholders and a duty of fidelity to their employees. What happens when action

requires a trade-off between these duties? Which duty takes precedence? Is one universal more absolute than another? What about the duty of motherhood for a female employee versus loyalty to the job and company?

Contract-Based Theories

Social contract theory is based on the most fundamental considerations for maintaining social order and harmony, that is, that individuals must generally agree to abstain from preying on each other and that, to ensure that this does not happen, rules and a mechanism to enforce them are required. For marketers, social contract theory has special implications for relationships among competitors and for transactions with less powerful or vulnerable buyers and sellers, especially those who are dependent on a marketer as either a customer or a supplier. By implication, social contract theory demands obedience to laws and adherence to the provisions of business contracts.

Integrative Social Contracts Theory

A hypothetical social contract takes into account ethical standards developed by groups through real social contact and based on their mutual interest in supportive or, at least, benign interaction. In other words, managers both desire and expect that there be ethical rules to govern their marketplace transactions. They envision global humanity coming together to work out a rational arrangement for ethics in economic life. The rational humans at this global convention would recognize that moral rationality is bounded in the same way that economic rationality is bounded. Thus, Donaldson and Dunfee, two chief advocates of the social contract theory approach, conclude that they would want business communities or groups to have moral free space. People, including managers, would want to have moral free space because they want to keep their moral options open until they confront the full context and environment of a decision.[21]

In theory, there may be norms that condone murder as a method of enforcing contracts or that endorse racial or sexual discrimination. As a consequence, it can be assumed that the vast majority of people would want to *restrict* the moral free space of communities by requiring that, before any community norms become ethically obligatory, they must be found to be compatible with hypernorms. Hypernorms (the norms by which all other norms are to be judged) entail principles so fundamental to human existence that we would expect them to be reflected in a convergence of religious, philosophical, and cultural beliefs. A list of hypernorms would surely include the following:

- An obligation to respect the dignity of each human person
- Core human rights, such as personal freedom, physical security and well-being, and the ownership of property
- Equity, or the fair treatment of similarly situated persons
- Avoiding unnecessary injury to others

The notion that "acceptable standards" of business or industry practice cannot violate hypernorms is one of the basic contributions of this approach. Integrative social contracts theory has been applied to international bribery and corruption and "establishes a means for displaying the ethical relevance of existing norms in industries, corporations, and other economic communities, even as it limits the acceptable range of such norms. It . . . advocates much closer scrutiny of existing ethical beliefs and practices in institutions as dissimilar as the European Community, the Sony Corporation, the international rubber market, and Muslim banks."[22]

Rawlsian Theory

Another contemporary theory that is contract based in its approach was formulated by the late professor John Rawls.[23] Rawls proposed two principles of justice that, like Kant's categorical imperative, are never to be violated. These principles are the *liberty principle* and the *difference principle*. The liberty principle states that each person is to have an equal right to the most extensive basic liberty compatible with a similar liberty for others. The difference principle states that social and economic equalities are to be arranged so that they are to the greatest benefit of the most disadvantaged.

The liberty principle is fairly understandable in light of the American political tradition. It implies that people have inherent rights, such as freedom of speech, to vote, to due process of law, and to own property, and that they have a right to exercise these liberties to the extent that they do not infringe on the fundamental liberties of others. The Patient's Bill of Rights (incorporated in the McCain-Kennedy Bill), represents a good illustration of the liberty principle. All patients have the right to the following:

- To choose their own doctors
- To independent, external reviews of medical decisions made by their health plans
- To sue their health plans in state court for medical decisions that result in injury or wrongful death
- To sue their health plans for up to $5 million in punitive damages over decisions resulting in injury or death

The difference principle is a bit more complicated. Basically, it states actions should not be taken that will further disadvantage those groups in society which are currently the least well off. In other words, corporate actions should be formulated in such a way that their social and economic effects are of most benefit to the least advantaged. This somewhat controversial principle is basically a call for *affirmative action* on behalf of the poor and politically underrepresented groups in society, comparable to the *preferential option for the poor,* enunciated in recent papal pronouncements.[24] Over time, it is an egalitarian principle that should make those least well off better off. The difference principle also emphasizes that it would be unethical to exploit one group for the benefit of others. In the example discussed earlier of the public relations firm considering whether to accept a foreign government with a questionable civil rights record as a client, the difference principle would suggest the agency should forgo that opportunity because the implementation of a public relations campaign could add legitimacy to the (presumably corrupt) ruling foreign government. Furthermore, it might exacerbate the position of a worse-off group, namely, citizens in a country where human rights are systematically violated. More generally, it suggests that marketers have superordinate duties to consumers who are illiterate in the workings of the marketplace.

Virtue-Based Ethics

Virtue Ethics

A final comprehensive theory of ethics is referred to as *virtue ethics*. It has a long tradition and is currently receiving renewed support. In part, virtue ethics is a contemporary reaction to the rampant relativism wherein society seems to lack a way of reaching moral agreement about ethical problems. The relativistic approach to morality seems to be based on the strength of persuasive appeals and intuitionism whereby when interests collide, one opinion is as good as another. It is almost a one-person, one-vote method to establishing what is ethical. Virtue ethics has been resurrected to counteract modern relativism.

What exactly is virtue ethics? Its key criterion is seeking to live a virtuous life. In many ways, it is a renaissance of the Greek ideal suggesting that the guiding purpose of life should be the quest for goodness and virtue. In philosophical circles, one of the most prominent proponents of this position is Alasdair MacIntyre of the University of Notre Dame. MacIntyre basically defines virtue as acquired human qualities that enable persons to achieve "the good" in their chosen vocations, that is, the development of personal character.[25]

Virtue ethics differs from consequence-, duty-, and contract-based ethics in that the focus is on the individual and not the decision to be made or the principle to be followed. As such, virtue ethics is fundamentally different from the other theories. Advocates of virtue ethics suggest that one problem with contemporary organizations is that when they do look at situations with ethical implications, they are preoccupied with what the public thinks. Put another way, today's corporations may be entirely too reactive, wondering at times whether their actions will be perceived as "opportunistic," as "exploitative," or in "bad taste" by the general public. This may be a misdirected effort that can be rectified through virtue ethics. Thus, organizations should instead focus on questions such as "What kind of organization *should* we be?" and "What constitutes the ideally ethical organization?" Companies that know what they stand for and then embody these beliefs in a company credo or values statement are following this approach to ethics. In short, the virtue ethics perspective seems to imply that the question of *understanding* virtue precedes the discussion and development of rules of conduct. Once management understands the nature of a virtuous organization, ethical decision rules are much easier to develop.

Believers in this approach find much value in the writings of Aristotle.[26] While the essence of virtue ethics cannot easily be captured in a few sentences, there are some key elements that reflect this mode of thinking. First, virtues are essentially good habits. In order to flourish, these habits must be practiced, and the uninitiated managers in the organization must learn these virtues. This point has powerful implications for managers, including the notion that (1) firms can become virtuous only by engaging in ethical activities and that (2) organizations have to teach managers precisely what the appropriate virtues are. In other words, companies have the responsibility to foster ethical behavior. Wharton professor Thomas Donaldson says that, "Aristotle tells us that ethics is more like building a house than it is like physics. You learn to be an ethical manager by managing, not by reading textbooks on philosophy." Professional philosophers sometimes view the practice of business ethics as a theoretical pursuit, continues Donaldson. "It's not. It is an art. It can't be reduced to a science." For an Aristotelian, it's impossible for a company to be too ethical.

A second dimension of virtue ethics is that admirable characteristics are most readily discovered by witnessing and imitating widely acclaimed behavior. Aristotle, while focusing on the individual rather than the organization, listed such virtues as truthfulness, justice, generosity, and self-control as characteristics to which the noble person should aspire. In the theory of virtue, much attention is placed on role models. The insight here is that to be an ethical person is not simply an analytical and rational matter. It takes virtuous people to make right decisions, and virtue is learned by doing. Put another way, the ultimate test and source of ethical conduct is the character of the actor. Aristotle often discussed the lives of obviously good Athenians in order to teach ethics. One learned the right thing to do by observing good people and by doing what they did. Such lessons reinforce the importance of top management serving as role models in the formation of an ethical corporate climate. Who has been a mentor or role model in your life?

Companies that are acclaimed for their ethical corporate culture most often can trace their heritage back to founders intent on developing an organization that respected human dignity and insisted on a humane way of life. Founders of such companies as Johnson & Johnson shaped their organization so that they embodied the values and virtues that proved personally rewarding. The way of life in the company was not a result of an abstract code of conduct; rather, such statements were later used to spell out exactly what was at the heart of the existing corporate culture. For example, the top management of Levi Strauss has recently put forth four guiding values/virtues—empathy, originality, integrity, and courage. (For a complete discussion, visit www.levistrauss.com.)

Third, a key to understanding virtue ethics and the discipline it requires is based on the *ethic of the mean.* Applied to virtue ethics, the mean is an optimal *balance* of a quality that one should seek. An excess or deficiency of any of the key virtues can be troublesome, as Aristotle effectively argued.[27] For example, an excess of truthfulness is boastfulness. A deficiency of truthfulness is deception. Both of these outcomes (the excess or the deficiency) are unacceptable. The Swedish language has a word, *lagom,* that means "not too much, not too little, but just enough." The virtuous marketing manager, then, strives for a balance among the qualities it takes to be an effective manager. For example, she should not be so directive as to be authoritarian or so easygoing as to abdicate her leadership role. Golfers may appreciate the analogy that one's goal in the sport is to stay in the fairway and out of the rough. This is the way a marketing manager should behave, that is, by not going to extremes.

Obviously, there is disagreement about exactly which characteristics should appear on a list of virtues to which an organization should aspire. Over the years, different philosophers have compiled many different lists. Business executives and professors have enumerated virtues (Exhibit 1-5) that they feel are most important for international marketing.[28] Whether a particular corporation elects to foster those virtues is another issue.

EXHIBIT 1-5   Virtue Ethics for International Marketing

Virtue	Definition	Related Virtues	Applications to Marketing
Integrity	Adherence to a moral code and completeness	Honesty Moral courage	• Conveying accurate and complete information to consumers
Fairness	Marked by equity and free from prejudice or favoritism	Justice	• Selling and pricing products at a level commensurate with benefits received
Trust	Faith or confidence in another party	Dependability	• Confidence that salespeople or suppliers will fulfill obligations without monitoring
Respect	Giving regard to views of others	Consideration	• Altering products to meet cultural needs and refusing to sell unsafe products anywhere
Empathy	Being aware of and sensitive to the needs and concerns of others	Caring	• Refraining from selling products to consumers who cannot afford them

Source: Patrick E. Murphy, "Character and Virtue Ethics in International Marketing,"
Journal of Business Ethics, (January 1999): 113.

However, let's assume for a moment that an organization accepts the virtue ethics approach to corporate conduct. In other words, they subscribe to the belief that an organization should be "all that it can be" in an ethical sense. Then, with regard to the scenarios discussed earlier, one might conclude that (1) the virtuous organization has no need to provide gifts to purchasing agents in order to secure product orders, (2) the virtuous organization should be totally truthful so that it has no problem with disclosing a change of components as well as updating consumers with regard to the reliability of all their brands, and (3) the virtuous organization will not stoop to fear-generating, emotional appeals to sell its products—manipulation is wrong, so almost all fear appeals would be inappropriate.

One logical objection to the application of virtue ethics in an organizational context is that it would sometimes be very difficult to agree on what in fact constitutes "the good." What virtues should an organization emulate, and how should those virtues be operationalized in company policy? The contemporary philosopher MacIntyre and other recent proponents of virtue ethics seem to deal with this situation in the following way. First, they recognize that a great diversity of virtues exists in society. However, in many cases, particular organizations are self-contained. It is within the context of individual companies that the notion of appropriate virtues should be explored. Second, consistent with Aristotle, they assume that these virtues will be "other directed" (i.e., undertaken for the good of the community rather than in a self-serving manner). Third, this theory assumes that people aspire to a higher level of ethics. Unfortunately, we know that this is not always the case. Hence, virtue ethics is sometimes criticized as being too idealistic.

It is important to note that we find the corporation among the more controlled communities in modern society. Each corporation has its own *corporate character,* often rooted in religious values (discussed next). It is within the context of corporate culture that a particular firm can seek virtues appropriate for that organization. All of this, of course, underscores the importance of developing an ethical corporate culture that facilitates appropriate managerial behavior. The idea of a corporate culture rooted in ethics follows from the "shared community" worldview.

RELIGIOUS MODELS OF MARKETING ETHICS

The various ethical schools of thought presented previously are properly characterized as mostly *secular* or *civic.* They are the product of moral reasoning, based on human experience, and can be viewed as applying to and derived from nature or the world as opposed to any religious or sectarian source. While these ethical theories have, directly or indirectly, been embraced over time by religious teachings and traditions, it is important to establish their independence.

However, it is also relevant to recognize the extent to which religion contributes to the ethical standards observed in the world. Because of the historical importance of trade, both within and between communities, it was natural for people to seek moral guidance from religious sources—and for religious leaders to provide such guidance as representing divine instruction. In particular, Judeo-Christian, Confucian, Jewish, Islamic, and Buddhist religions have ethical precepts at their core. All have supported a variation of the golden rule for centuries (see Exhibit 1-6). Although the religious perspective is sometimes expressed as opposing business institutions, the world's religions have much to offer in terms of ethical guidance to marketers. In recognizing cultural influences over human behavior, regardless of their own religious heritage, students of marketing (particularly global marketing) are well advised to become familiar with such primary rules and principles from religious sources. They continue to be a dominant force in the development and maintenance of social norms.

Religious leaders have often preached that the answers to the majority of moral questions, business related or otherwise, could be found in the Bible. There has also been considerable debate about the level of guidance generated by religious principles. On the one hand, proscriptions like "thou shalt not steal" are fairly unambiguous. On the other hand, many situations that the contemporary corporate manager is faced with are exceedingly complex and defy the simple application of biblical precepts. Despite the difficulty of applying religious teachings, often rooted in centuries-old social conventions, to contemporary marketplace problems, to ignore them would be a serious omission. (We discuss a sample of religious traditions next and use Catholic

EXHIBIT 1-6   The Golden Rule across Religions

Judaism and Christianity (Old Testament)	*You shall love your neighbor as yourself.* Bible, Leviticus 19:18
Judaism	*When he went to Hillel, he said to him, "What is hateful to you, do not do to your neighbor: that is the whole Torah; all the rest of it is commentary; go and learn."* Talmud, Shabbat 31a
Christianity (New Testament)	*Whatever you wish that men would do to you, do so to them.* Bible, Matthew 7:12
Islam	*Not one of you is a believer until he loves for his brother what he loves for himself.* Forty Hadith of an-Nawawi 13
Confucianism	*Try your best to treat others as you would wish to be treated yourself and you will find that is the shortest way to benevolence.* Mencius VII.A4 *Tsetung asked, "Is there one word that can serve as a principle of conduct for life?" Confucius replied, "It is the word shu—reciprocity: Do not do to others what you do not want them to do to you."* Analects 15.23
Hinduism	*One should not behave towards others in a way which is disagreeable to oneself. This is the essence of morality. All other activities are due to selfish desire.* Mahabharata, Anusasana Parva 113.8
Buddhism	*Comparing oneself to others in such terms as "Just as I am so are they, just as they are so am I," he should neither kill nor cause others to kill.* Sutta Nipata 705
African traditional religions	*One going to take a pointed stick to pinch a baby bird should first try it on himself to feel how it hurts.* Yoruba Proverb (Nigeria)

Source: Adapted from Tom Dalla Costa, *The Ethical Imperative: Why Moral Leadership Is Good Business* (Reading, Mass.: Addison-Wesley, 1998), 141–142.

social thought as our example of Christianity, knowing that several prominent [and fairly compatible] Protestant approaches also exist.)

Roman Catholic Social Thought

Beginning in the late nineteenth century, in a belated response to the challenges posed by the Industrial Revolution, popes and bishops of the Roman Catholic Church began to seek scriptural wisdom and to interpret it in light of modern circumstances. One notable attempt to inject moral values into the marketplace was the pastoral letter authored by the American Catholic Bishops.[29] Drawing on Scripture and Catholic social teaching, this document attempted to derive propositions with useful current applications. For example, among the ethical precepts implied by this document are the following:[30]

- When considering trade-offs between labor and technology, managers have the responsibility to give special weight to human resources because of the *primacy of labor over capital* doctrine.
- When making strategic marketing decisions, managers have a special duty to consider the effect of those actions on economically vulnerable members of the community because of the *preferential option for the poor* doctrine.
- When making business decisions that may negatively impact the physical environment, managers have a special obligation to strongly consider possible external costs on the ecological environment because of the *stewardship* doctrine.

Jewish Ethical Tradition

The Hebrew Torah also offers substantial guidance to marketers.[31] One business executive publicly proclaimed that his Jewish faith led him in 1995 to continue paying his employees after a disastrous fire destroyed his operations facility.[32] A Halakic Code of Ethics has been formed by the Center of Business Ethics and Social Responsibility in Israel. Among the stakeholders specifically mentioned in this code are investors and executive officers, employees, customers, competitors, suppliers, investors, and the community. Two specific statements relate directly to customers and marketing:

Pricing: We will not charge customers for the goods we are selling or the services we are providing by any amount greater than its market value, unless customers are aware of the additional benefits they are receiving in paying a higher price. Care will be taken not to exploit any short-term difficulties encountered by our customers. To not act in this manner would be in breach of *ona'ah* (price oppression).

Selling practices: Our firm does not accept the principle of "buyer beware." Instead, we will ensure that the buyer has accurate and full information regarding the nature and quality of the goods sold or services provided, without any concealment of defects or deficiencies. All goods sold or services provided will be according to those specified in the contract or as advertised.

Islamic Ethical Tradition

The Islamic religious tradition has received much closer examination after the tragic events of September 11, 2001. In fact, the mainstream Muslim religious tradition is rich in the moral precepts it espouses. Muslim business executives have followed several axioms of Islamic ethical philosophy for centuries. Muslims observe the values of *equity* and *justice*. Among the most prominent are *unity, equilibrium, free will, responsibility,* and *benevolence.*[33] These axioms are defined and related both to marketing ethics and to the traditional philosophical ethical theories in Exhibit 1-7. What, in your opinion, are the most significant items of ethical advice from this exhibit?

Confucian Ethics

The Confucian conception of business ethics is most closely akin to virtue ethics. *Trust*—and *trustworthiness*—are central to the Confucian ethos.[34] An early Confucian philosopher, Mencias, noted that three interrelated concepts are central to what virtue is all about. These three notions are extensions (*t'ui* or *ta*), attention (*ssu*), and intelligent awareness (*chih*). Virtue is actualized by individuals when they learn to extend knowledge from one situation to other, similar ones. From a marketing standpoint, product and advertising managers should learn the appropriate ethical norms in their dealings with advertising agencies and other external consultants. For the attention concept, Mencias pithily commented, "If one attends, one gets it; if one does not, one does not." Thus, ethical training depends on the individual perceiving clearly, identifying corresponding actions, and responding only after careful reflection. Finally, intelligent awareness is expressed by the middle way between two extremes: "intelligence should guide our actions, but in harmony with [the] texture of the situation at hand, not in accordance [only] with a set of rules or procedures."[35]

Buddhist Ethical Imperatives

Trade and industry are viewed as comparatively recent developments in those nations where Buddhism is a prominent religious tradition. Nonetheless, the writings attributed to the Buddha address a number of issues that are relevant to marketers, particularly at the "macro" level.[36] Among these are the need to provide for basic needs (in the context of a simple lifestyle); the need for agricultural/rural development (as opposed to concentrating development efforts in urban areas); respect for the preservation of the resource endowment and beauty of nature; encouragement of private enterprise, self-reliance, and economic freedom; and the personal and social value of full employment with a living wage. (Certain business enterprises are also frowned on, such as those involving armaments, intoxicating drink, poisons, animal slaughter, gambling, and slavery.) There are five Buddhist principles that cannot be broken while working: (1) one cannot cause harm to another, (2) one may not cheat, (3) one may not lie, (4) one cannot promote intoxication, and (5) one cannot engage in sexual exploitation.

Hindu Ethics

The Hindu religion also contains directions for spiritual fulfillment. The Hindu scripture give insights into how to balance priorities to attain true success:

> Generating wealth (*artha*) is to be pursued within the larger priority of contributing to the well-being of society (*dharma*). Satisfying desires (*Kama*) is to be pursued within the larger priority of spiritual fulfillment (*moksha*). In accord with the wisdom of these spiritual teachings, we can see that business success naturally emphasizes contribution to society and spiritual fulfillment. When traditional measures of business success—shareholder return, market share, industry power, and so on—are subordinate to these higher priorities,

EXHIBIT 1-7   Axioms of Islamic Ethical Philosophy

Axiom	Definition	Relationship to Marketing Ethics	Similarities to Other Ethical Theories
Unity	Related to the concept of *tawhīd*. The political, economic, social, and religious aspects of man's life form a homogeneous whole, which is consistent from within, as well as integrated with the vast universe without. This is the vertical dimension of Islam.	Muslim business executives will not: • Discriminate among stakeholders on issues of race, color, sex or religion. • Be coerced into unethical practices.	Kantian/duty-based ethics, second formulation
Equilibrium	Related to the concept of `adl. A sense of balance among the various aspects of a man's life mentioned above in order to produce the best social order. This sense of balance is achieved through conscious purpose. This is the horizontal dimension of Islam.	• A balanced transaction is equitable and just. • Islam attempts to curb a business executive's property for covetousness and love for possession. • Will seek a moderate profit.	Virtue ethics Very similar to "ethic of the mean"
Free will	Man's ability to act without external coercion within the parameters of Allah's creation and as Allah's trustee on earth.	• Muslim executive has freedom to make a contract and either honor it or break it. • Muslims do choose a code of conduct (either ethical or unethical).	Social contract
Responsibility	Man's need to be accountable for his actions.	• Business executive bears ultimate moral responsibility for one's actions. • All obligations must be honored unless morally wrong.	Kantian/duty-based Universality
Benevolence	*Ihsān*, or an action that benefits persons other than those from whom the action proceeds without any obligation.	• Kindness is encouraged by Islam. • Responsibility to less fortunate. • Modest profit, debtors should have time to pay, return policies.	Virtue ethics Similar to empathy

Source: Adapted from Rafik Issa Beekun, *Islamic Business Ethics* (Herndon, Va.: International Institute of Islamic Thought, 1997).

wealth can be generated and desires can be satisfied while naturally promoting well-being rather than harm, service rather than greed, and an uplifted spirit rather than unscrupulous competition.[37]

A practical example comes from Isaac Tigret, the founder of Hard Rock Café. One of his objectives was to open an "absolutely classless" (aiming at all social classes) restaurant in London. While on a spiritual pilgrimage in India, he heard the saying "Love All, Serve All." To him, it embodied the ultimate goal of life: to love people and to serve from that place. That became the spiritual source of the company culture:

> All I did was put spirit and business together in that big mixing bowl and add love. I didn't care about anything but people . . . just cherish them, look after them, and be sensitive to them and their lives.[38]

OTHER THEORETICAL DEVELOPMENTS IN MARKETING ETHICS

Because of the difficulty of applying general theories and principles to specific case situations, a number of scholars have begun to investigate what particular factors account for ethical marketing decisions. In an effort to aid their investigations, some of these researchers have begun to formulate *models* that stipulate the factors contributing to ethical decisions.

The Moral Development Model

The concept of moral development is mostly derived from the work of educational psychologist Lawrence Kohlberg, who studied moral development in adolescents.[39] Kohlberg postulated that, over time, individuals develop moral systems that are increasingly complex, although there is no guarantee that any particular individual evolves beyond the initial and most fundamental stage of moral development. Essentially, he saw three broad levels of cognitive moral development:

1. *The preconventional stage:* Here, the abiding concern of the individual is to resolve moral situations, with the individual's own immediate interests and consequences firmly in mind. An individual at the preconventional level gives strong weight to external rewards and punishments. Normally, this stage includes a strong emphasis on literal obedience to rules and authority because of the penalties attached to deviation.

2. *The conventional stage:* Individuals at the conventional stage have progressed to a level where their ethical decision-making mode takes into consideration the expectations of significant reference groups and society at large. This mostly reflects what we have come to term *enlightened self-interest,* that is, a recognition of the longer-term and indirect effects of actions that may injure others or otherwise depart from social norms. What constitutes moral propriety follows a concern for others but is still influenced most directly by explicit, especially organizational, rules. Observance of rules is often tempered by keeping loyalties and doing one's duty to society.

3. ***The principled stage:***   This is the highest level of moral development. Individuals who reach this level solve their ethical problems in a manner that goes beyond the norms and laws applicable to a specific situation. Proper conduct certainly includes upholding the basic rights, values, and legal contracts of society, but beyond that, such individuals seem to subscribe to universal ethical principles that they believe all members of society should follow in similar situations. It is significant that principled actors are typically less bound by procedural rules when circumstances call for a response that may, when rules and principles conflict, violate those rules.

The moral development model implies that the ethical sophistication of managers can increase over time with maturity and experience. The major difference among the various stages of moral development is that, as managers advance to higher levels of moral development, they are able to take more factors into consideration, especially those that go beyond personal self-interest. Two significant implications of the moral development model are the following:

1.   Some managers are less sophisticated than others in terms of the considerations they bring to bear on a decision with potentially moral consequences. Some managers still operate at the most basic level, almost totally from the standpoint of egoistic self-interest.
2.   Interventions such as training programs, particularly in combination with organizational sanctions (related to continuing employment, compensation, and advancement opportunities), can be brought to bear that may compel managers toward higher levels of moral development—assuming that this is a goal seen to be in the company's interest.

This model has spawned significant academic and applied research. Among the most pertinent to marketing managers and students is the work of Narváez and Rest.[40] They have proposed a model that leads to "acting morally." It has four components:

Moral Characteristic	Ability	Most Important Virtue
Moral sensitivity	To interpret the situation in terms of how one's actions affect the welfare of others	Empathy
Moral judgment	To formulate what a moral course of action would be; to identify the moral ideal in a specific situation	Fairness Social responsibility
Moral motivation	To select among competing value outcomes of ideals, the one to act on; deciding whether to try to fulfill one's moral ideal	Altruism Integrity
Implementation	To execute and implement what one intends to do	Persistence Character

For an illustration of characters in fiction, politics, and movies that are strong and weak in these components, see Exhibit 1-8. Marketing managers should strive to be

**EXHIBIT 1-8 Real and Fictional Characters
That Represent the Four Components of Moral Action**

Component	Strong in Component	Weak in Component
Moral sensitivity	Mother Teresa Ralph Nader Bill Moyers The Tin Man (*Wizard of Oz*)	Archie Bunker Spock Bart Simpson
Moral judgment	King Solomon The Scarecrow (*Wizard of Oz*)	Snow White Homer Simpson Lucy (*I Love Lucy*)
Moral motivation	The biblical Paul Don Quixote Eleanor Roosevelt	Stalin Saddam Hussein Osama bin Laden Mr. Burns (*Simpsons*) Scrooge
Implementation	Moses Hercules John Wayne characters Dirty Harry Scarlett O'Hara	Many Woody Allen characters Garfield Cathy

Source: Partially adapted from D. Narváez and J. Rest, "The Four Components of Acting Morally," in *Moral Development: An Introduction*, ed. W. M. Kurtines and J. L Gewirtz (Boston: Allyn and Bacon, 1995), 385–99.

strong in each but may need mentors, superiors, and even subordinates to support them on dimensions where they are not as strong.

Ethical Behavior in Marketing

Against the background of a growing literature in marketing ethics devoted mostly to the application of teleological, deontological, and other normative models to marketing problems, Shelby Hunt and Scott Vitell proposed a behavioral or positive model of ethical behavior that has been extensively tested.[41] This complex model takes into account, in sequence, (1) such environmental factors as the industry and organizational environment; (2) the recognition of an ethical problem, optional solutions to the problem, and the likely consequences of the various solutions and their desirability and probability; (3) deontological norms that might "trump" any of the solution alternatives; (4) an ethical judgment based on these steps; (5) the formation of intentions; and (6) actual behavior. The separation of these components recognizes the prospect that, while the components are connected, they are distinct and, for example, an ethical judgment may still be followed by an unethical act. This model also provided for experiential feedback or learning such that the consequences of an act might inform future assessments and actions.

IDEAS FOR ETHICAL MARKETING

The call to apply a specific ethical theory to a particular marketing situation is easier given than implemented. Philosophers who study moral theory and reasoning regularly argue among themselves about what constitutes the *best* way to analyze and solve ethical issues. Once again, ethics is not an easy area to understand or control. While ethical theory for its own sake is important, theory in action is what makes for ethical marketing practice. Thus, marketing managers can vitalize ethical reasoning in their organizations by the following:

1. Identify the issues most likely to lead to moral or ethical conflict in your firm.
2. Develop a list of questions that reflect various ethical theories that can aid managers in determining whether a particular contemplated action or decision is unethical.
3. Recognize that there are sometimes conflicts among the various ethical principles that imply different (sometimes contradictory) decisions. Moreover, realize that these conflicts increase as the number of relevant stakeholders in a decision increases.

These points can be elaborated on:

First, a sequence of questions to improve ethical reasoning should be asked. One approach to deal more normatively with ethical issues is to require managers to proceed through a sequence of questions that tests whether an action they are contemplating is ethical or has possible ethical consequences. A battery of such questions might include the following:

Question 1 (the legal test):   Does the contemplated action violate the law?

Question 2 (the duties test):   Is this action contrary to widely accepted moral obligations? Such moral obligations might include *duties of fidelity,* such as the responsibility to remain faithful to contracts, to keep promises, and to tell the truth; *duties of gratitude,* which means that special obligations exist between relatives, friends, partners, cohorts, and employees; *duties of justice,* which basically have to do with obligations to distribute rewards based on merit; *duties of nonmaleficence,* which consist of duties not to harm others; and *duties of beneficence,* which rest on the notion that actions should be taken that improve the situation of others—if this can be readily accomplished.

Question 3 (the special obligations test):   Does the proposed action violate any other special obligations that stem from this type of marketing organization? (For example, the special duty of pharmaceutical firms to provide safe products, the special obligation of toy manufacturers to care for the safety of children, and the inherent duty of distillers to promote responsible drinking are all special obligations of this sort.)

Question 4 (the motives test):   Is the *intent* of the contemplated action harmful?

Question 5 (the consequences test):   Is it likely that any *major* damages to people or organizations will result from the contemplated action?

Question 6 (the virtues test):   Does this action enhance the ideal of a moral community, and is it consonant with what the marketing organization wants to be?

> ***Question 7 (the rights test)***:   Does the contemplated action infringe on property rights, privacy rights, or the rights of the consumer (the right to information, the right to be heard, the right to choice, and the right to remedy)?
>
> ***Question 8 (the justice test)***:   Does the proposed action leave another person or group less well off? Is this person or group already a member of a relatively underprivileged class?

These questions need not be pursued in lockstep fashion. If none of the questions uncover any potential conflicts, clearly the action being contemplated is quite likely to be ethical. However, if the sequence of queries does produce a conflict, this does not necessarily mean that the action being proposed is unethical per se. Unusual intervening factors may be present that would still allow the action to ethically go forward. For example, suppose it is determined that the contemplated action is a violation of the law. Perhaps the law is unjust and thus that there could be a moral impetus for an organization to transgress the law. Some companies follow a decision-making model somewhat similar to this one. Exhibit 1-9 shows the ethical decision model that bp (British Petroleum) expects employees to follow in its far-flung operation. For example, bp has acquired Amoco and ARCO in the United States along with several other oil companies and Russian oil fields. The model combines both rights and virtues in its commitments statement as well as a number of the same ethical questions that were listed previously.

Second, the stakeholder concept should be linked to marketing ethics. As the previous sections showed, several comprehensive theories can be utilized to guide the reasoning of managers as they try to reach moral conclusions. The difficulty, of course, is applying these theories to specific marketing situations and then resolving conflicts among principles. Sometimes, these conflicts will take the form of two competing duties owed to different stakeholder groups. For example, there is a fiduciary responsibility on the part of managers to render to stockholders a fair return. At times, this might involve taking steps that are clearly counterproductive to another stakeholder group, such as employees. This may occur in the case of a plant closing. The judgmental difficulty, then, is deciding which of the two duties takes precedence. Utilitarianism (and the cost-benefit analysis it often implies) is an extremely useful tool if one looks at a problem only from the standpoint of one or two stakeholder groups. However, when multiple stakeholders are introduced into the situation, the use of consequence-based theories is complicated considerably. In different instances, we would expect marketing managers to draw from various and multiple ethical theories.

Similarly, duty-based or virtue ethics approaches are also complex. There are often contradictory duties, such as in Scenario 2, where management has the right to point out their truthful strategic competitive advantage (i.e., benefits of weight-loss drug) while at the same time perhaps violating the duty not to unfairly manipulate the receivers of their promotional messages by using incomplete information. Frequently, however, most conflicts between stakeholders can be resolved through compromise or by broadening how the problem is framed. The existence of competing claims suggests that management must face up to the challenge of creating new alternatives that result in a better balance of obligations.

EXHIBIT 1-9 BP's Decision Model

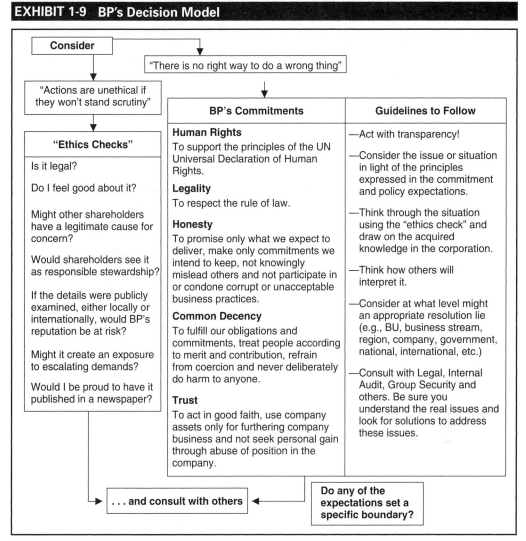

Source: BP, Ethical Conduct Policy: Guidelines on Business Conduct, 2000, 6–7.

In the end, weighing the concerns of multiple stakeholder groups becomes the essence of appropriate ethical decision making. Multiple claims on the organization are at the root of the complexity of such decision making. The stakeholder concept (and the multiple responsibilities it implies) provides the necessity for sensitizing managers to ethical implications and teaching them to reason from the standpoint of moral theory. In the final analysis, ethics still requires considerable prudential judgment that comes from the intuition of the marketing manager (grounded, it is hoped, in virtue ethics), but it is tempered by a knowledge of ethical theory and standards.

Notes

From *Ethical Marketing* (Upper Saddle River, N.J.: Prentice Hall, 2005), 1–47. Reprinted with permission.

1. Gerry Khermouch and Jeff Green, "Buzz Marketing," *BusinessWeek,* July 30, 2001, 50–56.

2. Chris Adams, "Xenical Ads Avoid Listing Unpleasant Side Effects," *Wall Street Journal,* April 3, 2001, B1, B6. For a follow-up, see Vanessa Fuhrman, "Roche Attempts to Beef Up Sales of Diet-Drug Xenical," *Wall Street Journal,* February 21, 2002, B3.

3. Patrick E. Murphy, *Eighty Exemplary Ethics Statements* (Notre Dame, Ind.: University of Notre Dame Press, 1998), 106–7.

4. Thomas A. Klein and Robert W. Nason, "Marketing and Development: Macromarketing Perspectives," in *Handbook of Society and Marketing,* ed. Paul N. Bloom and Gregory T. Gundlach (Thousand Oaks, Calif.: Sage, 2001), 263–97.

5. Robert C. Solomon and Fernando Flores, *Building Trust in Business, Politics, Relationships, and Life* (New York: Oxford University Press, 2001), 40–43.

6. James M. Carman and Luis V. Dominguez, "Organizational Transformations in Transition Economies: Hypotheses," *Journal of Macromarketing* 21, no. 2 (December 2001): 164–80.

7. One of the most persistent twentieth-century critics of the marketing system was John Kenneth Galbraith; his influential books were *The Affluent Society* (New York: Houghton Mifflin, 1958) and *The New Industrial State* (New York: Houghton Mifflin, 1967).

8. Edward R. Freeman, *Strategic Management: A Stakeholder Approach* (Boston: Pitman, 1984), 46. See also Kenneth E. Goodpaster, "Business Ethics and Stakeholder Analysis," *Business Ethics Quarterly* 1, no. 1 (January 1991): 53–73.

9. Archie B. Carroll and Ann K. Buchholtz, *Business and Society: Ethics and Stakeholder Management,* 5th ed. (Cincinnati: South-Western, 2003). For a similar approach to classifying stakeholders, see John A. Weber,

"Integrity in Selling," Special session, American Marketing Association Summer Educators' Conference (August 18, 2003).

10. Lawrence G. Foster, *Robert Wood Johnson: The Gentleman Rebel* (State College, Pa.: Lillian Press, 1999).

11. Robert C. Solomon, *The New World of Business: Ethics and Free Enterprise in the Global 1990s* (Lanham, Md.: Rowman & Littlefield, 1994).

12. See *The Shell Report,* www.shell.com (accessed December 31, 2003).

13. Patricia H. Werhane, *Moral Imagination and Management Decision Making* (New York: Oxford University Press, 1999).

14. Patrick E. Murphy, "Corporate Ethics Statements: An Update," in *Global Codes of Conduct: An Idea Whose Time Has Come,* ed. O. Williams (Notre Dame, Ind.: University of Notre Dame Press, 2000), 295–304.

15. James Rachels, "The Challenge of Cultural Relativism," in *Moral Relativism,* ed. P. K. Moser and T. L. Carson (New York: Oxford University Press, 2001), 53–65; Norman Bowie, "Relativism, Cultural and Moral," in *Encyclopedic Dictionary of Business Ethics,* ed. P. H. Werhane and R. E. Freeman (Malden, Mass.: Blackwell, 1997), 551–55.

16. Joseph Des Jardins, *An Introduction to Business Ethics* (New York: McGraw-Hill, 2003), 18–19.

17. Norman E. Bowie, "Challenging the Egoistic Paradigm," *Business Ethics Quarterly* 1, no. 1 (January 1991): 1–21.

18. Jeremy Bentham, *An Introduction to the Principles of Morals and Legislation* (New York: Hafner, 1984); John Stuart Mill, *Utilitarianism* (Indianapolis: Hackett, 1979).

19. Immanuel Kant, *Grounding for the Metaphysics of Morals* (Indianapolis: Hackett, 1981). [Originally published in 1785]

20. Norman E. Bowie, "A Kantian Approach to Business Ethics," in *A Companion to Business Ethics,* ed. R. E. Fredrick (Malden,

Mass.: Blackwell, 1999), 3–16; see also Norman E. Bowie, *Business Ethics: A Kantian Perspective* (Malden, Mass.: Blackwell, 1999).

21. Thomas Donaldson and Thomas W. Dunfee, *Ties That Bind: A Social Contracts Approach to Business Ethics* (Boston: Harvard Business School Press, 1999).

22. Thomas W. Dunfee, "Business and Ethics," in *Modern Business Law and the Regulatory Environment* (New York: McGraw-Hill, 1996), 137–160.

23. John Rawls, *A Theory of Justice* (Cambridge, Mass.: Harvard University Press, 1971).

24. John Paul II, "Centesimus Annus," *Origins* 21, no. 1 (May 16, 1991): 1, 3–24.

25. Alasdair MacIntyre, *After Virtue*, 2nd ed. (Notre Dame, Ind.: University of Notre Dame Press, 1984).

26. Aristotle, *Nicomachean Ethics* (New York: Macmillan, 1962).

27. Aristotle, *Ethics* (London: Penguin, 1976), 94.

28. Patrick E. Murphy, "Character and Virtue Ethics in International Marketing: An Agenda for Managers, Researchers and Educators," *Journal of Business Ethics* 18, no. 1 (1999): 107–24.

29. American Catholic Bishops, "Economic Justice for All: Catholic Social Teaching and the U.S. Economy," *Origins* 16, no. 4 (November 27, 1986): 409–55.

30. A more thorough examination of the marketing implications of the U.S. Bishops' economic letter may be found in Thomas A. Klein, "Prophets and Profits: Macromarketing Implications of the 'Pastoral Letter on Catholic Social Teaching and the U.S. Economy,'" *Journal of Macromarketing* 7, no. 1 (fall 1987): 59–77. For more information on Catholic social thought and business, see H. J. Alford and M. J. Naughton, *Managing as if Faith Mattered* (Notre Dame, Ind.: University of Notre Dame Press, 2001).

31. See, e.g., Meir Tamari, *In the Marketplace: Jewish Business Ethics* (Southfield, Mich.: Targum Press, 1991); Moses L. Pava, "The Substance of Jewish Business Ethics," *Journal of Business Ethics* 17, no. 6 (1998): 603–17; David Vogel, "How Green Is Judaism?—Exploring Jewish Environmental Ethics," *Business Ethics Quarterly* 11, no. 2 (April 2001): 349–63; and Hershey H. Friedman, "The Impact of Jewish Values on Marketing and Business Practices," *Journal of Macromarketing* 21, no. 1 (June 2001): 74–80.

32. Matthew W. Seeger and Robert R. Ulmer, "Virtuous Responses to Organizational Crisis: Aaron Feuerstein and Milt Cole," *Journal of Business Ethics* 31, no. 8 (2001): 369–76.

33. Mohammad Saeed, Zafar U. Ahmed, and Syeda-Masooda Mukhtar, "International Marketing Ethics from an Islamic Perspective: A Value-Maximization Approach," *Journal of Business Ethics* 32, no. 2 (2001): 127–42; see also Rafik Issa Beekun, *Islamic Business Ethics* (Herndon, Va.: International Institute of Islamic Thought, 1997).

34. Daryl Koehn, "Confucian Trustworthiness and the Practice of Business in China," *Business Ethics Quarterly* 11, no. 3 (July 2001): 415–29.

35. Francisco J. Varela, *Ethical Know-How: Action, Wisdom, and Cognition* (Stanford, Calif.: Stanford University Press, 1999).

36. Victor Wee, "Buddhist Approach to Economic Development," in *Buddhist Perspective in the Face of the Third Millennium*, Proceedings of the Year 2000 Global Conference on Buddhism (Buddhist Fellowship, 2001); see also Bodhipaksa, "Reinventing the Wheel: A Buddhist Approach to Ethical Work" in *Spiritual Goods: Faith Traditions and the Practice of Business*, ed. Stewart W. Herman with A. G. Schaefer (Bowling Green, Ohio: Philosophy Documentation Center, 2001), 33–54.

37. Debra Miller and William Miller, "Defining Business Success," www.spirituality. indiatimes.com/articleshow/37572573.cms (accessed December 22, 2003).

38. Miller and Miller, "Defining Business Success."

39. L. Kohlberg, "Stage and Sequence: The Cognitive Development Approach to

Socialization," in *Handbook of Socialization Theory and Research,* ed. D. A. Goslin (Chicago: Rand McNally, 1969), 347–480; Kohlberg's approach has been challenged by Carol Gilligan, *In a Different Voice: Psychological Theory and Women's Development* (Cambridge, Mass.: Harvard University Press, 1993).

40. D. Narváez and J. Rest, "The Four Components of Acting Morally," in *Moral Development: An Introduction,* ed. W. M. Kurtines and J. L. Gewirtz (Boston: Allyn and Bacon, 1995), 385–99.

41. Shelby D. Hunt and Scott Vitell, "A General Theory of Marketing Ethics," *Journal of Macromarketing* 6, no. 1 (spring 1986): 5–16; Shelby D. Hunt and Scott Vitell, "The General Theory of Marketing Ethics: A Retrospective and Revision," in *Ethics in Marketing,* ed. N. Craig Smith and John A. Quelch (Burr Ridge, Ill.: Irwin, 1993), 775–84; S. J. Vitell, G. P. Paolilla, and J. L. Thomas, "The Perceived Role of Ethics and Social Responsibility: A Study of Marketing Professionals," *Business Ethics Quarterly* 13, no. 1 (January 2003): 63–86.

CHAPTER

Contemporary Readings in Marketing Ethics

CONTEMPT OF CONSUMER: IT'S A REAL CRIME[1]

Seth Godin

The Fuller Brush Man[2] knew what he was doing. In the old days, Fuller's door-to-door salesmen learned a basic rule: After you ring the bell, take a step or two backward. That way, the woman of the house won't feel intimidated opening the door for a stranger.

It wasn't just a tactic, though. It was a strategy—one designed to help the company grow by treating people with respect, in contrast to rival salesmen who were taught to jam a foot in the door.

Imagine the Fuller Brush Man trying to make a living today as a telemarketer or a spammer or any of the high-pressure salespeople who jam their electronic feet in people's doors. He'd last about three minutes. He's not selfish enough, not eager enough to steal the customer's time. It's a shame, but in the battle to make our businesses grow, we've forgotten how to respect the people who pay our bills.

We're making those people—our customers—angry. In our race to make as much money as possible (as fast as possible), we take time and resources and esteem and careers and use them up as fast as we can. We've lost sight of what it means to treat customers with respect. We also disrespect our shareholders, our employees, and our government—but it's all part of the same problem.

And we're running out of time to do something about it. Ironically, the obsolete tactics of the Fuller Brush Man may be exactly what we need.

The amazing thing is that respect doesn't cost anything. Taking two steps back after you ring the bell isn't just free, it's profitable. Instead of spamming the globe, market to people who want to hear from you. It's not just good manners, it's profitable.

---

[1]*Fast Company*, September 2003, p. 114. Reprinted with permission.
[2]Between 1906 and 1956, it was estimated that Fuller representatives (the "Fuller Brush Men") called on nearly nine out of every ten American homes, selling more than $8 million dollars worth of cleaning products. Fuller Brush became a leader in the home care industry because of its relentless focus on product quality and customer service.

Everyone wants to be treated with respect—all the time. In fact, when we treat people with respect, they're more likely to do what we want.

Some will tell you that treating people with respect is just an old-fashioned notion. Business ethics may be an oxymoron—is respectful marketing the same? Don't we need to call people at home during dinner or trick them with fine print in order to make a profit?

In fact, I believe that the only way to make a long-term profit is by respecting people. There's growing evidence that the old, shortsighted ways of making a profit are getting less effective. People are fending off marketing assaults with TiVo and Telezappers. More than 12 people a second signed up for the Federal Trade Commission's Do Not Call list on its first day. Consumers axe voting with their pocketbooks, choosing to visit the retailers that treat them with respect, not avarice.

Some marketers may understand how strip-mining consumer trust is costing them, but most don't want to take two steps back to the good old days. Instead, they're fighting the wrong fights. They're getting ready to sue TiVo, because the device makes it too easy to skip commercials. They're faking the headers on the spam that they send out to get past filters. They're lobbying Congress to stop the Do Not Call list.

But when a business spams, it has made its lack of respect clear. When an airline puts the "gotcha" into the fine print of a full-page ad, it's disrespecting consumers' intelligence. Running a business that can survive only by deception and disrespect is not our right—our right is to realize our dead-end path and pick a better, more respectful business.

I believe that it's all about to come crashing down on slash-and-burn marketers. Consumers (especially the business-to-business buyers) are getting ever smarter, cagier, and more sophisticated. They won't sit quietly as marketers steal their time and attention and money. Ask yourself a simple question: If all of our customers were well-informed, would we do better—or worse? For many companies, the answer is grim. McDonald's was stung when it was caught slipping beef flavoring into its supposedly all-vegetable french fries. And Kmart went bankrupt for committing contempt of consumer—telling its shoppers, "Hey, it's cheap. What do you expect?"

Karl Marx (probably being quoted for the first time ever in *Fast Company*) asked a simple question. "Who benefits?" It is, I think, the key question. Companies that work to benefit their customers will have no trouble treating the newly picky consumer with respect. It's a natural by-product for marketers who aim to serve. Those who work to trick and coerce their customers, on the other hand, have everything to lose and very little to gain.

1. Is respecting consumers an ethical issue? Why or why not?
2. Can you give an example of where a marketer showed "respect" for you?
3. How does respect relate to Chapter 1? (Hint: virtue ethics and Exhibit 1-3).

KID NABBING[1]

Melanie Wells

Caitlin Jones is Hollywood's kind of pitch gal. Several months ago the 16-year-old received an e-mail announcing DreamWorks SKG's new teen flick, *Win A Date With Tad Hamilton!*, and was asked to help the studio pick the movie's logo. A few weeks later when she went to a movie theater, she was thrilled to see a trailer for the film and discover that they'd picked the logo she liked. "Oh, my God," she told a friend who was sitting next to her, "I voted for that logo!" She beamed. "So they do listen. It does matter."

Jones, a junior at St. Joseph Hill Academy in Staten Island, N.Y., couldn't wait to spread the word. "I told a bunch of friends at school," she recalls. "I told my next door neighbor. I told well over 10 or 20 people." And, of course, she plans to see the film, taking a handful of pals with her.

Gina Lavagna was tapped through snail mail. After receiving a $2 minidisc for Sony's Net MD and six $10-off coupons, she rushed four of her chums to a mall near her home in Carlstadt, N.J., to show them the digital music player, which sells for $99 and up. "I've probably told 20 people about it," she says, adding, "At least 10 are extremely interested in getting one." Her parents got her one for Christmas.

Madison Avenue was once known for men in gray flannel suits. Today some of its most credible foot soldiers wear T-shirts and sneakers. They are 280,000 strong, ages 13 to 19, all of them enlisted by an arm of Procter & Gamble called Tremor. Their mission is to help companies plant information about their brands in living rooms, schools and other crevices that are difficult for corporate America to infiltrate. These kids deliver endorsements in school cafeterias, at sleepovers, by cell phone and by e-mail. They are being tapped to talk up just about everything, from movies to milk and motor oil—and they do it for free.

Manipulation? To some extent. Some kids aren't even aware that they're participating in a word-of-mouth marketing effort on an unprecedented scale. Roughly 1% of the U.S. teen population is involved.

They are selected and organized by P&G, which has kept many details about Tremor, created in 2001, under wraps until now. It is a remarkable little business, partly because P&G helped pioneer traditional TV advertising—soap operas were sponsored by Tide—and partly because it has unleashed Tremor's forces on brands it doesn't make including AOL, Coca-Cola, Kraft Foods and Toyota Motor. (A third of Tremor's activities are devoted to P&G products—Pantene shampoo, CoverGirl cosmetics and Pringles potato chips among them.) It's taken two years to build a national network. The kids, natural talkers, do the work without pay, not counting the coupons, product samples and the thrill of being something of an "insider." Without being asked, Lavagna, the New Jersey teen, hosted a gathering last year so her gal pals could try P&G beauty products, including Clairol Herbal Essences Fruit Fusions Shampoo and Noxzema face wash.

The effort grows out of a profound dissatisfaction among advertisers with conventional media, particularly network TV. Audiences are fragmented, and ever more

[1] *Forbes*, February 2, 2004, pp. 84–88. Reprinted with permission.

viewers are using devices like TiVo to zap commercials. Teens, in particular, are maddeningly difficult to reach and influence through advertising, even though they are a consumer powerhouse that will spend $175 billion on products this year. When they do catch TV commercials or print ads, these jaded consumers often ignore the marketing message. Hence the emphasis on friendly chatter among peers to deliver targeted messages. "The mass-marketing model is dead," says James Stengel, P&G's global marketing officer. "This is the future."

He's getting a little ahead of the story; Tremor's revenues this year might top $12 million, a drop in the $266 billion U.S. advertising market. But P&G seems to be onto something. Valvoline, the motor products unit of Ashland, is using Tremor as part of its marketing push for SynPower premium oil. Spending around $1 million—P&G charges that and more for a national campaign—Valvoline will focus on guys and gals who are 16-plus, or 65% of the Tremor empire. "This generation is much more influenced by peer behavior than baby boomers were," says Walter Solomon, senior vice president at Valvoline. "If we can make an impression, it will have tremendous long-term effect."

P&G used Tremor to make a sensitive point about Head & Shoulders it couldn't have broached in mainstream ads: that the dandruff shampoo kills the fungus that causes dandruff. "That's a message that won't survive in the mass market," says Ted W. Woehrle, Tremor's chief executive. "But it's perfectly appropriate to give it to 1% of teen boys and let them talk about it."

Some of this is old wine in new bottles. Word-of-mouth marketing, after all, predates even the apostles. It explains a large part of the rapid diffusion of hybrid corn seed among Iowa farmers from 1928 to 1941. Distillers and pharmaceutical companies have long understood the usefulness of bartenders and physicians. The Internet has been an ideal medium for the proliferation of promotional blather, especially among nonexperts. Word of mouth helped make *My Big Fat Greek Wedding* a much bigger hit than dozens of heavily advertised films.

Focus groups aren't exactly new, either; P&G has lived by them for decades. But Tremor combines the virtues of both—testing the likely acceptance of products and sending out thousands of eager missionaries to secure converts—on an epic scale. A lot is hit-or-miss. While P&G screens the kids it taps, it doesn't coach them beyond encouraging them to feel free to talk to friends; it does follow up with random phone interviews to monitor changes in brand awareness and image. Other, smaller companies keep tighter tabs on their acolytes. [See Cross-Pollinators, p. 48.]

Sony Electronics, which stopped promoting Net MD in print ads and radio spots late last year in favor of Tremor, is still tallying the results of the campaign. The International Dairy Foods Association is a believer. Last spring P&G worked with association member Shamrock Farms of Phoenix on its launch of a new chocolate-malt-flavored milk. The dairy monitored sales of the new product in Phoenix and Tucson where the plan and expenditures were the same, with one exception: In Phoenix, 2,100 Tremorites received product information, coupons and stickers. After 23 weeks, Shamrock says, sales of the drink were 18% higher in Phoenix than in Tucson. Surprisingly, overall milk sales rose, too, in Phoenix—4%. Coupon redemption was an impressive 21%, the highest the dairy has ever seen, says Sandy K. Kelly, marketing chief at Shamrock. "The remarkable thing about the multiplier effect is that so few kids can affect the attitude of so many," says Thomas Nagle Jr., vice president of marketing for the dairy association, the group behind the "Got Milk?" ads.

Tremor will launch perhaps 20 U.S. campaigns this year, up from 15 in 2003. Woehrle says it will turn a profit by the end of the fiscal year, June 30. Faster expansion doesn't make sense because P&G recognizes that its stealth sales force can get bored too easily. "Sometimes it's a hassle if you get more than one e-mail, and they want you to fill things out," says Jill Markowitz, 18, a freshman at New York University, who reports she has received some 30 solicitations.

Who gets tapped? Tremor looks for kids with a wide social circle and a gift of gab. Using e-mail invitations and Web banner ads, the company trolls for members and offers them a chance to register to win a free product, like a DVD player. To register, kids fill out a questionnaire, which asks them, among other things, to report how many friends, family members and acquaintances they communicate with every day. (Tremorites have an average 170 names on their buddy lists; a typical teen has 30.) Only the most gregarious prospects, about 10% of respondents, are invited to join the network, which is billed as a way for kids to influence companies and find out about cool new products before their friends do. To help keep them interested, P&G sends them exclusive music mixes and other trinkets, like shampoo and cheap watches. The Valvoline participants just get a few car-care tips. (Like this: For a lint-free shine, use a cloth diaper.)

The network includes kids like Glendan Lawler, a freshman at UC, Berkeley, who says he talks to everyone, even strangers on the bus. He has been tapped for DreamWorks and Coke. "My friends will usually agree with me. They say, 'That sounds good; I'll look into it.'" Nicholas Smith, another Berkeley freshman, got introduced to the Toyota Matrix through Tremor. "I'd never seen a car with that kind of sound system," he says. "I'd definitely consider buying one." Jared McCullough of Newnan, Ga., acted on his enthusiasm. The high school senior bought a Tombstone Pizza and passed out Tremor coupons for the frozen Kraft product.

Information can spread like the flu in small towns. There are nine Tremor recruits in Glendive, Mont., and these aren't necessarily the coolest kids in school. That's one reason P&G likes them. Why? The hipsters who are the first to try something new don't want everyone copying them. "A lot of companies, including our own, chased early adopters for a long time, frankly, with mixed business results," says Steve J. Knox, Tremor's vice president of business development. "They adopt a product early in its life cycle, but that doesn't mean they talk about it."

What makes kids want to discuss company products? "It's cool to know about stuff before other people," says Staten Islander Jones. Last May CoverGirl sent a group of gals a booklet of makeup tips in a thin round tin with some $1-off coupons. Nothing fancy, but CoverGirl wanted to see if it would give its lipstick, mascara and foundation a boost in Hartford, Conn., Jacksonville, Fla., and Norfolk, Va. It did. Claimed purchases, based on P&G interviews with teens before and after the program, rose 10% among teens in those cities.

"Teens are one of the most disempowered groups out there," says Tremor's Knox. "They are filled with great ideas, but they don't think anyone listens to them."

Coca-Cola Co., for one, does. In a recent campaign to boost sagging sales of Vanilla Coke, it asked Tremor kids for ideas of "smooth and intriguing" messages for cans it is rolling out this summer. The gimmick: As it warms in a drinker's hand, a heat-sensitive can might display such sayings as, "You are what you ride" and "Fashion is required. Taste is acquired." "That's a great thing, to talk about tomorrow at lunch," says Andrew Schrijver, a freshman at Poly Prep Country Day School in Brooklyn, N.Y., one of 21,000 Tremor members in the New York metropolitan area.

George Silverman, author of *The Secrets of Word-of-Mouth Marketing* and an Orangeburg, N.Y., consultant, offers a caution: "It's like playing with fire: It can be a positive force when harnessed for the good, but fires are very destructive when they are out of control. If word-of-mouth goes against you, you're sunk." Says David Godes, a business professor at Harvard: "If it gets too pervasive, there could be a consumer backlash. It needs to stay on the periphery."

Another risk: Some kids may like to talk, but not to push products on their friends. Laura Skladzinski, a freshman at NYU, admits she keeps goodies and coupons to herself when she likes them and passes them on when she's not crazy about them. Her friend Jill Markowitz conceded she feels awkward hawking products. When she handed out some samples of Clairol Herbal Essences Shampoo to pals last year, "I felt a little weird."

Tremor executives admit they need to learn more about people in the network. There have been mismatches of products and pitchfolk. In May 2002 a feminine care "learner's kit" by Tampax went out to Tremor teen girls who were too old for such hand-holding; the effort fell flat. Fifteen-year-old Andrew Schrijver recently got the come-on from Valvoline—even though he doesn't have a learner's permit. His dad, Robert, is upset that Tremor portrays itself as a forum for opinion sharing when it's really trying to hawk products: "If they're going to try to sell things to kids, they need to make it explicit that this is a selling channel."

P&G can't afford to alienate parents. The $43 billion (fiscal 2003 sales) packaged-goods giant is starting to build a new network of equal or greater size, one that will focus on moms—a much bigger and more affluent target than teens—who will be asked to help flog Tide, Pampers and Bounty paper towels, among other brands. Says Stengel, P&G's marketing chief: "The possibilities are almost limitless."

Cross-Pollinators

Christopher Harris has spent 30 hours doling out 25 copies of *Ode*, a New Age publication for yoga buffs and soy lovers, in recent months. Nearly every day Harris, 34, dutifully files an online report to a company in Boston called BzzAgent coach in Boston immediately responded. "Keep up the great job!"

BzzAgent's community of 20,000 adult hypesters (all nonpaid) is much smaller than P&G's loose teen group, but it is a more closely monitored bunch. While Tremor members receive few marching orders, "buzz agents" get a word-of-mouth primer when they volunteer to pitch products. They also get copious personalized feedback about their activities for Anheuser-Busch, Estée Lauder and publisher Penguin Group. "We feel like people need to understand how powerful their voice really is," says BzzAgent Founder Dave L. Balter, 32. "We also want to steer and control what happens in the marketplace."

"When Joe [the bike messenger] came in today, I asked him: 'Do you like your job?' And of course he hated it!" reports one of 3,300 folks who recently signed up to plug Monster Networking, an online schmoozefest. "It's like Match.com for your career!" the 27-year-old Philadelphian told the hapless messenger. "There is nothing but good that can come of checking it out."

The give-and-take gives BzzAgent useful information. It knows, for instance, that people who like a book will have three 5- to-7-minute conversations about it over a 12-week period. It knows agents' incomes, broadband usage, and brand preferences for jeans, beer and more. In a recent 12-week campaign for Rock Bottom Restaurant & Brewery, sales of the chain's 100,000-strong frequent-diner program grew by $1.2 million above the baseline after 400 members became buzz agents.

BzzAgent charges clients according to the number of agents used and the length of a campaign. An eight-week effort with 1,000 agents costs $85,000. Balter professes to be amazed at how willing people are to be agents: "I would never do this, but I'm not everybody."

1. What marketing technique mentioned at the beginning of Chapter 1 is being used by P&G and other companies? Explain.
2. Is using teenagers as product spokespersons ethical? Why or why not?

DANGEROUS TERRAIN[1]

John J. Fialka

MORGANTOWN, W.Va.—The last time Jessica Adams's mother saw her alive, she was spread-eagle on a gravel embankment along a rural road here. Jessica looked like she was sleeping, but her neck was broken. By the time she arrived at the hospital, she was dead. Jessica, a petite 13-year-old, and another girl, age 14, had borrowed an adult-size all-terrain vehicle and sped off down a paved road to a nearby Boy Scout camp. Witnesses saw Jessica sitting behind the driver. Police say she died after the ATV veered out of control, climbed a 5-foot embankment and hit a tree.

Sales of ATVs—the four-wheel, motorcycle-like vehicles made to navigate rough terrain at speeds as high as 70 mph—climbed 89% between 1997 and 2002. In 2002, the latest year for which figures are available, manufacturers say they sold 825,000 ATVs in the U.S., exceeding sales of small pickup trucks. Kawasaki Motors Corp., Honda Motor Co., Arctic Cat Inc., Polaris Industries Inc., Yamaha Motor Corp. and other ATV makers that previously focused on selling snowmobiles say they've found a juicier market in ATVs.

But as ATV sales have expanded to more than $3 billion a year, so have deaths and injuries, particularly among children. According to the federal Consumer Product Safety Commission, Jessica was one of 357 people to die in ATV crashes in 2002, up 67% from 1997. Serious injuries more than doubled in the same period, with 113,900 riders hurt in 2002.

Since 1992, a third of the injured have been under 16, and children under 12 have accounted for 14% of deaths. ATV injuries are 12 times as likely to be fatal to children as bicycle accidents, says the National Safe Kids Campaign, a nonprofit that tracks childhood deaths.

Judging the relative danger of ATVs is tricky. There were more deaths and injuries on ATVs than on snowmobiles or personal watercraft in 2002. ATV use results in more injuries per vehicle than cars, though there are more deaths per vehicle in cars. A more meaningful measure might be deaths and injuries per mile traveled, but those figures aren't available for ATVs, snowmobiles or personal watercraft. Cars travel many more miles than the other vehicles.

When problems first cropped up with ATVs in the 1980s, federal regulators prodded the industry to stop making three-wheel versions. But today, their four-wheel cousins operate in a virtual regulatory void. Unlike cars, trucks and motorcycles, they aren't subject to regulation by the National Highway Traffic Safety Administration because they're not designed for highway use. The CPSC is investigating allegations of safety problems but hasn't found any evidence of improper design. Since the agency only regulates products, not their potential misuse, the agency's chairman says states are in a better position to deal with ATV accidents.

---

[1]"As ATVs Take Off in Sales, Deaths and Injuries Mount," *Wall Street Journal*, February 10, 2004, A1, A12. Reprinted with permission.

Yet state regulation is minimal. Only 10 states require that ATV drivers have a driver's license. While 27 states set a minimum age for ATV drivers, two-thirds allow 12-year-old drivers and, in Utah, 8-year-olds are legal. Only 20 states require riders to wear helmets. Thirty-four bar most uses of ATVs on paved roads, but those laws are frequently ignored. In West Virginia, with the nation's highest ATV-related per capita death rate, legislators have debated rules for seven years without passing any.

With little pressure from the government, the industry has had internal fights over how much to regulate itself, if at all. Alarmed by increased deaths and injuries and concerned about potential liability, manufacturers have proposed laws in West Virginia, Pennsylvania and other states that would require riders to wear helmets, bar ATVs from paved roads, prohibit passengers on ATVs, and keep children under 16 off adult-size vehicles. The industry "really has a comprehensive plan in place and states are implementing pieces of that in varying degrees," says Tim Buche, president of the Specialty Vehicle Institute of America in Irvine, Calif., which represents ATV makers.

But ATV makers have encountered resistance from some dealers who favor allowing passengers on ATVs and want to open more paved roads to the vehicles. Meanwhile, consumer advocates criticize manufacturers' proposals as being designed merely to shift responsibility from companies to consumers and state law enforcement authorities. These advocates prefer a federal ban on sales of ATVs for use by kids under 16.

"Self-regulation by the ATV industry has led to larger and faster ATVs and more children being killed and injured," says Rachel Weintraub, an attorney for the Consumer Federation of America in Washington.

Manufacturers also are resisting some state regulation. In Maine, for example, legislators are preparing to address ATV safety and trespassing problems. The industry has countered with less-stringent proposals. "Industry is more focused on this than they have been in a long time," says Paul Jaques, head of an ATV task force appointed by Maine's governor. "They recognize that if somebody doesn't do something about these things, this whole thing's going to blow up."

The first ATV was a small, motorized tricycle developed by a Honda engineer around 1970. The machines were first popular among farmers, foresters and others who put them to work. Recreational users began to boost U.S. sales in the 1980s.

But the three-wheel vehicles were difficult to handle, especially for untrained drivers. After more than 260 ATV users died in accidents in 1987, the CPSC sued the five largest manufacturers, asking a federal court to halt production and sales because ATVs were "imminently dangerous consumer products."

The manufacturers, who had already planned to switch to four-wheel vehicles, agreed to stop production of three-wheelers. They also agreed to stress more prominently warnings that are now bolted onto today's vehicles. The warning labels say drivers should wear helmets; passengers shouldn't be allowed; the vehicles are hard to steer on paved roads because the low-inflated balloon tires are made to grip uneven terrain; and children under 16 should ride only smaller, less-powerful machines under parental supervision.

Four-wheel ATVs, which are more stable, soon grew more popular than their predecessors, especially with recreational users. Sales over the last 10 years have increased five-fold, and 70% of users now ride ATVs as a "family recreational activity," according to the ATV manufacturers group.

In recent years, the industry has rolled out hot-rod-like "high performance" ATVs capable of higher speeds and quicker acceleration. Marketing pitches revel in speed and power. In sales brochures for its Predator ATV line, Polaris says "survival of the fittest is the rule. . . . And like all dominant beasts, Predator continues to evolve. That's a good thing. Because out here, you're either Predator or you're prey." The line includes adult models and smaller versions built for children as young as 6.

A Yamaha brochure for one of its less-powerful models says, "The whole point of the ATV movement is to get out there and experience Mother Nature; the pace at which you experience it is, of course, entirely up to you. Tear along when the mood strikes you."

Manufacturers say they don't market adult-size models to youngsters. In brochures, the industry shows family groups wearing goggles and helmets, with parents supervising children, who ride smaller machines. "Riding an ATV is an exercise in responsibility," says a Honda brochure.

However, children often use adult-size ATVs. Jeff DeVol, a dealer in Parkersburg, W. Va., says he and his salesmen tell customers that children can't safely handle adult-size machines, which cost $3,000 to $6,000 apiece, and urge parents to buy child-size models, which run as high as $3,000. But some buyers don't believe him, he says, and many can't afford more than one machine. Buyers sometimes fib about the recipient and get a "household ATV" that winds up being used by teens, he says.

The Consumer Federation and several medical and environmental groups have petitioned the CPSC to ban the sale of adult-size ATVs for use by children under 16. Ms. Weintraub of the Consumer Federation says the ban would enable the agency to fine or bring criminal charges against manufacturers who don't police dealers. It would also send "a powerful message to parents," she says.

The CPSC has the power to impose a ban or order vehicles redesigned if it finds they pose substantial harm, says Hal Stratton, the commission's Republican chairman. But after months of research and public hearings in West Virginia, New Mexico and Alaska, the agency hasn't found design flaws so much as "behavior problems" in how people ride, he says.

Even consumer advocates haven't cited design flaws in ATVs. And because the CPSC regulates products, not how people use them, it may not be able to act, Mr. Stratton says. However, agency staffers haven't completed their investigation or decided what could be done. One possibility is suggesting model legislation to states, Mr. Stratton says.

West Virginia's experience suggests why state regulation is piecemeal or nonexistent. The rural, mountainous state is one of six with no ATV regulations. It counts about 200,000 of the vehicles, or about one for every nine persons.

The number of deaths and injuries among young people "is an epidemic in terms of what we previously experienced," says Jim Helmkamp, an epidemiologist for the Center for Rural Emergency Medicine at West Virginia University. Since 1990, West Virginia has averaged 15 ATV deaths per year, at least 35% of them on paved roads. Last year, there were 27, the center says. Mr. Helmkamp has conducted studies showing that states with helmet-use and other regulations have lower death and injury rates.

Julian Bailes, head of the neurosurgery department at West Virginia University Hospital, where Jessica Adams was pronounced dead, says the hospital's emergency staff has seen 238 ATV-related injuries and deaths over the last decade. About a third of the victims were under 18 and 80% weren't wearing helmets, he says.

"What stands out is the stupidity of some of these accidents," he says. The worst involve parents carrying young children as passengers. The kids are "almost always thrown off and sometimes the vehicle rolls over on them."

But efforts to regulate ATV use, including that by children, have gone nowhere. "The local bubba wants to ride on the roads," says Leff Moore, lobbyist for West Virginia's Recreational Vehicle Association, a group of 14 dealers who have been pushing the manufacturers' proposed legislation since 1996. It would codify into law the warnings already bolted onto vehicles, requiring helmet use and barring children under 16 from riding on adult-size ATVs.

The legislation has never gotten close to a decisive vote, largely because of opposition by a splinter group of ATV dealers led by Mr. DeVol, the Parkersburg dealer. He says safety problems have less to do with the vehicles than with the people who use them. "My customers tell me that if the law results in a blanket statement that ATVs are prohibited from all paved roads in the state, basically you're making criminals out of them," he says.

Each year, Mr. DeVol's group has succeeded in persuading enough lawmakers to oppose the manufacturers' favored legislation. The group's lobbyist, Sam Love, says he makes a practice of reminding legislators how many of their constituents use ATVs. "When you have 200,000-plus people in the state, this is something legislators need to know before they enact restrictive legislation."

Last year, as the bill moved through the Senate, Mr. Love persuaded lawmakers to add an amendment that would have explicitly opened 20,000 miles of rural roads— many of them paved—to ATVs. (Currently, West Virginia law is ambiguous about whether ATVs are legal on paved roads.)

At that point, the manufacturers pulled their support, killing the bill. Mr. Moore, the industry lobbyist, says encouraging ATV users to use more paved roads could raise the state's "body count" and spur federal regulators to take more drastic steps.

Last month, the ATV manufacturers prodded West Virginia legislators with an open letter published in local newspapers demanding that the stalemate finally be broken. Now Democratic Gov. Bob Wise is trying to broker a compromise between the opposing dealer groups that would impose safety education, helmets and a no-passenger rule on children under 18.

As state police and Jessica's family have pieced together her Sept. 30, 2002, accident, the seventh-grade honor student had just finished supper and done her homework. It was around 6 p.m. She went for a walk in "Healthy Heights," the trailer park where she lived. Cynthia Lefever, her mother, says she felt little reason for concern. "She was very health and safety conscious," Ms. Lefever says.

Jessica went down the street to see a fellow seventh-grader, who wasn't home. But his 17-year-old brother rolled out the family ATV, a 2002 Honda Rancher that showroom dealers say is capable of speeds up to 50 mph. A spokesman for American Honda Motor Co. says Jessica's death was a "tragedy" beyond the manufacturer's control. "We try to make vehicles as safe as possible, but it requires supervision of the parents as well," he says.

Ms. Lefever says Jessica had never shown much interest in the machines. But another friend, a 14-year-old girl, jumped on the driver's seat and Jessica climbed on behind.

An hour later, someone heard moaning coming from the nearby woods. It was the 14-year-old, who had been thrown off. She suffered a punctured lung and bruised ribs. Jessica was lying quietly nearby.

Jessica's friends fashioned a tribute of her stuffed toys and favorite candy next to the tree the ATV struck. Mr. Helmkamp, of the state's Center for Rural Emergency Medicine, is preparing a more lasting memorial: a video describing her death that he hopes to distribute among state schools. "This was an event that could have been prevented," he says.

Meanwhile, teenagers in Jessica's neighborhood still get out to joyride. Jessica's mother can hear them revving their ATV engines at night. Sometimes she sees them collecting at a nearby gas station, comparing their shiny machines. "A lot of them are boys," she says. "They think they're invincible."

1. Which statistics in this article do you find most compelling?
2. What ethical responsibilities do the manufacturers of ATVs have to consumers?
3. Which of the ethical theories from Chapter 1 relates most closely to the ATV situation?
4. Is there a way to legislate the safer use of ATVs, especially by young people?

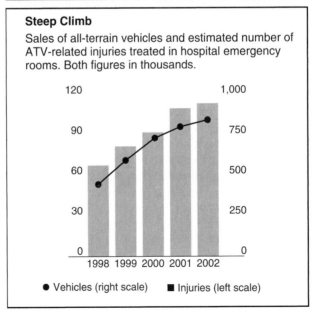

EXHIBIT 2-1 "Steep Climb" All-Terrain Vehicles

Steep Climb

Sales of all-terrain vehicles and estimated number of ATV-related injuries treated in hospital emergency rooms. Both figures in thousands.

● Vehicles (right scale)   ■ Injuries (left scale)

Sources: Motorcycle Industry Council Retail Sales Reporting System; U.S. Consumer Product Safety Commission

FIRST THE TARGET WAS TOBACCO. THEN BURGERS. SO HOW HAS BIG ALCOHOL STAYED OUT OF THE LAWYERS' SIGHTS?[1]

Adam Jones

First the target was tobacco. Then burgers. So how has Big Alcohol stayed out of the lawyers' sights?—When branding the message.

A century or more ago, tortured aesthetes would express their exquisite yearning for death with an unfiltered French cigarette in one hand and a shot of hard liquor in the other. Today, rising concern about obesity would seem to make a chocolate bar a more lethal choice than a measure of absinthe.

While tobacco remains the most vilified of the legal vices, makers of fattening foods are now also being besieged by hostile lobby groups, lawyers, politicians and the media, all seeking to hold them to account for their customers' poor eating habits. In the latest sign of the pressure food producers are under, Kraft, the multinational, has announced it is to cut portion sizes and reduce fat and sugar content.

In contrast—and to the private amazement of some food and tobacco executives—makers of alcoholic drinks have escaped the same level of scrutiny. This is perhaps surprising: drinkers after all cause or suffer a broader range of social ills than over-eaters, including road accidents, violent crime, unwanted pregnancies, marital breakdowns, disease and absenteeism.

Moreover, globally, alcohol consumption has been rising. Average per capita consumption around the world rose 12 percent between 1990 and 2001, according to *World Drinks Trends*, a standard industry data source. The broadest surge has been in the emerging markets of Latin America and eastern Europe, where it has often gone hand in hand with economic growth.

According to the World Health Organization, 140 million people suffer from alcohol dependence.

Even in the US—where many of the legal threats to tobacco and food manufacturers have emerged—alcohol is getting easier to buy. Some states have loosened rules forbidding Sunday sales and rolled back laws that stopped residents buying direct from out-of-state winemakers. In South Carolina there is momentum to get rid of one of the oddest licensing quirks in the US: the rule that says all spirits served in the state's bars have to be poured from the sort of mini-bottles found on aircraft.

Several states have recently legalized in-store tastings of spirits, which is great news for Big Alcohol's profits. Frank Coleman, of the Distilled Spirits Council of the United States, says: "To get people to buy up from a $20 bottle of Scotch to a $40 bottle, you have to get them to taste it."

So has Big Alcohol—the loose grouping of spirits, beer and wine multi-nationals such as Diageo, Allied Domecq, Brown-Forman, Anheuser-Busch, SABMiller and Heineken—really succeeded in presenting itself as just another manufacturing industry? Not quite. But it has shown an ability to influence the public health debate in ways that could be instructive to beleaguered food executives.

---

[1]*Financial Times*, July 8, 2003. Reprinted with permission.

One reason the alcohol industry has largely escaped tobacco-style litigation is that consumption in some rich nations is declining. The British may show an increased thirst for wine; beer consumption has risen in Ireland. But in the US—in spite of the emergence of *Modern Drunkard*, a magazine and website that smirkingly celebrate alcoholic excess—consumption has fallen. The average American consumed the equivalent of 6.7 litres of pure alcohol in 2001, down from 8.3 litres in 1980. The French also drink much less than they used to 30 years ago, as do the Italians.

A second reason, argues John Banzhaf, the George Washington University law professor who was a pioneer of smoking lawsuits and is now at the forefront of obesity litigation, is that it may be harder for drinkers to plead ignorance in court. "The dangers associated with over-consumption of alcohol are arguably far better known."

Last month a TGI Fridays restaurant franchisee from Ohio paid $21 million to settle a lawsuit brought by the parents of two teenagers killed in a car crash caused by a drunk customer. But this is a threat to retailers, not directly to producers of alcoholic drinks.

Third, Big Alcohol has benefited precisely because of the growing concern with tobacco use and obesity. The Robert Wood Johnson Foundation, one of the industry's most powerful critics, which has given $5 billion to health causes, says childhood obesity is now its main concern. Although treatment for alcohol abusers is still a funding priority, the foundation has decided that prevention is no longer a primary goal.

Similarly, the World Health Organization has concentrated its recent efforts on cutting tobacco use. In the 1980s its European arm made one of the boldest experiments since Prohibition to cut general drinking, calling for per capita consumption to dwindle in Europe to just 75 percent of 1980 levels by 2000. But, despite some success in France, the goal was not achieved, and the WHO has not committed itself to any new targets for reducing consumption in Europe or worldwide. The last time the assembly of WHO member nations adopted a resolution on alcohol was 1983. Since then there have been many resolutions on tobacco.

Derek Yach, the WHO executive director in charge of its work on tobacco, alcohol and bad diet, admits that Gro Harlem Brundtland, its director-general, "hasn't really engaged substantially in the alcohol area" for fear of compromising the WHO's work in cutting tobacco use. The WHO was worried the tobacco and alcohol lobbies would join forces to oppose it if Dr. Brundtland opened a second front against alcohol, Dr. Yach said. Rather, the WHO has been seeking a dialogue with industry. Drinks companies complained after they were not invited to a May 2002 meeting that led the WHO to claim that young people were being aggressively wooed. Representatives of some of the biggest drinks companies were then invited to meet WHO officials in February—the first such meeting.

The WHO remains concerned about the marketing of alcohol to the young and about the "ubiquity" of drinks advertisements. At a conference in Stockholm, Dr. Brundtland railed against the targeting of the young by marketers, likening this "manipulation" to an incident she experienced as a student when her drink was spiked with 96 percent proof medical alcohol.

Dr. Yach is pragmatic about involving industry in a way that would be unthinkable for the WHO on tobacco. Alcohol does not have "anywhere near the lethality of tobacco," he said; "The nature of the product lends itself to having a more flexible approach."

Drinks companies have succeeded in much of the above for two reasons. First, they have shown a willingness to submit to responsible self-regulation—something largely missing from the food industry. Second, they have successfully encouraged a distinction between overall consumption and the need to curtail patterns of excessive drinking.

Big increases in drinking have tended to attract the attention of public health campaigners, thanks to an influential school of thought that directly links higher average consumption to a higher incidence of alcohol-related harm. If countries reduce per capita consumption through curbs on advertising and availability, alcohol-related problems will also decline, the thinking goes. The alcohol lobby has long claimed that this is a discredited, "neo-prohibitionist" theory that punishes responsible drinkers with higher taxes and shorter bar hours.

The balance of power between these two viewpoints—one leaning toward across-the-board cuts in boozing, the other seeking to limit action to specific problems such as binge drinking—varies around the world. But there are signs that Big Alcohol may have neutralized the worst of the threat posed by the control-of-consumption theory.

A warning shot was fired by David Byrne, the European Union commissioner for health and consumer protection, who challenged the drinks industry to prove that voluntary codes of conduct can work. However, the commissioner's office now says no crackdown is planned.

Self-regulation in Britain is carried out through the Portman Group. Its independent complaints panel bared its teeth in May in what was described as a "landmark" decision against an alcopop called fcuk Spirit. This sugary, fruit-flavored drink—made by Constellation Brands, the world's biggest wine company—borrowed the name of a popular clothing brand and had to be withdrawn after it was deemed more likely to appeal to under-18s than to adults.

Although fcuk Spirit launched in the autumn of 2001, the panel acted only in May 2003 because it had to wait for the public to complain first. By this time the UK alcopop sector was declining anyway.

Individual companies have also found ways of showing that they are serious about fighting alcohol abuse. Internal codes of conduct have been strengthened. Messages about responsible drinking are creeping into mainstream advertising outside the US, where they have been incorporated for a long time.

Diageo, the world's biggest spirits company, is launching television adverts for Smirnoff vodka that exhort drinkers in the UK and Ireland to know when to stop. It also bankrolled an African feature film based round Michael Power, a fictional hero who features in its Guinness adverts. The film contains sensible drinking messages as well as product placement.

Alcohol's cause is helped by the fact that so many governments rely on the tax revenue it brings in. Scientific claims that moderate drinking can be good for your health have been another factor in the argument.

Big Alcohol has also emphasized the limitations of its power in order to placate opponents. The leading producers stress that much of the world's alcohol is made by small operators that would register on few regulatory radar screens, not least because many are illegal producers.

Even so, the alcohol industry faces some degree of backlash. In Ireland, a task-force on alcohol abuse found last year that drastic measures had to be taken after consumption increased 41 percent between 1989 and 1999. Ireland liberalized its licensing laws in 2000, stretching the basic trading hours to 12.30 am, Thursday to Saturday. Police statistics suggest that this coincided with a big rise in public drunkenness and disorderly or violent behavior.

Revised legislation bans "happy hours" and imposes an 11.30 pm closing time on Thursdays to ensure that young drinkers show up for lectures or work on Fridays. The taskforce has recommended an increase in taxes to reduce average consumption.

Ireland's toughening stance on general alcohol consumption contrasts with plans in England and Wales where an overhaul of licensing laws will clear the way for 24-hour pub opening. Hand in hand with this planned liberalization, the government is drawing up a long-awaited strategy for limiting alcohol abuse. But some public health experts are dismayed by the direction of reform.

Griffith Edwards, the founder of the National Addiction Centre at King's College London, says: "The more you make drink available, the more people will actually drink and the more harm will be done to health."

The contradictions in the UK reflect the paradox of alcohol. While many individuals believe it is a commodity that enriches their lives, it all too clearly ruins the lives of a few. The same is true of fattening foods, seen as a legitimate indulgence by many but a debilitating habit for others.

The modern tendency for policymakers to seek dialogue with Big Alcohol rather than call for aggressive cuts in general consumption will continue to disappoint those seeking a harder line. But a similar pattern of collaboration rather than confrontation may well emerge in the food industry—leaving tobacco as a lonely public health pariah.

With hindsight, it may have not been a wise idea to ask Frank Skinner, a former alcoholic, to host an awards dinner for the British pub industry. The comedian's first-hand experience with addiction contributed to an awkward moment for Carlsberg, the Danish brewer. Mr. Skinner treated the audience to a dark, satirical riff about Carlsberg Special Brew, the super-strength lager often associated with vagrants.

What sort of marketing gimmicks could be used to promote such a product, Mr. Skinner wondered aloud: a string dog-leash free with every six-pack? And who needs conventional advertising when a few empty cans left on a pavement next to a puddle of urine speak so eloquently?

The public face of some alcoholic drinks can be very different from what their makers originally intended.

For instance, in the 1950s, E&J Gallo, the family-controlled California wine company, marketed Thunderbird, a fortified wine, to appeal to American suburbanites.

The product was initially a success—but nowadays it is more likely to be associated with vagrants. Meanwhile, Gallo says it no longer advertises Thunderbird.

Buckfast Tonic Wine was a medicinal drink made by monks in Devon, England, from a recipe obtained in 1897. Yet now it is often linked with alcohol abuse among young people in Scotland, particularly in Lanarkshire.

Tony Joyce, managing director of J. Chandler & Co, the company that bottles and distributes the tonic wine, dismisses the criticism as media "prejudice" against the product, which is not advertised anywhere in the UK. He says indignantly: "It is drunk by all sorts of people."

Like all consumer goods companies, even the most conscientious makers of alcoholic drinks cannot be in control of their target market all the time.

Supermarkets have enormous and growing purchasing power and are particularly eager to discount lager, Britain's national drink. This, in turn, manages to bring even some carefully nurtured premium brands within reach of the desperate.

Carlsberg, which is controlled by a Danish charitable foundation that supports the arts and sciences, insists that Special Brew does not deserve its park bench image, regardless of what Mr. Skinner says.

Indeed, the 9 percent alcohol by volume beer was brewed in 1950 to commemorate the first visit of Winston Churchill, then prime minister, to Copenhagen. Carlsberg maintains that its core consumers include wealthy beer connoisseurs as well as respectable, older drinkers.

Nonetheless, the brewer was teased in 1999 when it tried to reinvent Special Brew as "the beer of the gods" in a rare advertising campaign. Carlsberg's hopes of giving Special Brew a more rounded personality finally got a bizarre boost earlier this year when Maggi Hambling, the eccentric British artist, produced a series of 34 portraits of the beer, which she described as a long-standing friend.

The paintings depict the golden cans in various situations, such as visiting Japan in the snow, sunbathing by the sea, climbing a mountain and even having sex.

But even then Special Brew was unable to rid itself of its old associations: about half of the proceeds from the auction of the paintings went to the Depaul Trust, a charity that helps young homeless people.

1. Why has "Big Alcohol" not received as harsh a treatment as other marketers?
2. What is your view of the ethics of alcohol marketing? Give an example to support your point of view.
3. How does this article relate to Chapter 1?

WHEN DOES A GIFT BECOME A BRIBE?[1]

Kirk Davidson

The marketing of prescription drugs is the subject of ongoing attention from business ethicists, consumer activists, and government regulators. The interactions between drug companies' sales representatives and representatives of the medical profession are the most often scrutinized activities. The focus is on gifts and incentives and on the question: When does a gift become a bribe?

At the heart of the marketing is the relationship between buyer and seller. In the prescription drug industry, however, that relationship is quite complex, and it differs significantly from other industries such as toothpaste or automobiles. Consider these three important differences:

- Buyers/patients and seller/drug companies are not the only parties involved: Doctors, pharmacists, and insurance companies play critical roles as well. Because the choice of products is made by the doctor who prescribes them, drug companies aim much of their marketing strategies at doctors, who are technically intermediaries, rather than at the patients, who are the actual end users.
- Patients have little or no knowledge about the product, and this is unlikely to change because the product category is too technologically complex. They have no way to judge the value of one competing product over another, not to mention the health risks involved.
- Although toothpaste and automobiles represent varying degrees of importance to their purchasers, a prescription drug may mean the difference between life and death. Thus, health care marketing is unique.

Long ago, pharmaceutical companies realized that doctors are the key to success in their marketing strategies. In most cases, doctors play more than a simple consulting role because they are the only participant in the complex marketing process with knowledge of both the drug's benefits and properties and the patient's needs and medical condition. Although drug companies can now direct some of their marketing efforts directly at consumers, doctors are still their most important target.

The selling practice that has raised the most concern among ethicists and watchdog groups involves giving gifts to doctors. The danger is that a gift can become a bribe. Drug manufacturers give all sorts of things to doctors. They give them samples of their products, especially new products. How else can a doctor learn about the new drug's benefits and side effects and compare them with those of competing drugs? Few critics question the practice of giving samples, though there have been isolated cases of abuse.

Giving promotional items such as pens, pads, address books, and key rings is also common in the industry. This is acceptable to most ethicists, who assume that gifts of only modest value do not influence doctors' decisions.

[1]*The Moral Dimension of Marketing: Essays on Business Ethics* (Chicago: American Marketing Association, 2002), pp. 99–101. Reprinted with permission.

Pharmaceutical representatives often provide meals for doctors and their staff. In this case, the value of the gift is far greater than a pen or a key ring, and it generates proportionately more ethical concern. Representatives and their companies defend the practice by arguing that it is often the only feasible way to get the doctor's time and attention, and in many cases, the doctor asks that the company host the meal as a convenience. However, there is at least a possibility that the free meal influences the doctor's choice of prescriptions.

Next on the ascending scale of questionable gifts is sending a doctor to conferences and seminars. Invariably, such conferences are held in attractive vacation spots—think of Palm Springs or Key West—and the time spent on actual business-related education, as opposed to time spent playing golf or tennis, is minimal. The line separating work from play, a learning experience from boondoggle, becomes fuzzy. After being sent to a conference, the doctor may feel some real obligation to reciprocate by directing prescriptions to the company hosting the trip.

What is wrong with these practices? Why do ethicists and consumer activists find at least some of them unethical and unacceptable? Outright bribes are unethical in any industry, but the unique structure and circumstances of the pharmaceutical marketing situation make these practices especially suspect. Buyers and sellers are supposed to come together in the marketplace with somewhat equal standing, that is, equal knowledge of the product. Because that is impossible with prescription drugs, the patient *must* rely on the physician for professional advice. That advice must not be tainted by the incentives that are dangled in front of the doctor by drug manufacturers. It is absolutely imperative in this industry, given the possible life-and-death consequences, that patients be able to trust their physicians' prescription choices.

Five things are necessary to keep the system above reproach and maintain the public's confidence:

1. Drug makers must exercise restraint in their promotions and selling practices. If they take advantage of the unequal power they have in the marketing relationship with patients—because they have all the knowledge about the product and patients have little or none—they invite even more serious regulations than now exist.
2. Doctors must also exercise restraint and reject unreasonable incentives when they are proffered. This is easier said than done because almost every doctor would state, and perhaps actually believe, that the trip to Palm Springs did not really influence his or her choice of prescription drugs. Doctors must at all times act as the patient's counselor and advocate, not as a profit center.
3. Insurance companies must increase their oversight of doctors' prescription patterns, both to hold down costs and to ensure fairness.
4. Patients can help themselves by taking advantage of the increasing amount of information about prescription drugs that is available from advocacy groups such as Public Citizen and the American Association of Retired Persons (AARP).
5. Some degree of government regulation must continue. The government must be involved to ensure fairness in cases in which the buyer-seller relationship

does not work perfectly and in which there is a more complex relationship such as when doctors act as intermediaries.

Although the public good can tolerate marketing practices that are ethically questionable in some industries, it cannot tolerate them in others. Prescription drugs fall into the latter category, and all parties to the marketing process in this critical industry—drug manufacturers, doctors, patients, insurance companies, and government regulators—must share in the responsibility of maintaining the highest level of ethical standards and preserving public confidence.

1. How does a bribe differ from what the government calls a "facilitating payment"?
2. What makes bribery questionable from an ethical perspective?
3. In what other industries do buyers have little or no knowledge about the product and are, therefore, at the mercy of the seller?

THE WAL-MART YOU DON'T KNOW: WHY LOW PRICES HAVE A HIGH COST[1]

Charles Fishman

A gallon-sized jar of whole pickles is something to behold. The jar is the size of a small aquarium. The fat green pickles, floating in swampy juice, look reptilian, their shapes exaggerated by the glass. It weights 12 pounds, too big to carry with one hand. The gallon jar of pickles is a display of abundance and excess; it is entrancing, and also vaguely unsettling. This is the product that Wal-Mart fell in love with: Vlasic's gallon jar of pickles.

Wal-Mart priced it at $2.97—a year's supply of pickles for less than $3! "They were using it as a 'statement' item," says Pat Hunn, who calls himself the "mad scientist" of Vlasic's gallon jar. "Wal-Mart was putting it before consumers, saying, This represents what Wal-Mart's about. You can buy a stinkin' gallon of pickles for $2.97. And it's the nation's number-one brand."

Therein lies the basic conundrum of doing business with the world's largest retailer. By selling a gallon of kosher dills for less than most grocers sell a quart, Wal-Mart may have provided a service for its customers. But what did it do for Vlasic? The pickle maker had spent decades convincing customers that they should pay a premium for its brand. Now Wal-Mart was practically giving them away. And the fevered buying spree that resulted distorted every aspect of Vlasic's operations, from farm field to factory to financial statement.

Indeed, as Vlasic discovered, the real story of Wal-Mart, the story that never gets told, is the story of the pressure the biggest retailer relentlessly applies to its suppliers in the name of bringing us "everyday low prices." It's the story of what that pressure does to the companies Wal-Mart does business with, to U.S. manufacturing, and to the economy as a whole. That story can be found floating in a gallon jar of pickles at Wal-Mart.

Wal-Mart is not just the world's largest retailer. It's the world's largest company, bigger than Exxon Mobil, General Motors, and General Electric. The scale can be hard to absorb. Wal-Mart sold $244.5 billion worth of goods last year. It sells in three months what number-two retailer Home Depot sells in a year. And in its own category of general merchandise and groceries, Wal-Mart no longer has any real rivals. It does more business than Target, Sears, Kmart, J.C. Penney, Safeway, and Kroger combined. "Clearly," says Edward Fox, head of Southern Methodist University's J.C. Penney Center for Retailing Excellence, "Wal-Mart is more powerful than any retailer has ever been." It is, in fact, so big and so furtively powerful as to have become an entirely different order of corporate being.

Wal-Mart wields its power for just one purpose: to bring the lowest possible prices to its customers. At Wal-Mart, that goal is never reached. The retailer has a clear policy for suppliers: On basic products that don't change, the price Wal-Mart will pay, and will charge shoppers, must drop year after year. But what almost no one outside the world of Wal-Mart and its 21,000 suppliers knows is the high cost of those low prices. Wal-Mart has the power to squeeze profit-killing concessions from vendors. To

---

[1]*Fast Company*, December 2003, pp. 68–80. Reprinted with permission.

survive in the face of its pricing demands, makers of everything from bras to bicycles to blue jeans have had to lay off employees and close U.S. plants in favor of outsourcing products from overseas.

Of course, U.S. companies have been moving jobs offshore for decades, long before Wal-Mart was a retailing power. But there is no question that the chain is helping accelerate the loss of American jobs to low-wage countries such as China. Wal-Mart, which in the late 1980s and early 1990s trumpeted its claim to "Buy American," has doubled its imports from China in the past five years alone, buying some $12 billion in merchandise in 2002. That's nearly 10% of all Chinese exports to the United States.

One way to think of Wal-Mart is as a vast pipeline that gives non-U.S. companies direct access to the American market. "One of the things that limits or slows the growth of imports is the cost of establishing connections and networks," says Paul Krugman, the Princeton University economist. "Wal-Mart is so big and so centralized that it can all at once hook Chinese and other suppliers into its digital system. So—wham!—you have a large switch to overseas sourcing in a period quicker than under the old rules of retailing."

Steve Dobbins has been bearing the brunt of that switch. He's president and CEO of Carolina Mills, a 75-year-old North Carolina company that supplies thread, yarn, and textile finishing to apparel makers—half of which supply Wal-Mart. Carolina Mills grew steadily until 2000. But in the past three years, as its customers have gone either overseas or out of business, it has shrunk from 17 factories to 7, and from 2,600 employees to 1,200. Dobbins's customers have begun to face imported clothing sold so cheaply to Wal-Mart that they could not compete even if they paid their workers nothing.

"People ask, 'How can it be bad for things to come into the U.S. cheaply? How can it be bad to have a bargain at Wal-Mart?' Sure, it's held inflation down, and it's great to have bargains," says Dobbins. "But you can't buy anything if you're not employed. We are shopping ourselves out of jobs."

There is no question that Wal-Mart's relentless drive to squeeze out costs has benefited consumers. The giant retailer is at least partly responsible for the low rate of U.S. inflation, and a McKinsey & Co. study concluded that about 12% of the economy's productivity gains in the second half of the 1990s could be traced to Wal-Mart alone.

There is also no question that doing business with Wal-Mart can give a supplier a fast, heady jolt of sales and market share. But that fix can come with long-term consequences for the health of a brand and a business. Vlasic, for example, wasn't looking to build its brand on a gallon of whole pickles. Pickle companies make money on "the cut," slicing cucumbers into spears and hamburger chips. "Cucumbers in the jar, you don't make a whole lot of money there," says Steve Young, a former vice president of grocery marketing for pickles at Vlasic, who has since left the company.

At some point in the late 1990s, a Wal-Mart buyer saw Vlasic's gallon jar and started talking to Pat Hunn about it. Hunn, who has also since left Vlasic, was then head of Vlasic's Wal-Mart sales team, based in Dallas. The gallon intrigued the buyer. In sales tests, priced somewhere over $3, "the gallon sold like crazy," says Hunn, "surprising us all." The Wal-Mart buyer had a brainstorm: What would happen to the gallon if they offered it nationwide and got it below $3? Hunn was skeptical, but his job was to look for ways to sell pickles at Wal-Mart. Why not?

And so Vlasic's gallon jar of pickles went into every Wal-Mart, some 3,000 stores, at $2.97, a price so low that Vlasic and Wal-Mart were making only a penny or two on a jar, if that. It was showcased on big pallets near the front of stores. It was an abundance of abundance. "It was selling 80 jars a week, on average, in every store," says Young. Doesn't sound like much, until you do the math: That's 240,000 gallons of pickles, just in gallon jars, just at Wal-Mart, every week. Whole fields of cucumbers were heading out the door.

For Vlasic, the gallon jar of pickles became what might be called a devastating success. "Quickly, it started cannibalizing our non-Wal-Mart business," says Young. "We saw consumers who used to buy the spears and the chips in supermarkets buying the Wal-Mart gallons. They'd eat a quarter of a jar and throw the thing away when they got moldy. A family can't eat them fast enough."

The gallon jar reshaped Vlasic's pickle business: It chewed up the profit margin of the business with Wal-Mart, and of pickles generally. Procurement had to scramble to find enough pickles to fill the gallons, but the volume gave Vlasic strong sales numbers, strong growth numbers, and a powerful place in the world of pickles at Wal-Mart. Which accounted for 30% of Vlasic's business. But the company's profits from pickles had shriveled 25% or more, Young says—millions of dollars. The gallon was hoisting Vlasic and hurting it at the same time.

Young remembers begging Wal-Mart for relief: "They said, 'No way,'" says Young. "We said we'll increase the price"—even $3.49 would have helped tremendously—"and they said, 'If you do that, all the other products of yours we buy, we'll stop buying.' It was a clear threat." Hunn recalls things a little differently, if just as ominously: "They said, 'We want the $2.97 gallon of pickles. If you don't do it, we'll see if someone else might.' I knew our competitors were saying to Wal-Mart, 'We'll do the $2.97 gallons if you give us your other business.' Wal-Mart's business was so indispensable to Vlasic, and the gallon so central to the Wal-Mart relationship, that decisions about the future of the gallon were made at the CEO level."

Finally, Wal-Mart let Vlasic up for air. "The Wal-Mart guy's response was classic," Young recalls. "He said, 'Well, we've done to pickles what we did to orange juice. We've killed it. We can back off.'" Vlasic got to take it down to just over half a gallon of pickles, for $2.79. Not long after that, in January 2001, Vlasic filed for bankruptcy although the gallon jar of pickles, everyone agrees, wasn't a critical factor.

By now, it is accepted wisdom that Wal-Mart makes the companies it does business with more efficient and focused, leaner and faster. Wal-Mart itself is known for continuous improvement in its ability to handle, move, and track merchandise. It expects the same of its suppliers. But the ability to operate at peak efficiency only gets you in the door at Wal-Mart. Then the real demands start. The public image Wal-Mart projects may be as cheery as its yellow smiley-face mascot, but there is nothing genial about the process by which Wal-Mart gets its suppliers to provide tires and contact lenses, guns and underarm deodorant at everyday low prices. Wal-Mart is legendary for forcing its suppliers to redesign everything from their packaging to their computer systems. It is also legendary for quite straightforwardly telling them what it will pay for their goods.

John Fitzgerald, a former vice president of Nabisco, remembers Wal-Mart's reaction to his company's plan to offer a 25-cent newspaper coupon for a large bag of Lifesavers in advance of Halloween. Wal-Mart told Nabisco to add up what it would spend on the promotion—for the newspaper ads, the coupons, and handling—and then just take that amount off the price instead. "That isn't necessarily good for the manufacturer," Fitzgerald says. "They need things that draw attention."

It also is not unheard of for Wal-Mart to demand to examine the private financial records of a supplier, and to insist that its margins are too high and must be cut. And the smaller the supplier, one academic study shows, the greater the likelihood that it will be forced into damaging concessions. Melissa Berryhill, a Wal-Mart spokeswoman, disagrees: "The fact is Wal-Mart, perhaps like no other retailer, seeks to establish collaborative and mutually beneficial relationships with our suppliers."

For many suppliers, though, the only thing worse than doing business with Wal-Mart may be not doing business with Wal-Mart. Last year, 7.5 cents of every dollar spent in *any store in the United States* (other than auto-parts stores) went to the retailer. That means a contract with Wal-Mart can be critical even for the largest consumer-goods companies. Dial Corp., for example, does 28% of its business with Wal-Mart. If Dial lost that one account, it would have to double its sales to its next nine customers just to stay even. "Wal-Mart is the essential retailer, in a way no other retailer is," says Gib Carey, a partner at Bain & Co., who is leading a yearlong study of how to do business with Wal-Mart. "Our clients cannot grow without finding a way to be successful with Wal-Mart."

Many companies and their executives frankly admit that supplying Wal-Mart is like getting into the company version of basic training with an implacable Army drill sergeant. The process may be unpleasant. But there can be some positive results.

"Everyone from the forklift driver on up to me, the CEO, knew we had to deliver [to Wal-Mart] on time. Not 10 minutes late. And not 45 minutes early, either," says Robin Prever, who was CEO of Saratoga Beverage Group from 1992 to 2000, and made private-label water sold at Wal-Mart. "The message came through clearly: You have this 30-second delivery window. Either you're there, or you're out. With a customer like that, it changes your organization. For the better. It wakes everybody up. And all our customers benefited. We changed our whole approach to doing business."

But you won't hear evenhanded stories like that from Wal-Mart, or from its current suppliers. Despite being a publicly traded company, Wal-Mart is intensely private. It declined to talk in detail about its relationships with its suppliers for this story. More strikingly, dozens of companies contacted declined to talk about even the basics of their business with Wal-Mart.

Here, for example, is an executive at Dial: "We are one of Wal-Mart's biggest suppliers, and they are our biggest customer by far. We have a great relationship. That's all I can say. Are we done now?" Goaded a bit, the executive responds with an almost hysterical edge: "Are you meshuga? Why in the world would we talk about Wal-Mart? Ask me about anything else, we'll talk. But not Wal-Mart."

No one wants to end up in what is known among Wal-Mart vendors as the "penalty box"—punished, or even excluded from the store shelves, for saying something that makes Wal-Mart unhappy. (The penalty box is normally reserved for vendors who don't meet performance benchmarks, not for those who talk to the press.)

"You won't hear anything negative from most people," says Paul Kelly, founder of Silvermine Consulting Group, a company that helps businesses work more effectively with retailers. "It would be committing suicide. If Wal-Mart takes something the wrong way, it's like Saddam Hussein. You just don't want to piss them off."

As a result, this story was reported in an unusual way: by speaking with dozens of people who have spent years selling to Wal-Mart, or consulting to companies that sell to Wal-Mart, but who no longer work for companies that do business with Wal-Mart. Unless otherwise noted, the companies involved in the events they described refused even to confirm or deny the basics of the events.

To a person, all those interviewed credit Wal-Mart with a fundamental integrity in its dealings that's unusual in the world of consumer goods, retailing, and groceries. Wal-Mart does not cheat suppliers, it keeps its word, it pays its bills briskly. "They are tough people but very honest; they treat you honestly," says Peter Campanella, who ran the business that sold Corning kitchenware products, both at Corning and then at World Kitchen. "It was a joke to do business with most of their competitors. A fiasco."

But Wal-Mart also clearly does not hesitate to use its power, magnifying the Darwinian forces already at work in modern global capitalism.

What does the squeeze look like at Wal-Mart? It is usually thoroughly rational, sometimes devastatingly so.

John Mariotti is a veteran of the consumer-products world—he spent nine years as president of Huffy Bicycle Co., a division of Huffy Corp., and is now chairman of World Kitchen, the company that sells Oxo, Revere, Corning, and Ekco brand housewares.

He could not be clearer on his opinion about Wal-Mart: "It's a great company, and a great company to do business with. Wal-Mart has done more good for America by several thousand orders of magnitude than they've done bad," Mariotti says. "They have raised the bar, and raised the bar for everybody."

Mariotti describes one episode from Huffy's relationship with Wal-Mart. It's a tale he tells to illustrate an admiring point he makes about the retailer. "They demand you do what you say you are going to do." But it's also a classic example of the damned-if you-do, damned-if-you-don't Wal-Mart squeeze. When Mariotti was at Huffy through-out the 1980s, the company sold a range of bikes to Wal-Mart, 20 or so models, in a spread of prices and profitability. It was a leading manufacturer of bikes in the United States, in places like Ponca City, Oklahoma; Celina, Ohio; and Farmington, Missouri.

One year, Huffy had committed to supply Wal-Mart with an entry-level, thin-margin bike—as many as Wal-Mart needed. Sale of the low-end bike took off. "I woke up May 1"—the heart of the bike production cycle for the summer—"and I needed 900,000 bikes," he says. "My factories could only run 450,000." As it happened, that same year, Huffy's fancier, more-profitable bikes were doing well, too, at Wal-Mart and other places. Huffy found itself in a bind.

With other retailers, perhaps, Mariotti might have sat down, renegotiated, tried to talk his way out of the corner. Not with Wal-Mart. "I made the deal up front with them," he says. "I knew how high was up. I was duty-bound to supply my customer." So he did something extraordinary. To free up production in order to make Wal-Mart's cheap bikes, he gave the designs for four of his higher-end, higher-margin products to rival manufacturers. "I conceded business to my competitors, because I just ran out of capacity," he says. Huffy didn't just relinquish profits to keep Wal-Mart happy—it handed those profits to its competition. "Wal-Mart didn't tell me what to do," Mariotti says. "They didn't have to." The retailer, he adds, "is tough as nails. But they give you a chance to compete. If you can't compete, that's your problem."

In the years since Mariotti left Huffy, the bike maker's relationship with Wal-Mart has been vital (though Huffy Corp. has lost money in three out of the last five years). It is the number-three seller of bikes in the United States. And Wal-Mart is the number one retailer of bikes. But here's one last statistic about bicycles: Roughly 98% are now imported from places such as China, Mexico, and Taiwan. Huffy made its last bike in the United States in 1999.

As Mariotti says, Wal-Mart is tough as nails. But not every supplier agrees that the toughness is always accompanied by fairness. The Lovable Company was founded in 1926 by the grandfather of Frank Garson II, who was Lovable's last president. It did business with Wal-Mart, Garson says, from the earliest days of founder Sam Walton's first store in Bentonville, Arkansas. Lovable made bras and lingerie, supplying retailers that also included Sears and Victoria's Secret. At one point, it was the sixth-largest maker of intimate apparel in the United States, with 700 employees in this country and another 2,000 at eight factories in Central America.

Eventually Wal-Mart became Lovable's biggest customer. "Wal-Mart has a big pencil," says Garson. "They have such awesome purchasing power that they write their own ticket. If they don't like your prices, they'll go vertical and do it themselves—or they'll find someone that will meet their terms."

In the summer of 1995, Garson asserts, Wal-Mart did just that. "They had awarded us a contract, and in their wisdom, they changed the terms so dramatically that they really reneged." Garson, still worried about litigation, won't provide details. "But when you lose a customer that size, they are irreplaceable."

Lovable was already feeling intense cost pressure. Less than three years after Wal-Mart pulled its business, in its 72nd year, Lovable closed. "They leave a lot to be desired in the way they treat people," says Garson. "Their actions to pulverize people are unnecessary. Wal-Mart chewed us up and spit us out."

Believe it or not, American business has been through this before. The Great Atlantic & Pacific Tea Co., the grocery-store chain, stood astride the U.S. market in the 1920s and 1930s with a dominance that has likely never been duplicated. At its peak, A&P had five times the number of stores Wal-Mart has now (although much smaller ones), and at one point, it owned 80% of the supermarket business. Some of the antipredatory-pricing laws in use today were inspired by A&P's attempts to muscle its suppliers.

There is very little academic and statistical study of Wal-Mart's impact on the health of its suppliers and virtually nothing in the last decade, when Wal-Mart's size has increased by a factor of five. This while the retail industry has become much more concentrated. In large part, that's because it's nearly impossible to get meaningful data that would allow researchers to track the influence of Wal-Mart's business on companies over time. You'd need cooperation from the vendor companies or Wal-Mart or both—and neither Wal-Mart nor its suppliers are interested in sharing such intimate detail.

Bain & Co., the global management consulting firm, is in the midst of a project that asks, How does a company have a healthy relationship with Wal-Mart? How do you avoid being sucked into the vortex? How do you maintain some standing, some leverage of your own?

Bain's first insights are obvious, if not easy. "Year after year," Carey, a partner at Bain & Co., says, "for any product that is the same as what you sold them last year, Wal-Mart will say, 'Here's the price you gave me last year. Here's what I can get a competitor's product for. Here's what I can get a private-label version for. I want to see a better value that I can bring to my shopper this year. Or else I'm going to use that shelf space differently.'"

Carey has a friend in the umbrella business who learned that. One year, because of costs, he went to Wal-Mart and asked for a 5% price increase. "Wal-Mart said, 'We were expecting a 5% decrease. We're off by 10%. Go back and sharpen your pencil.'" The umbrella man scrimped and came back with a 2% increase. "They said, 'We'll go with a Chinese manufacturer'—and he was out entirely."

The Wal-Mart squeeze means vendors have to be as relentless and as microscopic as Wal-Mart is at managing their own costs. They need, in fact, to turn themselves into shadow versions of Wal-Mart itself. "Wal-Mart won't necessarily say you have to reconfigure your distribution system," says Carey. "But companies recognize they are not going to maintain margins with growth in their Wal-Mart business without doing it."

The way to avoid being trapped in a spiral of growing business and shrinking profits, says Carey, is to innovate. "You need to bring Wal-Mart new products—products consumers need. Because with those, Wal-Mart doesn't have benchmarks to drive you down in price. They don't have historical data, you don't have competitors, they haven't bid the products out to private-label makers. That's how you can have higher prices and higher margins."

Reasonable advice, but not universally useful. There has been an explosion of "innovation" in toothbrushes and toothpastes in the past five years, for instance; but a pickle is a pickle is a pickle.

Bain's other critical discovery is that consumers are often more loyal to product companies than to Wal-Mart. With strongly branded items people develop a preference for—things like toothpaste or laundry detergent—Wal-Mart rarely forces shoppers to switch to a second choice. It would simply punish itself by seeing sales fall, and it won't put up with that for long.

But as Wal-Mart has grown in market reach and clout, even manufacturers known for nurturing premium brands may find themselves overpowered. This July, in a mating that had the relieved air of lovers who had too long resisted embracing, Levi Strauss rolled blue jeans into every Wal-Mart doorway in the United States: 2,864 stores. Wal-Mart, seeking to expand its clothing business with more fashionable brands, promoted the clothes on its in-store TV network and with banners slipped over the security-tag detectors at exit doors.

Levi's launch into Wal-Mart came the same summer the clothes maker celebrated its 150th birthday. For a century and a half, one of the most recognizable names in American commerce had survived without Wal-Mart. But in October 2002, when Levi Strauss and Wal-Mart announced their engagement, Levi was shrinking rapidly.

The pressure on Levi goes back 25 years—well before Wal-Mart was an influence. Between 1981 and 1990, Levi closed 58 U.S. manufacturing plants, sending 25% of its sewing overseas.

Sales for Levi peaked in 1996 at $7.1 billion. By last year, they had spiraled down six years in a row, to $4.1 billion; through the first six months of 2003, sales dropped another 3%. This one account—selling jeans to Wal-Mart—could almost instantly revive Levi.

Last year, Wal-Mart sold more clothing than any other retailer in the country. It also sold more pairs of jeans than any other store. Wal-Mart's own inexpensive house brand of jeans, Faded Glory, is estimated to do $3 billion in sales a year, a house brand nearly the size of Levi Strauss. Perhaps most revealing in terms of Levi's strategic blunders: In 2002, half the jeans sold in the United States cost less than $20 a pair. That same year, Levi didn't offer jeans for less than $30.

For much of the last decade, Levi couldn't have qualified to sell to Wal-Mart. Its computer systems were antiquated, and it was notorious for delivering clothes late to retailers. Levi admitted its on-time delivery rate was 65%. When it announced the deal with Wal-Mart last year, one fashion-industry analyst bluntly predicted Levi would simply fail to deliver the jeans.

But Levi Strauss has taken to the Wal-Mart way with the intensity of a near-death religious conversion—and Levi's executives were happy to talk about their experience getting ready to sell at Wal-Mart. One hundred people at Levi's headquarters are devoted to the new business; another 12 have set up in an office in Bentonville, near Wal-Mart's headquarters, where the company has hired a respected veteran Wal-Mart sales account manager.

Getting ready for Wal-Mart has been like putting Levi on the Atkins diet. It has helped everything—customer focus, inventory management, speed to market. It has even helped other retailers that buy Levis, because Wal-Mart has forced the company to replenish stores within two days instead of Levi's previous five-day cycle.

And so, Wal-Mart might rescue Levi Strauss. Except for one thing. Levi didn't actually have any clothes it could sell at Wal-Mart. Everything was too expensive. It had to develop a fresh line for mass retailers: the Levi Strauss Signature brand, featuring Levi Strauss's name on the back of the jeans.

Two months after the launch, Levi basked in the honeymoon glow. Overall sales, after falling for the first six months of 2003, rose 6% in the third quarter; profits in the summer quarter nearly doubled. All, Levi's CEO said, because of Signature.

But the low-end business isn't a business Levi is known for, or one it had been particularly interested in. It's also a business in which Levi will find itself competing with lean, experienced players such as VF and Faded Glory. Levi's makeover might so improve its performance with its non-Wal-Mart suppliers that its established business will thrive, too. It is just as likely that any gains will be offset by the competitive pressures already dissolving Levi's premium brands, and by the cannibalization of its own sales. "It's hard to see how this relationship will boost Levi's higher-end business," says Paul Farris, a professor at the University of Virginia's Darden Graduate School of Business Administration. "It's easy to see how this will hurt the higher-end business."

If Levi clothing is a runaway hit at Wal-Mart, that may indeed rescue Levi as a business. But what will have been rescued? The Signature line—it includes clothing for girls, boys, men, and women—is an odd departure for a company whose brand has long been an American icon. Some of the jeans have the look, the fingertip feel, of pricier Levis. But much of the clothing has the look and feel it must have, given its price (around $23 for adult pants): cheap. Cheap and disappointing to find labeled with Levi Strauss's name. And just five days before the cheery profit news, Levi had another announcement: It is closing its last two U.S. factories, both in San Antonio, and laying off more than 2,500 workers, or 21% of its workforce. A company that 22 years ago had 60 clothing plants in the United States—and that was known as one of the most socially responsible corporations on the planet—will, by 2004, not make any clothes at all. It will just import them.

In the end, of course, it is we as shoppers who have the power, and who have given that power to Wal-Mart. Part of Wal-Mart's dominance, part of its insight, and part of its arrogance, is that it presumes to speak for American shoppers.

If Wal-Mart doesn't like the pricing on something, says Andrew Whitman, who helped service Wal-Mart for years when he worked at General Foods and Kraft, they simply say, "At that price we no longer think it's a good value to our shopper. Therefore, we don't think we should carry it."

Wal-Mart has also lulled shoppers into ignoring the difference between the price of something and the cost. Its unending focus on price underscores something that Americans are only starting to realize about globalization: Ever-cheaper prices have consequences. Says Steve Dobbins, president of thread maker Carolina Mills: "We want clean air, clear water, good living conditions, the best health care in the world—yet we aren't willing to pay for anything manufactured under those restrictions."

Randall Larrimore, a former CEO of MasterBrand Industries, the parent company of Master Lock, understands that contradiction too well. For years, he says, as manufacturing costs in the United States rose, Master Lock was able to pass them along. But at some point in the 1990s, Asian manufacturers started producing locks for much less. "When the difference is $1, retailers like Wal-Mart would prefer to have the brand-name padlock or faucet or hammer," Larrimore says. "But as the spread becomes greater, when our padlock was $9, and the import was $6, then they can offer the consumer a real discount by carrying two lines. Ultimately, they may only carry one line."

In January 1997, Master Lock announced that, after 75 years making locks in Milwaukee, it would begin importing more products from Asia. Not too long after, Master Lock opened a factory of its own in Nogales, Mexico. Today, it makes just 10% to 15% of its locks in Milwaukee—its 300 employees there mostly make parts that are sent to Nogales, where there are now 800 factory workers.

Larrimore did the first manufacturing layoffs at Master Lock. He negotiated with Master Lock's unions himself. He went to Bentonville. "I loved dealing with Wal-Mart, with Home Depot," he says. "They are all very rational people. There wasn't a whole lot of room for negotiation. And they had a good point. Everyone was willing to pay more for a Master Lock. But how much more can they justify? If they can buy a lock that has arguably similar quality, at a cheaper price, well, they can get their consumers a deal."

It's Wal-Mart in the role of Adam Smith's invisible hand. And the Milwaukee employees of Master Lock who shopped at Wal-Mart to save money helped that hand shove their own jobs right to Nogales. Not consciously, not directly, but inevitably. "Do we as consumers appreciate what we're doing?" Larrimore asks. "I don't think so. But even if we do, I think we say, Here's a Master Lock for $9, here's another lock for $6— let the other guy pay $9."

1. Is Wal-Mart an ethical marketer? Why or why not?
2. The title of this article contrasts low prices with high costs. What does this mean?
3. Are you a Wal-Mart shopper (most Americans are)? What is your experience with the company? Would you recommend it to others?

A MATTER OF TRUST[1]

Jennifer Gilbert

In the aftermath of highly publicized corporate scandals, all eyes are on company executives and the way they do business. Here's how some are leveraging their salespeople as the first line of defense against skeptics.

Gary Welch was hoping his early December meeting with a prospective business partner, a local builder, would go well. What he didn't expect was that he'd all but closed the deal in that one meeting on the strength of his company's ethical reputation.

"We were just wanting to build a relationship with him where we would act as his exclusive lender," says Welch, vice president of HomeBanc Mortgage Corporation, an Atlanta-based retail mortgage lender. For HomeBanc, prospective business partners are essentially prospective customers. When a deal is signed, HomeBanc becomes a builder's preferred lender—allowed to put marketing materials in the builder's homes and offices, and recommended to the builder's home buyers.

What sealed the deal in the meeting wasn't some knock 'em dead presentation— it was an article the builder had read in *The Atlanta Journal-Constitution* the previous day about HomeBanc's new chief people officer: Dwight "Ike" Reighard, an ordained minister. HomeBanc hired Reighard in December to maintain the quality of its workforce as the company expands.

"The builder said that if HomeBanc was willing to invest its money and its human capital in keeping employees happy, he had no questions as to how we would treat his customers," Welch says.

Such an example supports Welch's belief that customers do care about companies' ethical standards—and that it's in a company's best interest to have salespeople make such standards known. "That value has been heightened by all the negative things that have happened; it's a growing appreciation," Welch says. "If you can provide people with service and trust, they are willing to pay for that."

It's an issue that's coming up more and more during sales calls: An increasing number of sales managers are telling their reps to address the issues of ethics, corporate responsibility, and even financial viability in interactions with clients. In this business climate, some experts say, touting ethics during sales meetings is a golden opportunity to bolster a company's image. While most companies have ethics codes already in place, some are taking a second look at them, says John Boatright, professor of business ethics at Loyola University Chicago and executive director of the Society for Business Ethics, in Chicago. "But they're also looking at the need to increasingly focus on the code and use that code in decision making."

One potential use of the code, Boatright says, is "to make customers aware of it and to transmit this through the sales force. If companies are failing to do this, they are missing a good opportunity, because it increases the credibility of the company."

According to a recent *SMM*/Equation Research survey, 83 percent of 220 respondents said they train their reps to sell their companies' ethics and integrity along with

---

[1]*Sales & Marketing Management*, March 2003, pp. 30–35. Reprinted with permission.

their products and services. Nearly 70 percent said they believe their clients consider a company's ethical reputation when deciding whether to make a purchase. And while 48 percent said their companies haven't changed their emphasis on ethics and values in this economic climate, another 48 percent said they are placing somewhat more or much more emphasis on ethics.

"If corporations are not trying to promote, advertise, and sell their integrity through customers, employees, investors, and potential investors, then they are really missing a tremendous opportunity," says W. Michael Hoffman, executive director of the Center for Business Ethics at Bentley College, in Waltham, Massachusetts. Companies that develop strategies to convince those stakeholders to trust them will have a major competitive advantage over those that cannot, he says. "We are in an economic environment in which trust is at a premium. It's like air: When it's present, you don't think about it. When it's not present, you think about it all the time," Hoffman says. "We're in a financial market where there isn't a lot of air."

SPEAKING UP

Salespeople today are being told by their managers that a company's integrity can be as much of a selling point as low prices. So they talk about it.

HomeBanc's salespeople, for example, like to speak at length with customers about the company's commitment to keeping its employees happy. They hope that in every interaction, clients ask, "Why should we do business with you?" Welch says. HomeBanc's mission statement is: "To enrich and fulfill lives by serving each other, our customers and communities . . . as we support the dream of homeownership." The company's list of values includes, "We have integrity—do the right thing, always!" and "We deliver world-class service—serve all customers as they wish to be served." The company's mission and values are printed on cards that marketing materials sales associates carry with them to pass out to potential customers, and HomeBanc's marketing packages include reprints of newspaper articles highlighting the company's ethical initiatives.

Welch, who manages 10 salespeople and also engages in direct selling, says he has experienced a customer's appreciation for a company's integrity and ethical reputation and how that affects his or her buying decision. "There's been a real awakening to the question of, 'Who can we trust?'" in the wake of recent corporate scandals, he says. "What we're finding is that as people learn and see us live by our mission statement, they are attracted to doing business with us, because we fall in line with what their mission statement is."

Nancy Sparks, vice president of sales and marketing for Marietta, Georgia–based builder Homes by Williamscraft Inc., says her company chose HomeBanc as its exclusive lender for that reason. "We wanted to be associated with just them," she says. "They deliver as promised." Sparks says HomeBanc also promotes itself positively in the community through its advertising and salespeople and clearly sends the message that it is a well-established, reputable company. "In the corporate climate that we're in right now, any kind of business is suspect," she says. "Companies have to get out there

EXHIBIT 2-2   Dens of Iniquity

What aspects of corporate culture foster unethical behavior among employees, particularly salespeople?

An environment in which employees don't have a clear understanding of what is expected of them "The ideal approach is for an organization to have a written code of conduct that everyone receives and reads," says Jim Eskin, a public affairs consultant in San Antonio, Texas. It doesn't have to be formal; expectations regarding ethical conduct can be effectively communicated in meetings, orientation, bulletins, and e-mail. "The employer is asking for trouble when there is no communication at all," he says.

A communication breakdown Employees need to feel comfortable talking to supervisors. Otherwise, they will be less inclined to report ethics violations.

Rules dictated from the top down Smart employers bring their people together to talk about common issues, such as gifts and entertainment and the use of e-mail and other company resources. "The most effective rules result from employee input and feedback," Eskin says.

A win-at-any-price attitude from management Management leads by example, and if executives send signals that grabbing short-term profits is desirable regardless of the consequences, workers throughout the organization will reflect that attitude in their behavior.

A commission-centric environment Commissions can be tricky and run the risk of distorting judgment, especially when they put salespeople's personal interests at odds with those of the customer or client.

The cog-in-the-wheel trap If employees are proud of their organization and feel a sense of loyalty, their conduct is far more likely to be ethical. "But if they feel management is making profits at their expense, there could be a mindset of getting even," Eskin says.

—*J.G.*

every day and prove themselves. You don't want to be associated with any company that might not be doing that."

A big part of HomeBanc's ethical agenda is keeping employees honest and satisfied. It's on the right track, at least according to one expert: "The best indicator of how sales organizations are going to treat their clients is how they treat their employees," says Brian Clapp, managing principal of the mid-Atlantic region for Right Management Consultants, based in Philadelphia.

HomeBanc stages day-long orientation programs for new salespeople, during which reps learn about how to best treat customers—by providing service guarantees and full refunds for unsatisfactory services, for example. Training is a seven-week process that teaches salespeople how to identify the best loans for customers. And to make sure all reps are behaving ethically, HomeBanc set up a hotline eight years ago that salespeople can use to report behavior that would reflect negatively on the company.

"We've been Atlanta's number-one mortgage lender for eleven straight years and if we weren't ethically responsible, I don't think we'd be here," HomeBanc's Chief People Officer Reighard says.

Another company, Memphis, Tennessee–based Inventory Locator Service (ILS), also tries to promote its ethical standards—inside and out. "When I saw some of our new dot-com competitors come out in 1999, one of the things I developed for our sales team was a white paper that focused on integrity, because at the time, the competitors were using less-than-ethical business practices," says James Sdoia, vice president of sales and service at the company, which runs an electronic marketplace for the aviation, marine, and industrial gas turbine industries and the U.S. Department of Defense.

Salespeople give the two-page sheet to customers. It addresses ILS's fiscal integrity, data integrity, and client integrity, Sdoia says, and has been "quite effective in several cases—even more so when the competitors started using high-pressure tactics such as those you'd get from a door-to-door salesman."

Recently revised, the two-pager details the company's new products and services and has been reformatted into a question-and-answer structure. The handout answers questions such as, "What makes up your financial strength and stability?" And while his company's business-to-business customer base hasn't been rocked by corporate scandals reported in the news to the extent that he believes consumers have, Sdoia insists that his salespeople address the issue of ethics.

"Certainly, the corporate integrity of any company should be reflected by the salespeople when they talk about the company," he says. "You don't have to come out and say 'Our company's trustworthy'; you show how long you've been in business, that you are financially stable, and that you have long-term relationships with clients. Salespeople should say those things in pitches."

Bill Morales, president of Tracer Corporation, a Milwaukee-based aircraft parts company, says he's proud to be a 10-year ILS customer because of its ethical and professional reputation. "They back up what they say they can do," he says. "From an ethics standpoint, they are extremely open and forward-thinking. They are willing to stand behind their product."

LOOSE LIPS SINK SHIPS?

Some experts, of course, caution managers against having their salespeople talk too much about their company's integrity and ethical responsibility in pitches, advocating a show-don't-tell approach. Broaching the subject, they argue, can actually backfire and raise suspicion.

"The least effective way to be seen as trustworthy is to say, 'I'm trustworthy.' You have to behave in a way that inspires confidence," Atkins says, rather than say, "'We're really honest.' It sounds a little disingenuous."

Like Atkins, Bill Cook, vice president of sales at Santa Clara, California–based Sun Microsystems, is an advocate of the actions-speak-louder-than-words philosophy.

A 17-year alumnus of Sun's sales team, Cook says his company's ethical reputation has been built over time through its employees' actions.

Indeed, it's the small stuff that often means more to customers than words, Right's Clapp says. These include following up on commitments, not being cavalier, honoring noncompetes, and not selling empty promises.

Still, Cook acknowledges that the latest corporate scandals have shed new light on the issues of corporate and financial responsibility. Last October, Sun rolled out the Fiduciary Boot Camp, a special training program for all senior-level managers worldwide. The boot camp is designed to educate executives on the new rules and regulations included in the Sarbanes-Oxley Act of 2002, which holds companies to higher corporate governance standards, and informs them of Sun's view of ethical leadership. Executives who attend share the lessons with salespeople.

Sun's boot camp has boosted reps' recognition of the issues. But salespeople still interact with customers as they always have, Cook says. Customers do perceive Sun to be an ethical company with which to do business, Cook says, but that's because of the way its salespeople conduct themselves. "You just show it, day in and day out," he says. "We tell our customers about our products and offerings, and then we make sure we deliver against those. It's part of Sun's culture."

1. Which company example discussed in this article did you find most persuasive? Why?
2. How does trust relate to Chapter 1?
3. Have your personally experienced any of the "Dens of Iniquity?" Explain.

CHAPTER

Short Cases

TOY WARS[1]

Manuel Velasquez

Early in 1986, Tom Daner, president of the advertising company Daner Associates, was contacted by Mike Teal, the sales manager of Crako Industries. Crako Industries is a family-owned company that manufactures children's toys and had long been a favorite and important client of Daner Associates. The sales manager of Crako Industries explained that the company had just developed a new toy helicopter. The toy was modeled after the military helicopters that had been used in Vietnam and that had appeared in the "Rambo" movies. Mike Teal explained that the toy was developed in response to the craze for military toys that had been sweeping the nation in the wake of the Rambo movies. The family-owned toy company had initially resisted moving into military toys because members of the family objected to the violence associated with such toys. However, as segments of the toy market were increasingly taken over by military toys, the family came to feel that entry into the military toy market was crucial for their business. Consequently, they approved development of a line of military toys, hoping that they were not entering the market too late. Mike Teal now wanted Daner Associates to develop a television advertising campaign for the toy.

The toy helicopter Crako designers had developed was about one and one-half feet long, battery operated, and made of plastic and steel. Mounted to the sides are detachable replicas of machine guns and a detachable stretcher modeled on the stretchers used to lift wounded soldiers from a battlefield. Mike Teal explained that they were trying to develop a toy that would be perceived as "more macho" than the top-selling "G.I. Joe" line of toys. According to the sales manager, if the company were to compete successfully in today's toy market, it would have to adopt an advertising approach that was even "meaner and tougher" than what other companies were doing.

Consequently, he continued, the advertising clips developed by Daner Associates would have to be "mean and macho." Television advertisements for the toy, he suggested, might show the helicopter swooping over buildings and blowing them up. The more violence and mayhem the ads suggested, the better. Crako Industries was relying heavily on sales from the new toy, and some managers felt that the company's future might depend on the success of this toy.

Tom Daner was unwilling to have his company develop television advertisements that would increase what he already felt was too much violence on television aimed at children. In particular, he recalled a television ad for a tricycle with a replica machine gun mounted on the handle bars. The commercial showed the tricycle being pedaled through the woods by a small boy as he chased several other boys fleeing before him over a dirt path. At one point, the camera closed in over the shoulder of the boy, focused through the gunsight, and showed the gunsight apparently trying to aim at the backs of the boys as they fled before the tricycle's machine gun. Ads of that sort had disturbed Tom Daner and had led him to think that advertisers should find other ways of promoting these toys. Therefore, he suggested that instead of promoting the Crako helicopter through violence it should be presented in some other manner. When Teal asked what he had in mind, Tom was forced to reply that he didn't know. At any rate, Tom pointed out, the three television networks would not accept a violent commercial aimed at children. All three networks adhered to an advertising code that prohibited violent, intense, or unrealistic advertisements aimed at children.

This seemed no real obstacle to Teal, however. Although the networks might turn down children's ads when they were too violent, local television stations were not as squeamish. Local television stations around the country regularly accepted ads aimed at children that the networks had rejected as too violent. The local stations inserted the ads as spots on their non-network programming, thereby circumventing the advertising codes of the three national networks. Daner Associates would simply have to place the ads they developed for the Crako helicopter through local television stations around the country. Mike Teal was firm: If Daner Associates would not develop a mean and tough ad campaign, the toy company would move their account to an advertiser that would. Reluctantly, Tom Daner agreed to develop the advertising campaign. Crako Industries accounted for $1 million of Daner's total revenues.

Like Crako Industries, Daner Associates was also a family-owned business. Founded by his father almost 50 years ago, the advertising firm that Tom Daner now ran had grown dramatically under his leadership. In 1975, the business had grossed $3 million; 10 years later, it had revenues of $25 million and provided a full line of advertising services. The company was divided into three departments (creative, media, and account executive), each of which had about 12 employees. Tom Daner credited much of the company's success to the many new people he had hired, especially a group with MBAs who had developed new marketing strategies based on more thorough market and consumer analyses. Most decisions, however, were made by a five-person executive committee consisting of Tom Daner, the senior accountant, and the three department heads. As owner-president, Tom's views tended to color most decisions, producing what one member of the committee called a "benevolent dictatorship." Tom was an enthusiastic, congenial, intelligent, and well-read person. During college he had considered becoming a missionary priest, but had changed his mind and was now married and the father of three daughters. His personal heroes included Thomas Merton, Albert Schweitzer, and Tom Doley.

When Tom Daner presented the Crako deal to his executive committee, he found that they did not share his misgivings. The other committee members felt that Daner Associates should give Crako exactly the kind of ad they wanted: one with a heavy content of violence. Moreover, the writers and artist in the creative department were enthused with the prospect of letting their imaginations loose on the project, several feeling that they could easily produce an attention-grabbing ad by "out-violencing" current television programming. The creative department, in fact, quickly produced a copy script that called for videos showing the helicopter "flying out of the sky with machine-guns blazing" at a jungle village below. This kind of ad, they felt, was exactly what they were being asked to produce by their client.

After viewing the copy, Tom Daner refused to use it. He insisted they should produce an ad, he insisted, that would meet their client's needs but that would also meet the guidelines of the national networks. The ad should not glorify violence and war, but should somehow support cooperation and family values. Disappointed and somewhat frustrated, the creative department went back to work. A few days later, they presented a second proposal: an ad that would show the toy helicopter flying through the family room of a home as a little boy plays with it; then the scene shifts to show the boy on a rock rising from the floor of the family room; the helicopter swoops down and picks up the boy as if rescuing him from the rock where he had been stranded. Although the creative department was mildly pleased with their attempt, they felt it was too "tame." Tom liked it, however, and a version of the ad was filmed.

A few weeks later, Tom Daner met with Mike Teal and his team and showed them the film. The viewing was not a success. Teal turned down the ad. Referring to the network regulations that other toy advertisements were breaking as frequently as motorists broke the 55-mile-per-hour speed law, he said, "That commercial is going only 55 miles an hour when I want one that goes 75." If the next version was not "tougher and meaner," Crako Industries would be forced to look elsewhere.

Disappointed, Tom Daner returned to the people in his creative department and told them to go ahead with designing the kind of ad they had originally wanted: "I don't have any idea what else to do." In a short time, the creative department had an ad proposal on his desk that called for scenes showing the helicopter blowing up villages. Shortly afterwards, a small set was constructed depicting a jungle village sitting next to a bridge stretching over a river. The ad was filmed using the jungle set as a background.

When Tom saw the result, he was not happy. He decided to meet with his creative department and air his feelings. "The issue here," he said, "is basically the issue of violence. Do we really want to present toys as instruments for beating up people? This ad is going to promote aggression and violence. It will glorify dominance and do it with kids who are terrifically impressionable. Do we really want to do this?" The members of the creative department, however, responded that they were merely giving their client what the client wanted. That client, moreover, was an important account. The client wanted an aggressive "macho" ad, and that was what they were providing. The ad might violate the regulations of the television networks, but there were ways to get around the networks. Moreover, they said, every other advertising firm in the business was breaking the limits against violence set by the networks. Tom made one last try: Why not market the toy as an adventure and fantasy toy? Film the ad again, he suggested, using the same jungle backdrop. But instead of showing the helicopter shooting at a burning village, show it flying in to rescue people from the burning village. Create an ad that shows excitement, adventure, and fantasy, but no aggression. "I was trying," he said later, "to figure out a new way of approaching this kind of advertising. We have to follow the market or we can go out of business trying to moralize to the market. But why not try a new approach? Why not promote toys as instruments that expand the child's imagination in a way that is positive and that promotes cooperative values instead of violence and aggression?"

A new film version of the ad was made, now showing the helicopter flying over the jungle set. Quick shots and heightened background music give the impression of excitement and danger. The helicopter flies dramatically through the jungle and over a river and bridge to rescue a boy from a flaming village. As lights flash and shoot haphazardly through the scene, the helicopter rises and escapes into the sky. The final ad was clearly exciting and intense. It promoted the saving of a life instead of violence against life.

It was clear when the final version was shot, however, that it would not clear the network censors. Network guidelines require that sets in children's ads must depict things that are within the reach of most children so that they do not create unrealistic expectations. Clearly the elaborate jungle set (which cost $25,000 to construct) was not within the reach of most children, and consequently most children would not be able to re-create the scene of the ad by buying the toy. Moreover, network regulations stipulate that in children's ads scenes must be filmed with normal lighting that does not create undue intensity. Again clearly the helicopter ad, which created excitement by using quick changes of light and fast cuts, did not fall within these guidelines.

After reviewing the film, Tom Daner reflected on some last-minute instructions Crako's sales manager had given him when he had been shown the first version of the ad: The television ad should show things being blown up by the guns of the little helicopter and perhaps even some blood on the fuselage of the toy; the ad had to be violent. Now Tom had to make a decision. Should he risk the account by submitting only the rescue mission ad? Or should he let Teal also see the ad that showed the helicopter shooting up the village, knowing that he would probably prefer that version if he saw it? Was the rescue mission ad really that much different from the ad that showed the shooting of the village? Did it matter that the rescue mission ad still violated some of the network regulations? What if he offered Teal only the rescue mission ad and Teal accepted the rescue approach? What if the ad failed to sell the Crako toy? Was it right to experiment with a client's product, especially a product that was so important to the future of the client's business? Tom was unsure what he should do. He wanted to show Teal only the rescue mission commercial, but he felt he first had to resolve these questions in his own mind.

1. From a moral point of view, what in your judgment should Tom Daner's final decision be? Justify your answer. What should Tom do if he is asked to make the final ad more violent than the rescue ad he had filmed?
2. Answer the questions Tom Daner asked himself: Was the rescue mission ad really that much different from the ad that showed the shooting of the village? Did it matter that the rescue mission ad still violated some of the network regulations? Was it right to experiment with a client's product, especially a product that was so important to the future of the client's business?

TOY WARS CASE ANALYSES

Editors' note: We included the Toy Wars case because it is a "classic" in marketing ethics, and we wanted to share with you two different approaches to analyzing the rest of the cases. In the pages to follow, we first answer the questions posed at the end of the case. Then, we use a case analysis worksheet in analyzing "Toy Wars." Your instructor may want to use this format or another approach rather than having you complete the questions provided for case discussion. Finally, the "real" Tom Daner gives a short reflection on how this case was ultimately resolved and what happened to the Crako Company.

Question 1   Tom should resist showing the violent commercial and only recommend the rescue mission one. The violent commercial goes against both his personal and the agency's values. In justifying this answer, one could use the virtue ethics discussion in Chapter 1. He should probably be prepared to resign the account rather than give in to making the ad more violent. Although the Crako account is substantial in terms of billings, the agency could probably afford to lose it. This decision would send a signal to Tom's employees that the values he espouses are lived in a time of crisis.

Question 2   In Tom's mind the rescue mission ad was much different than the original violent version. He feels that children are exposed to too much violence in program content and commercials. He wants to promote the positive values/virtues of "excitement, adventure and fantasy, but no aggression." The second part of the question asks about the set. This mock-up, while not technically acceptable, helps create the atmosphere for the ad. Tom and his company seem to be using a utilitarian approach (see Chapter 1) in going with the new set. In other words, the benefits of portraying the situation realistically outweigh the higher costs. The third portion of this question is the hardest to answer. The student is encouraged to review the rights/duties discussion of Chapter 1. The instructor might want students to "debate" the answer to this question given that there appear to be merits on both sides of the issue.

CASE ANALYSIS WORKSHEET

Determine the Facts (who, what, where, when)   The major characters in this case are Tom Daner, chief executive officer (CEO) of the ad agency, and Mike Teal, of Crako Toys. This case deals with an ad agency that is asked to come up with a campaign to sell toy helicopters. Tom Daner's client—Crako—wants a violence-oriented ad because "war toys" were selling well at this time. The creative team at the agency complied with the client's request, but Daner resisted this approach. Crako represents a $1 million account in a $30 million business. It takes place somewhere in the United States, and the time period is the mid-1980s.

Ethical Issue (Make sure to identify precisely what the ethical issue is. For example, conflict involving rights, question over limits of obligation on safety responsibility to a certain stakeholder, and so on.)   The ethical issue primarily revolves around a conflict between the client's values and the owner of the ad agency. Another way to put it in question form is, Is it ethical for Tom Daner to violate the marketing concept and not give the client what he wants in terms of a commercial for the product?

Identify Major Principles or Theories (For example, what ethical theories relate most closely to this issue? Virtue ethics [integrity, fairness, respect for persons] duties [recall Kant's formulations], consequences—greatest good, rights and duties, and so on.)   This case appears to be one that deals primarily with virtue ethics. Tom resists the violence-oriented theme because it violates his personal and his organization's values. The other principle that could be applied is the rights of the client versus the agency.

Stakeholder Analysis (Who are the most important stakeholders? Distinguish between primary—those with direct contractual relationship; indirect—those with an abiding interest; and secondary—those with a potential or distant interest.)   The primary stakeholders in the case are Mike Teal of Crako, Tom Daner, and Tom's employees. They all have a stake in this decision in that losing the account could possibly affect the employees' future with the firm. Since both of these are private firms, they do not have to answer to stockholders. The financial viability of Crako may be at stake if they fail to sell the projected number of toy helicopters. Children who would play with the toy are also primary stakeholders.

Indirect stakeholders are parents, other toy manufacturers and other advertising agencies. All these have a vested interest in what Daner and Teal decide to do. Secondary stakeholders might be the media that report on violence-oriented subjects and social action groups that try to protect the rights of children. What others can you think of?

Specify the Alternatives (List the major alternative courses of action, including those that represent some form of compromise or point between simply doing or not doing something. Also list the pros and cons of each alternative.) This case is relatively straightforward in that there appear to be only two alternatives. First, Daner can give Crako the violent ad that Teal wants. The advantage of this alternative is that this is what the client has demanded, but the downside is that it flies in the face of Daner's values. Second, he can present only the "rescue" ad. Its advantages and disadvantages are just the opposite of the first alternative. Are there additional alternatives?

Compare Principles and Theories with Alternatives (Determine if there is one principle theory or value or combination thereof that is so compelling that the proper alternative is clear, such as correcting a defect that is almost certain to cause loss of life.) This case boils down to one of Daner sticking to his principles and rejecting the violent ad, even in the face of pressure from both his employees and Teal. His values and the virtue ethics approach suggest that he must follow his conscience.

Make and Justify Your Decision (Select the alternative that best fits your primary principles or values. How would you argue for *your* decision when others might disagree with you?) Daner should only present the rescue mission ad to Teal and Crako. If they reject it, he should be willing to resign the account. However, he should make every effort to convince them that such a rescue-oriented approach may "differentiate" Crako from the competitors, who are using a violence-oriented theme.

TOY WARS: THE REST OF THE STORY

Ron Nahser

Twenty years after the fact, it is an honor and pleasure to reveal the facts behind the Toy Wars case. Based on my experience, it captures the basic dilemma of how we present products to the public to interest them in their purchase.

To identify the characters, my name is F. Byron Nahser (better known as Ron, or Tom Daner in the case), and I have been president and CEO of the Nahser Agency since 1984. We are a family-owned agency, it being founded by my father in 1939 as an outgrowth of our family's Globe Engraving and Electrotype Company founded in 1889 by my grandfather in Chicago. So, we have a long history, and I have always attempted to take the long view.

The name of Crako Industries is Nylint Toys of Rockford, Illinois, founded in 1943. Mike Teal is a composite character representing Ted Klint, president and son of the founder, and the Nylint sales manager, Wayne Helfer. Since they both held the same view toward the ad, a decision was made to minimize the number of characters in the case.

The hero of the story, who is not mentioned because he comes in just after the conclusion of the case, is the founder of Nylint, a Swedish tool and die maker, Bernard Klint—known better as Barney. Since he will play a central role in how the case actually ended, a word of background is important.

Barney began the company to make cheese slicers for the Swedish population in Rockford, Illinois. In the evenings, he would bring home scrap metal and make metal toys for his two sons and neighbor children.

In classic American fashion, Barney's wife, Grace, would take extra toys and sell them door to door in Rockford. The business grew over the years, and Nylint and the much better-known Tonka Toys were the leaders who developed the steel toy industry. Tonka and Nylint eventually divided the market with Tonka taking the lead in "yellow goods"—construction toys—and Nylint with "red goods"—fire and rescue equipment.

Incidentally, Barney is the picture of what you would imagine a president of a toy company to be—a stern, round leader, with red cheeks that put you in mind of Santa Claus in charge of a workshop of elves—in a gray tool and die knee-length denim work coat with a red collar and "Barney" embroidered in red letters across the top of a pocket filled with micrometers and other tools of the trade. He had a stern look, but you could see right through the eyes to a warm and loving heart.

The rest of the facts in the case are accurate. One word of background: several years before this case, Nylint had planned to enter the military toy category with a jeep/machine gun attack vehicle. I had then suggested that they turn it into a forestry rescue vehicle with canoe, rope, ladder, and so on. So when I first saw the military helicopter as part of the new line, I suggested that it would make a great hospital or emergency chopper. There was a loud round of groans, and they said no, unless I wanted to buy all the forestry jeeps still languishing in the warehouse. This was going to be military, like in *Apocalypse Now*. I reminded them that the movie was profoundly antiwar, to which Ted responded, "I'm talking about the scene with Robert Duvall and the smell of napalm."

I would add that sales manager Wayne Helfer, when he presented the product and the first version of the commercial to the head toy buyer at the largest account Toys 'R Us, to his credit explained that they had kept all the regulatory guidelines and so on. After the showing, there was silence. Finally, the buyer looked over at Wayne and said, "That commercial goes 55 miles an hour. It needs to go 90."

Shortly after Wayne returned to Rockford, the final meeting to decide on the advertising was called. As we prepared for the meeting, I rehearsed the argument wondering if it would make any difference since it was a rehash of a now long and extensive conversation with Ted and Wayne.

I walked into the meeting in the mahogany toy-filled conference room, and quickly the meeting went downhill when I presented only the rescue version of the commercial. As we were heading for the inevitable decision to be fired or resign, just then the door of the conference room opened, and in walked Barney, who quietly took his place at the head of the table. I quickly summarized my case and finally said, mumbling my way to a conclusion, something like "I just didn't think it was right to present the war commercial" and Barney, in a very soft voice, said, "I agree. A company like ours doesn't do things like that." At that moment I felt something akin to grace, or the spirit, fill the room—or certainly me!

NEXT STEP

We ran the "rescue" commercial. It was beautiful, exciting, and a rescue mission. Unfortunately, the product turned out to be too complicated and too expensive and did not sell all that well.

We kept the account for the next 20 years. In the 1990s, Fisher Price successfully sold a series of products called "Rescue Heroes" on the same idea of nonviolent rescue figures and products.

THE AFTERMATH

Nylint, as many manufacturers have gone through, ran into great difficulty as cheaper imports in toys came from the Orient. They moved some of their production, in a joint venture, to Korea and through an agent into China. But they had a fierce loyalty to their Rockford employees.

Barney died several years later, and with Ted at the helm, he was reluctant to face the tough decision to let go long-standing employees in Rockford and face the inevitable move to cheaper production sourcing. As Nylint faced continuing tough competition and in the turmoil of the stock market and dot-com collapse that considerably weakened the economy, the company went into bankruptcy and sold for pennies on the dollar, owing the Nahser Agency a considerable amount of money.

The irony is that the bankruptcy occurred in May 2001, months before the fatal 9/11 attacks. Think for a moment of the opportunity for an ethically based company to market "red goods"—fire engines—to a grieving public where the image of brave firemen and their vehicles played such an inspirational part of the drama.

STRATEGY QUESTION

What does this little case say about Nylint Toys and its survival, the Nahser Agency and its survival, and American business and advertising in general?

The basic point, I would say, is that millions of executives all over the world are faced with tough decisions to be made every day in business. The sum total of all those decisions is what makes up our world.

In Nylint's case, you could say they were too focused on their own survival and not open to different ways to think about the business. That, to me, is the constant task that best is summed up in what Patricia Werhane has dubbed "moral imagination."

WHAT WOULD I HAVE DONE IF . . .

The obvious question is, What would I have done if Barney had not interceded?

In those blazing moments, when we faced the decision, I trust I would have said in an equally soft voice as Barney did, "No, we won't do it." But with Barney there, I realized the importance of a community and leaders to inspire the strength of others. I will never forget his simple logic and quiet voice to present his thoughts and heart.

FINAL PERSONAL NOTE

I believe that advertising has an enormous impact in shaping what can only be called "the common good" because it is through our purchases that we determine the shape of our society. Therefore, we've been guided by this purpose as we have refined it over some 60 years of business: "Our purpose is to create and implement outstanding ideas to help our clients' business grow, benefit the user, and contribute to the well-being of society." To achieve this, we activate our clients' sustainable competitive advantages to grow their market position: "Own Who You Are®."

We help each of our clients and think it's the task of every organization to figure out how best to serve the market, respond to authentic needs, and make the tough decisions based on the values of the character of the organization and of the individual for the sustainability of the company, the customer, and the society in which we live.

The lesson is that at times, we need, as Barney Klint showed, to say, quietly, "No, that isn't the kind of company, and people, we are."

THE COOKIE CASE[1]

Catherine Hart

Introduction

Within Hillside Mall's food court is Mrs. Fields Cookies, one of the cookie company's over 650 domestic locations. This particular franchise in a suburban mall is owned and operated by Sue and John Smith. Mrs. Fields Cookies prepares and sells cookies, brownies, muffins, and chocolate candies. The store also serves soda, coffee, and milk.

Upon opening, Sue and John made the decision to discount all mall employee soda purchases. Mall employees may receive any size soda they want (small, medium, or large) for the price of a small. This widely recognized discount draws many mall employees to Mrs. Fields when they are on their work breaks. Thus, Mrs. Fields consistently earns significant profits from mall employees and sees many repeat customers.

Sue and John are extremely easygoing bosses and put a lot of trust and responsibility into their employees, most of whom are teenage girls. The two of them are often gone from the location, and rely on in-store managers to run the store much of the time. Consequently, many activities in the store go unnoticed.

Free Treats

It is the summer of 1996, and 15-year-old Catherine has been working at Mrs. Fields for about two weeks. Usually about three to five people staff each shift. When Sue and John are not present, there is always an adult manager and then two or three other workers with Catherine. Each person is in charge of assisting customers, which includes giving them their food and/or drink and then ringing up their purchase at the register. During slow periods, employees restock the shelves and keep the countertops clean.

Catherine has noticed that many of the employees will often give customers food and drinks without making them pay. The customers receiving free food are often friends or family of the Mrs. Fields employee, but they are usually fellow mall employees. The typical encounter consists of a greeting between the two employees, a bit of small talk, occasional flirting, the selection of the mall employee's desired treat and/or beverage, more small talk, and then a goodbye. What happened to the exchange of money?

It is clear to Catherine that her coworkers do not find their actions to be that big of a deal. With all of the cookies that are dropped, squished, and eaten by Mrs. Fields workers (which Sue and John generously permit), the freebies are too difficult to account for anyway. There is no way Sue and John would truly know that their employees frequently do not charge visitors for food.

---

[1]This case was prepared by Catherine Hart under the direction of Patrick E. Murphy for classroom discussion, rather than to illustrate either effective or ineffective handling of an administrative, ethical, or legal decision by individuals or management.

Rachel's Reasons

Rachel, a 17-year-old who has been working at Mrs. Fields for almost a year, feels no guilt in giving free soda and treats to some of her "favorite" customers. She is a vivacious young girl who loves the attention that friendly visitors give to her. Rachel aims to please so that she will be known as the "likeable girl" from the food court.

One of her favorite customers is Ben, a young gentleman who works at Banana Republic. Rachel looks forward to his visits because of his good looks and charming compliments. Their interactions are always the same: a pleasant greeting, Rachel giving him his favorite order without him needing to ask, some playful talk and gestures, a then a goodbye. She never charges him, and he has become accustomed to this routine.

Rachel is overly gracious to everyone and thrives off the pleased responses she receives after giving treats away free of charge. She continues to do this for many people because she likes to make them happy and she wants people to think fondly of her in return.

Ashley's Alibi

Ashley, a 16-year-old who has been at Mrs. Fields for two months, gives mall employees free goodies with the hope that she will get store discounts from them in return. She repeatedly hands over free cookies and soda to people who work in some of her favorite clothing and accessory stores. When she makes visits to their stores, the employees remember her from the food court, and they often give her their employee discounts when they ring her up at the register. It is one favor for another.

Catherine's Conflict

Catherine is faced with these encounters during every shift of hers. Although she knows what the girls are doing is not right, she does not think too much of it until Rachel, Ashley, and some of the others start giving her a hard time for charging some of their favorite repeat customers. They explain to her that it is upsetting to the customers who have come to expect preferred treatment when they visit Mrs. Fields during their breaks. They feel Catherine is ruining the image they are creating for themselves. The other girls make it seem like it is an accepted way of doing work around there. Catherine knows Sue and John would not feel that way!

Many of the customers are even influential. Catherine can sense their surprise and/or disappointment when she charges some of the mall employees for their food. It makes her feel as though they will dislike her if she does not give them the preferred treatment as the other Mrs. Fields employees do.

The Dilemma

Catherine is unsure about what to do. She realizes Sue and John will never really know if she just gives a few of the mall employees food without charging them. Besides, if she just goes ahead and does this, her coworkers will be pleased with her and she will not get as many frowns from the repeat customers. Everyone will be happier with her, and Sue and John likely will not find out. However, Catherine knows that she should not partake in their dishonorable behavior. Furthermore, she knows her coworkers' habits should be stopped. Sue and John trust their employees, whose actions are not only disloyal but are costing Sue and John profits as well. Yet, if Catherine does not go along with the employees' pressures to give away free food, she will feel uncomfortable around them knowing that they are upset with her. It is likely to create an awkward working environment for her. She will also feel like she is just as much to blame if she does not report their behavior to Sue and John. It would be wrong for her to let such lack of trustworthiness go unnoticed. Catherine knows what is going on and has the choice to ignore it, participate in it, or attempt to stop it.

1. What should she do?

MAKING IT UP[1]

Raymond F. Keyes

Terry Peters was in a tough situation. His boss was asking him to do something that Terry believed bordered on dishonesty. However, if he refused to go along, he was pretty sure that his position as a sales representative with the Acme Instruments Corp. would be seriously jeopardized. As a new member of the Northeast Medical Instruments team, Terry was just beginning to learn the ropes regarding his responsibilities as a field sales rep calling on hospitals, medical laboratories, and other medical facilities. His job called for regular sales calls on each of his assigned accounts to provide product information and to take orders for new and replacement medical instruments products. Since he was one of five sales reps in the Northeast region, he, along with his fellow team members, traveled extensively from account to account in a widespread geographic area. Terry's territory covered western Massachusetts, northern New York, and Vermont. It was not unusual for him to be "on the road" for two and sometimes three nights a week. In order to properly cover his accounts, it was important for him to have a dependable, comfortable automobile. It was in the area of reimbursement for the automobile expenses and for other related travel costs that Terry was confronted with his ethical dilemma.

Before coming to work for Acme, Terry had worked as a sales representative for a pharmaceutical firm. Because of the nature of the job, all the salespersons were paid on a straight salary basis with modest end-of-year bonuses for accomplishment of corporate and regional sales objectives. In addition, the sales reps were supplied with leased cars and a fairly liberal reimbursement program for expenses related to sales calls and customer entertainment. While this job provided a good, safe income, it did not offer much of an opportunity for income growth in response to solid sales performance. Therefore, Terry had decided to go to work for Acme because of its excellent product line and its salary/commission sales plan. The salary portion of the plan provided adequate income for basic living expenses, while the commission component provided additional income in direct proportion to individual sales effectiveness and results. Terry favored this approach because he was confident that he could perform well and enjoy increased earnings as he mastered the job and generated increased sales returns for the company.

One significant difference in the new company was in the way they handled automobile and sales expense reimbursements. The company did not provide lease cars but rather gave each new sales rep a $10,000 signing bonus, primarily to cover the down payment on a new car. In addition, an ongoing mileage reimbursement plan was designed to cover gas, repairs and subsequent automobile payments. The logic of this plan was to position the salesperson to buy a car and to pay it off in three years. At the end of that time, the salesperson could buy a new car, using the turn-in value of his existing car to cover the new down payment. The mileage reimbursement would continue as before as

---

[1]This case was prepared by the late Professor Raymond F. Keyes of Boston College for classroom discussion rather than to illustrate either effective or ineffective handling of an administrative, ethical, or legal decision by individuals or management.

the source of funds for the continuing car payments. This plan seemed fair to Terry, and he appreciated the $10,000 signing bonus and the opportunity to purchase and own a car of his own choosing as opposed to using a leased one. It certainly seemed simpler this way for the company and for him.

After he had been on the job for six weeks, Terry's sales supervisor, Ralph Porter, took him aside to discuss a problem that the sales reps on the team were having with the company's expense reimbursement plan, especially in the automobile reimbursement area. Under the plan, sales reps were paid 35 cents per mile to cover their gasoline costs, upkeep repair of the cars, and ongoing car loan payments. According to Ralph, the 35 cents did not provide an adequate amount to position the sales reps to cover expenses and to position them to replace the cars at the end of three years. The reps had presented their case to company management, but the accountants insisted that the plan was fair, particularly insofar as the reps were allowed to use the cars for their personal use as well as for business purposes. According to Ralph's calculations, the sales reps should receive between 40 and 45 cents per mile in order to generate the necessary funds to cover automobile depreciation and replacement. In the face of management's refusal to increase the mileage rate, Ralph had come up with a simple plan to which his sales team had agreed. Each sales rep would add 100 miles to his or her weekly mileage figures, over and above the amount actually driven. The added miles would provide increased reimbursement, and according to Ralph's calculations, this would make up for the shortfall in the existing company plan. According to Ralph, this was the fair way to solve the problem in the face of the "damned accountants and their niggardly approach." All of the team members had agreed to this strategy, and Ralph presumed that Terry would agree as well. He said that it would look bad if one sales rep's mileage figures were significantly lower than the others in comparable territories. In fact, the sales rep who preceded Terry in the territory had used the 100-mile inflating device before being promoted to larger territory. Ralph pointed out that it would not look good to have Terry turn in mileage numbers that were significantly less than his predecessor's.

In this same meeting, Ralph had some other suggestions concerning expense reimbursements. Company policy allowed sales reps to be reimbursed for reasonable expenses for overnight accommodations and meals. It did not, however, allow for reimbursement of expenses related to entertainment or other nonbusiness out-of-pocket expenses. The accountants reasoned that the sales reps would be paying their own entertainment expenses if they were at home, and so should they do the same when traveling. "The company reimbursement plan is not designed to cover expenses not directly related to the business of doing business." Here again, Ralph believed that the "accountants" were being unrealistic and unfair. He felt that the sales reps should receive some compensation for the inconvenience and hardship of being away from home. "Are they expected to sit in their hotel rooms every evening reading the Bible?"

Ralph went on to explain that at the recent trade show in Chicago, he had advised his reps to build up their expense chits with extra charges for taxis and tips and other phantom expenses to make up for the $50 to $100 that they each spent on their evening out on the town. "How can you get people to work at these trade shows if there isn't some incentive in the form of entertainment and relaxation? You may think that this is simply padding the expense account, but I really believe that it is the fair way to handle things in the face of the unrealistic stance of the company's management."

It is now two weeks after his meeting with Ralph, and Terry is in the process of filling out his monthly expense reimbursement form. He is very uncomfortable with Ralph's plan involving the recording of extra mileage. In addition, he resists the idea that he should *make up* some business-related expenses to offset some of his non-business ones. However, it is not as easy as simply recording the correct figures. In his role as sales supervisor, Ralph sees every one of the expense forms. He will know that Terry has not built up his mileage or other travel-related expenses. This could create real problems for Terry in that it would be evident that he had acted against the instructions of his supervisor and against the wishes of the other members of the team. His actions would clearly be interpreted as a sign that he believed that they were acting unethically. Clearly, this would not get him off to a very good start in his new job. Ralph is in a position to do him genuine harm in his periodic performance evaluations and in his daily interactions with him. The other team reps can hurt Terry as well since the team concept requires that the people work together and assist one another in their various sales endeavors. Terry feels that he is confronted with the problem of "going along to get along" versus adherence to his own moral standards.

1. What is the ethical problem or dilemma here, and what moral standards are involved?
2. Who will be affected by Terry's action? How will these stakeholders be affected if Terry goes along with Ralph and if he does not go along?
3. What role does rationalization play in this situation? Does Ralph have any justification for his "making it up" approach?
4. What alternatives does Terry have? What are the ethical implications of the alternatives? What are the practical implications of the alternatives?
5. If Terry does go along with Ralph's approach, can he be absolved from responsibility because of Ralph's hold over him as his superior? If Terry goes along, can he claim that he is only following orders?
6. What would you do?

KROMBACHER—SAVE NATURE, DRINK BEER![1]

Eva Barcikowski and Johannes Brinkmann

In the summer of 2002, the most popular sporting event in Europe—the soccer World Cup—was about to begin. The venues for the matches were in Japan and Korea, but many, many fans throughout the world were expected to follow this event. Soccer, the national sport in Germany, is closely related to beer, the national drink.

For soccer fans, beer is the most popular drink in bars as they watch soccer games with their fellow fan-club members as well as at home, where they watch the games on TV with their friends. It is, therefore, understandable that an event like the World Cup, where even non–soccer–fans watch the games on TV and long for their country to be victorious, is the reason for an increase in advertising for virtually every beer producer. One German brewery developed an advertising campaign which gained special attention.

The Campaign

Krombacher is a brewery located in scenic Sauerland, an area in northwestern Germany.[2] It is the largest private brewery in Germany, and Krombacher Pils is the leading German lager in terms of market share. The company has advertised its beer as "the pearl of nature" (with a picture of Sauerland in each of its advertisements). For the brewery, its commitment to nature is an "obligation and challenge at the same time." Consequently, the advertising campaign built around the World Cup combined beer consumption with nature conservation.

Günther Jauch, Germany's favorite TV talkmaster, was hired as the spokesperson for the commercial spots. Günther is known for his informative TV shows, his extraordinary knowledge and high IQ, as well as for his passion for soccer. The success of the campaign, it was said, was in no small part due to Jauch being the presenter. He explained the motto "act and enjoy": purchasing one case of Krombacher beer will protect one square meter of the Dzanga-Shanga Rainforest in Central Africa, one of the world's richest areas in plants and animals (especially gorillas). Buying a 50-liter container (used in restaurants and bars) would protect five square meters of the rain forest. The protection of nature by drinking Krombacher beer was possible for everyone who purchased the product.

The campaign had strong and well-known partners. The German World Wildlife Fund (WWF—www.wwf.org) was supposed to channel most of the money (as was noted in the commercial spots) to train natives to become rangers in order to fight poaching and illegal woodcutting. In this way, the WWF would protect the collected amount of rain forest square meters. Another important partner of the campaign was the German Federal Department of Economic Cooperation and Development with its

---

[1]This case was prepared by Eva Barcikowski under the direction of Johannes Brinkmann for classroom discussion rather than to illustrate either effective or ineffective handling of an administrative, ethical, or legal decision by individuals or management.

[2]Two neighboring regions can be associated with the Krombacher brewery and its beer. The brewery is located in the community of Siegen. The city Krombach is a border municipality between the more well-known Sauerland and the previously more industrialized Siegerland. Sauerland fits better with the nature image, and the Krombacher brewery would probably claim that its water spring is located there.

"One World" initiative. With the help of the African secretary for environment and tourism, Constance Nathalie Gounebana, the Ministry used its part of the money for the development of a training camp for jobs related to ecological tourism (guides, trackfinders, and so on).

Nearly every day the TV spots reminded the World Cup broadcast viewers of the campaign's aim: to save 10 million square meters of rain forest. A few of the commercial spots also proposed alternative possibilities for donation (without buying a Krombacher beer). For example, a link on the Krombacher Web site to the WWF donation account number and the campaign partner ARCOR (a telephone company) offered a donation hotline.

In the updated commercials, Jauch informed the viewers about the ever-increasing square meters of protected land and demonstrated it for the soccer fans in the amount of soccer fields the square meters would make. Three weeks after starting the campaign, Krombacher helped protect 3,488,361 square meters of rain forest, an area nearly as big as 700 soccer fields. The halfway point of the campaign coincided with the preliminary round of the championship. At that time, three-fourths of the aspired area had been reached: 7,524,389 square meters, or 1,500 soccer fields. On June 25 (with two-thirds of the campaign completed), the protected area was about 8.6 million square meters. On that day, a legal action against Krombacher nearly stopped the campaign.

The Action

The Krombacher campaign was too successful for its competitors—achieving a historical production and turnover (sales) record (www.krombacher.com—under Facts, see Business Report). The competitors found it possible to sue Krombacher (by appealing to the consumer protection authorities) with a decade-old law against illegal competition—by alleging Krombacher used methods of "moral purchase constraint" (§1, §3 UWG, Unlauteres Wettbewerbs Gesetz). This law prohibits any combination of selling goods with promoting good causes if the way of support is not transparent to the consumer and/or the purchase is the only possibility to support the project. The statute led to an action against Krombacher on June 25 and forced it to stop all of the rain forest–commercial spots that did not offer alternative donation possibilities other than buying Krombacher beer, citing that the ads morally restrict the consumers' freedom to decide ("being against rainforest protection if not buying Krombacher beer"). This law was passed at a time when consumers were not used to commercial spots on German TV and could not be expected to understand message subtleties to the same extent as today. The intention was to protect consumers, when creating this law, against illegal competition. Basically, there is a presumption that, for example, in the case of Krombacher, the project needed to be explained much more in detail and that there must be several donation possibilities so consumers do not feel morally forced to buy beer in order to protect the rain forest. In other words, it must always be obvious how the consumer can support the social cause without the consumption of the product.

For Krombacher and its partners, this judgment was incomprehensible. Krombacher's argument was that consumers nowadays are different than when this law was passed. Contemporary consumers can analyze commercial messages and therefore can make a rational buying decision. The campaign was allowed to continue, but with the constraint of always having to offer an alternative way of supporting the African rain forest.

1. Was Krombacher's action ethical?
2. What ethical theories can you apply to this case?
3. Is it acceptable to appeal to a target group's environmental conscience without informing them about other initiatives covered by the donation?
4. Would you expect any minimum percentage of the whole campaign budget to be spent on the rain forest for justifying such a campaign? Where would you set such a percentage?
5. Is it defensible to promote a potentially harmful product (beer, alcohol) by referring to a good consequence (rain forest preservation)? Could the end justify the means?
6. Is it morally defensible for competitors to use the legal system to harass Krombacher rather than competing with similar or better campaigns?

Websites and Books with Further Information

General information: www.krombacher.com and www.wwf.org. For information about the campaign in German, see www.Krombacher.de, www.wwf.de, and http://admin. learnline.de/angebote/agenda21/archiv/02/04/WWF4P.HTM. Marconi, Joe. *Cause Marketing*, Chicago: Dearborn Publishing, 2002.

THE ETHICS OF SELLING VIOLENT VIDEO GAMES[1]

Trevor Prouty

Barry Gunderson, vice president of marketing at Take-Two Interactive Software, exhaled as he leaned back in his chair and stared at the ceiling. He reflected on how he had arrived at his current position and on the recent events that led him to reconsider his current line of business.

Barry was selected to his present position at Take-Two in 1999. He felt honored to have been chosen, as the job was in an incredible growth industry with an up-and-coming company. Prior to Take-Two, Barry worked at a major record house, promoting seven different labels during his time there. The job opening at Take-Two seemed like a breath of fresh air, though, and a perfect way into an industry with a brilliant future.

Take-Two Interactive Software

Take-Two Interactive Software designs, manufactures, and markets video games for both personal computers and home gaming consoles, such as the Sony Play Station 2 and the Microsoft X-Box. The recent explosion in the video gaming market has meant incredible profits for those who succeed in the industry, and Take-Two has been on the cutting edge for some time now. The company's stock has tripled in value since Barry joined, and its sales are steadily increasing. Take-Two's 10 largest video game titles make up 75 percent of their principal products sales. Their two current top games, *Grand Theft Auto 3* and *State of Emergency*, make up over 50 percent of the company's total sales.

The Video Games: Meeting Consumer Demand

The company has successfully marketed several genres of games, ranging from bass fishing simulations to role-playing games. In their recent hit *State of Emergency*, players take part in a citywide riot, destroying everything in their path. Take-Two has become infamous, however, for their recent series of *Grant Theft Auto (GTA)* games. These games allow players to wander through computer-generated towns, acting out the life of a mobster. With each new title, the violence becomes more realistic, the criticism grows louder, and sales increase. Antiviolence advocates have specifically criticized the *GTA 3* video-game player's ability to purchase sexual favors from a prostitute and then murder and rob her to receive their money back. In Take-Two's much anticipated upcoming release *GTA: Vice City*, players will be able to hijack cars, run over pedestrians and police officers, and utilize weapons of destruction, such as Molotov cocktails, rocket launchers, and assault rifles. The company willingly admits these games tend to be ultraviolent but points to the fact that all the games are marketed with a "Mature" ERSB rating. Take-Two's mature audience argument also relies on the fact that over 70 percent of Play Station 2 owners are over the age of 18.

While Barry does not like to think of games such as *GTA 3* in the hands of minors, he also believes that the growing video game market has a right to play a

---

[1]This case was prepared by Trevor Prouty under the direction of Patrick E. Murphy for classroom discussion, rather than to illustrate either effective or ineffective handling of an administrative, ethical, or legal decision by individuals or management.

violent video game if they so desire. R-rated movies have become an entrenched part of American culture, and Barry views "Mature"-rated video games in the same light.

Barry abruptly snapped back to reality when his secretary called to remind him of his meeting at 7:00 P.M. that night with the rest of the management team. Unfortunately, real-life events and video games fantasy have once again collided, and now Barry must weigh in on an incredibly important issue.

Video Games Meet Real Life

The date is October 15, 2002, and the Washington, D.C., area is in a state of panic. Since October 2, a sniper has been randomly targeting individuals in the area, and as of yet, few leads have been generated in the case. Besides the obvious tragedy, the case also weighs heavily on Barry's mind for other reasons. Take-Two has slated the release of *GTA: Vice City*, the latest in the line of *GTA* games, on October 25. Four million copies of the game have already been presold by retailers, and the projections indicate that sales could top 10 million copies. If these projections are correct, *GTA: Vice City* will generate $400 million for the company. As the critical holiday shopping period inevitably approaches, Take-Two is relying on this product to keep the company profitable in the coming year. The sale of *GTA: Vice City* has been planned for over a year.

However, even in light of the past controversy caused by the *GTA* series, a particular facet of *GTA: Vice City* troubles Barry in light of the recent events in D.C. The new game allows players to utilize a sniper scope and indiscriminately kill people in parks, on street corners, and at gas stations. This eerily coincides with the manner of the recent attacks by the D.C. sniper. Certain consumer and antiviolence groups have demanded the postponement of the game's release. Barry knows his input at the meeting will be critical in determining if Take-Two will push back the release date of the game. Barry also knows that if the company delays the release date of the game, the financial impact on the company will be enormous.

Criticism and Complaints

Barry contemplated the spotlight Take-Two's decision would attract whatever its outcome. The video game industry has recently been a hotbed of advocate protest and government intervention. The Australian government actually refused to allow the sale of *GTA 3* in the country. Barry can repeat the statistics in his sleep; he has heard them so many times from the antiviolence campaigns. By the time a typical child reaches the age of 18, that child will have seen 200,000 dramatized acts of violence and 40,000 dramatized murders, which advocates say can lead to a blurring of the line between fantasy and reality violence for vulnerable children. Also, the advocates maintain that if children do happen to see the sniper aspect of *GTA: Vice City*, they will revisit painful and potentially damaging memories of the D.C. sniper. Of course, Barry feels the critics unfairly place the blame squarely on the video game creators and manufacturers, even though all the *GTA* games are clearly marked as "Mature."

Barry is a father himself and can guarantee there is no way he would allow his 11-year-old son to play *GTA: Vice City*. Unfortunately, he also knows that in a recent government study, 85 percent of children aged 13 to 16 years were able to purchase violent video games that were ESRB rated "Mature" (only available for purchase to those over 17 years old). A policy analyst for the Culture and Family Institute had already spoken out against *GTA: Vice City* in light of the D.C. events, stating that, "It's a video game simulator that trains snipers. It's sick." Generally, Barry believes the advocates are simply searching for a scapegoat, but this time things felt slightly different.

The Decision

Barry sighs as he checks the time on his wristwatch. The conference room would be starting to fill with his peers, and they had a decision to make. He knows the release of a movie, *Phonebooth*, which centers on a sniper, has been postponed because of the D.C. attacks, but Barry doubts that movie accounted for over a third of the production company's revenue. As he slowly collects the papers scattered across his desk and stands up, Barry revisits the reasons for his decision in his head one last time.

1. Should Barry recommend that Take-Two go forward with the release of *GTA: Vice City*?
2. Given the contemplated video game is legal, is clearly marked as "Mature" for audiences over 17, and is targeted for audiences not particularly offended by the themes of *GTA: Vice City*, is there an ethical issue of any kind in this case?
3. Do video games producers bear any social responsibility whatsoever for the themes of gratuitous violence they reinforce or the messages they send about the treatment of women as sex objects?
4. If the answer to question 3 is yes, what steps do you recommend be taken to improve the current situation regarding the marketing of video games in the United States?

ABERCROMBIE & FITCH[1]

Meg Connolly

Abercrombie & Fitch (A&F) of today differs dramatically from the original waterfront shop in New York that carried high-quality clothing suitable for camping, fishing, and hunting. The A&F of 2002 can be found in virtually any major mall in America, and its target market includes preteens and teenagers. Indeed, the shift has been rather dramatic, and it could certainly be asserted that the direction A&F has recently headed strays substantially from the original vision of its founders.

The style of clothes offered by A&F could be described as worn, casual, and rather rugged. Some critics contend the merchandise at A&F is seemingly overpriced considering that it is arguably no more unique than any other store of its kind geared toward the same market. One aspect of A&F that *does* make it unique from other stores, however, is their catalog that was first published in 1997 and comes out four times a year with a spring break, summer, back-to-school, and Christmas issue. The *Quarterly* is a magazine-catalog hybrid that, in addition to the clothing portion of the catalog, has interviews with actors, musicians, directors, and even some famous scholars. Fashion legend Bruce Weber does many of the photographs that appear throughout the magazine, and "these photos depict young, healthy, presumably red-blooded Americans posing, frolicking, and generally living what could be considered 'the good life.' They do this in Abercrombie clothes, sometimes; other times, they do this *out* of Abercrombie clothes."[2]

As mentioned previously, the first publication of the *Quarterly* was released in 1997, and the catalog was immediately met with controversy and public outcry. The attorneys general of Illinois and Michigan as well as Mothers Against Drunk Driving denounced the 1998 "Back to School" issue for "encouraging underage drinking" with an article entitled "Drinking 101." Despite the fact that there was never any mention of pairing drinking with driving, A&F responded by placing a ban on any magazine material that could be viewed as encouraging underage drinking. It is interesting that the *Quarterly* even decided to write an article regarding drinking since the main target market is under the legal drinking age.

After this interchange with government officials and some angry mothers, A&F decided to switch gears and focus instead on sex as the theme of their quarterly publication. In addition to the magazine features discussed, interviews with porn stars as well as other actors who are dubious role models for preteens and teenagers were included. In a particular interview, one male porn star brags about his nearly 1,700 porn films and offers advice to those interested in entering his field. Furthermore, sex advice columns and other racy feature articles are sometimes part of the *Quarterly*.

---

[1]This case was prepared by Meg Connelly under the direction of Patrick E. Murphy for classroom discussion rather than to illustrate either effective or ineffective handling of an administrative, ethical, or legal decision by individuals or management.
[2]Sean T. Collins, "Quarterly Concern: The Boycott of Abercrombie & Fitch," Disinformation.com, July 29, 2001.

The Christmas 1999 issue titled "Naughty or Nice" included images of a sado-masochistic Santa and elves all clad in leather and posing in questionable positions. This issue led Illinois Lieutenant Governor Corinne Wood to call for a boycott of A&F. The boycott has gained nationwide support and is spearheaded by the American Decency Association (ADA). As a result of the actions taken by Lieutenant Governor Wood, A&F now packages its magazine in opaque shrink wrap, and there is a "You Must Be 18 Years of Age" sticker affixed to the cover. It retails for $6 an issue and can be received either by subscription or at an A&F retail outlet. While A&F took action to make sure that minors are not able to directly access the magazine, Wood is not satisfied.

Wood and others strongly believe that the clothing retailer is peddling soft porn in the form of a clothing catalog, which is completely inappropriate for the market that typically purchases the merchandise. She claims that "A&F is glamorizing indiscriminate sexual behavior that unsophisticated teenagers are not possibly equipped to weigh against the dangers of date rape, unplanned pregnancies and sexually transmitted diseases."[3] The publication displays page after page of partially nude young people, oftentimes in sexually explicit positions.

Others in favor of the boycott warn that A&F is manipulating young people into thinking that it is okay to take part in the behaviors that are depicted and written about and that in fact it will make one "cool." Adolescents at the preteen and teen levels are impressionable, and it is the fear of many of these outraged parents that their children will start to adopt these behaviors that are inappropriate for such a young age.

A&F does not appear to be overly concerned with the complaints; in fact, recent issues have had an increased amount of nudity, and the spring issue that had been rated "XXX."

At the heart of the debate lies the question, "Have the sales of A&F seen an increase since the racy publication started circulating?" Recently, an 18 percent dip in sales occurred that A&F Chairman and Chief Michael Jeffries attributes mainly as a result of the 9/11/01 national tragedy. President Bill Johnson of the ADA claims, "Eighteen percent is a heavy dip in sales to attribute solely to the September 11th attacks. Whatever was affecting their sales was going on long before then. So, while they may not admit it, I strongly believe our boycott was having an impact."[4]

After years of the boycotts and criticisms from lawmakers and concerned parents, A&F decided to cancel the 2001 issue of the *Christmas Quarterly*. Michael Jeffries claims that in light of the September 11 attacks, it would not be an appropriate move to publish the catalog for the Christmas season. While this may indicate that those opposing the disputed catalog have won, this may in fact not be true. A&F plans to pick up where it left off this past fall with the spring break issue of 2002 that will likely resemble past controversial catalogs.

In defense of the *Quarterly*, Jeffries does not feel as though "kids should be locked away in boxes until they're 50,"[5] and claims that he is not at all concerned with

---

3State.il.us/ltgov.htr.
4Martha Kleder, "Abercrombie & Fitch Cancels Holiday Quarterly," Culture and Family Institute, October 19, 2001.
5Kleder, "Abercrombie & Fitch Cancels Holiday Quarterly."

the criticisms both he and A&F have received. The chain's sales are beginning to pick up, and Jeffries is uncertain as to what decision to make about future issues of the *Quarterly*.

1. Is A&F really using the *Quarterly* to generate free publicity and to create a dimension of controversy and rebellion sometimes important to their youthful target market?
2. If you were called in as an advisor to Jeffries, what would you tell him to do about the *Quarterly*?
3. How does this case relate to the ethical theories/frameworks we have discussed?

CAN SHORT SKIRTS SELL SOFTWARE? AN ETHICAL DILEMMA[1]

Lori Lepp Corbett

Elizabeth smoothed her skirt as she crossed her legs. She was unsuccessful making eye contact with her customer, so she stared at the clock over his shoulder, squirming as the seconds slowly passed. Skip, one of her 60 customers and the CEO of the First Community Bank, was in the process of telling yet another story about "the good old days" when he was back in the fraternity at Georgetown University. He kept standing up, supposedly to point out souvenirs on his wall, although more likely to try and look down the front of her dress. He seemed to focus 100 percent of his attention on Elizabeth's chest instead of on her face or, more important, on the bid she had put in front of him over an hour ago. After what seemed like an eternity and easily four years' worth of frat boy antics, Skip decided he and Elizabeth should step across the street for a bite of lunch. Elizabeth stood up with relief, thinking that maybe a change of venue would help Skip regain some focus regarding the topic at hand—adding a debit card product to the First Community Bank line of retail banking service products.

Unfortunately, over lunch Elizabeth had another rude awakening. Instead of discussing business, Skip wanted to have drinks at lunch. For another three hours, the CEO continued to talk about the frolics of his college days while he slowly got drunk on vodka martinis. He continued to leer at Elizabeth, while he made innuendoes about his preference for younger women and his particular interest in 24-year-old blondes. Finally, at 4:00 P.M., after repeated attempts to leave, Elizabeth decided she didn't care anymore about the outcome of this sale. She stood up, thinking she could just walk out of the restaurant if he insisted *again* that she didn't really have to go back to her office. His last remark to her as she walked out the door was, "Liz, don't worry, I will sign that contract you left me, just as long as you are cuter than the little rep from ALS. You know I make all my decisions based upon the physical attributes of my vendors." Elizabeth was fuming as she pulled out of the parking lot. In fact, she bumped into another car because she was so distracted by Skip's final comment. Elizabeth sat on the side of the road, crying as she exchanged phone numbers with the other driver. She couldn't wait to get back to the office to tell one of her coworkers about this jerk (her local office was almost all women, which was typical for the entire firm).

Elizabeth's manager, Maria, was also her mentor—Maria was a saleswoman with a terrific reputation for closing deals. And she had been Skip's key contact until Elizabeth had been assigned the account. So once Elizabeth returned to the office, she practically ran into Maria's office to tell her about this creepy buyer and to propose letting him go as a customer. She was shocked as Maria started to nod her head knowingly, saying, "Oh sure, I know Skip loves to drink at lunch, and he loves the Superior Software girls. That's why we sent you out there, Elizabeth. As long as you go to see him once a month, wear a short skirt, let him gape at you for an hour or two, and buy him a few drinks, he will always extend his contract with us. He makes all of his decisions

---

[1]This case was prepared by Lori Lepp Corbett under the direction of Patrick E. Murphy for classroom discussion rather than to illustrate either effective or ineffective handling of an administrative, ethical, or legal decision by individuals or management.

based upon the appearance of his reps. So I want you to use your resources, go visit him occasionally, wear a short skirt, and don't get too hung up on his comments. Our management may be too conservative to use sex to advertise our software, but we sure can use our assets when calling on customers." Elizabeth went into her office thoroughly confused. She didn't want to ever see Skip again. But maybe Maria had a point: wearing a short skirt would be such an easy way to extend a contract. And surely the other companies were using the exact same tactics. Elizabeth knew she would have to make a very difficult decision—could she use her short skirt to sell software? Was this an ethical way to close a deal?

Facts about Superior Software

Superior Software is a subsidiary of First Bank, a large commercial Bancorp based in the Midwest. First Bank first opened their doors in 1863 when a group of businessmen started the bank inside a Masonic Temple. The goal of the original First Bank was to serve the Ohio River trade. First Bank grew rapidly through the next century, primarily through acquisitions, although the addition of innovative new products and services also helped add revenue as customers switched to the First Bank. In the early 1970s, First Bank reorganized in order to keep current with industry trends. As part of the restructuring, the bank switched their emphasis from commercial loans to consumer credit. As part of this new focus on the individual consumer, one of the senior officers of the bank realized that the future in retail banking was to move away from branches and introduce technology-oriented banking alternatives. This executive proceeded to develop his idea while having drinks with the First Bank CEO after a golf game. Their cocktail napkin sketch outlined a technology subsidiary that would support credit and debit card processing services. Out of their discussion came Superior Software, a data processing and information services resource.

By 1999, Superior Software had expanded into a dominant credit and debit card processor in the United States. Superior drove ATMs for more than 1,000 banks and credit unions and processed credit cards for over 20,000 merchants around the world. Their sales revenue had grown at a rate of 30 percent annually, an aggressive growth rate that the Superior team managed to maintain year after year. Additionally, the Superior profit margin was one of the highest in the industry. Superior provided 25 percent of total revenue for the bank in 1998, and the Bank profited $.25 for every dollar invested in Superior Software.

First Bank had an extremely aggressive executive vice president overseeing the technology subsidiary. He compensated his staff very well for their work; however, he demanded absolute dedication, 80- to 90-hour workweeks, weekend assignments, 24-hour on-call, and limited vacation. Elizabeth herself had already had one vacation cancelled because one of the executive's favorite customers asked to see her on a particular date, and the executive vice president "just couldn't say no." His staff was not happy with the work environment, but everyone was happy with their paychecks, which were significantly above industry average.

Employee Training and Compensation

Elizabeth had started work at Superior directly out of undergraduate school. She began a management training program that lasted for one year. During her training as a Superior associate, Elizabeth had the opportunity to learn about various aspects of the business, including legal, billing, sales, product development, and customer service. In each of these rotations, Elizabeth was able to refine her project management, problem-solving, and customer service skills. She learned how to calm down an irate customer as well as how to close the deal with a customer who was hesitant.

After her year of training, Elizabeth was promoted to consultant, and her responsibilities changed. She began to run system implementations, managing the entire six-month process. She coordinated the tasks for the programming staff, she trained new customers on the applications, and she went on-site to trouble shoot the implementation. It soon became clear to management that Elizabeth had a terrific ability to develop customer relationships. When she was done with an implementation, every customer wanted her to come back as the relationship manager. So, after six months, Elizabeth was promoted again to senior account manager. She handled key regional accounts, managing technical issues, billing complaints, and new product development. She also began to cross-sell and negotiate contracts. Skip, the CEO at the First Community Bank, was one of her first sales calls.

Elizabeth's compensation was based upon the following measures:

- Her base salary, $40,000, which was compensation for her day-to-day systems consulting tasks.
- A profit-sharing bonus, a percentage that was determined annually by the CEO of First Bank. The percentage was then applied to each employee's base salary to determine the dollar value of the bonus. The bank had been so successful in the past several years, that the 15 percent profit sharing had become an expectation, not a bonus.
- A bonus of $1000 per deal closed, plus a percentage of future earnings from the new sale (expectation of 0 to 10 deals per year—10 deals closed would be an outstanding year).
- Elizabeth did not receive stock options since she was not an officer in the bank, although this was a very valuable aspect of the compensation for officers. Elizabeth could expect to make officer (according to her manager) after being with the bank for four years.

So, Elizabeth's compensation as an employee with less than two years of work experience was a respectable $50,000 assuming $6000 in profit sharing and $4000 in closed deals. This was well above average for a 24-year-old employee with a liberal arts undergraduate degree in Economics.

The Ethical Dilemma

At this time, Elizabeth had a very difficult decision to make. She was uncomfortable using the sales tactics being recommended by her sales manager/mentor. While Maria seemed to think that sex could sell software, Elizabeth believed in the actual product. She didn't think she needed to use gimmicks such as short skirts and low-cut blouses to close a deal. Elizabeth thought this might be compromising her principles just for the sake of a few hundred bucks. On the other hand, Elizabeth did like her job. She was very busy, always learning new technology, traveling all over the United States, and meeting new people. And, of course, she was very well compensated for her work and on the fast track to management. When she sat down to review her alternatives, she decided she had three options:

1. Confront her manager and refuse to call on the customer.
2. Pull out that short skirt, run over to First Community Bank, and "close the deal."
3. Quit Superior Software and find a job somewhere where she would not have to compromise her ethics just to close a deal.

Elizabeth thought she would go home for the evening and sleep on it. But tomorrow she was going to have to make a decision.

1. Which option should she choose, and why?

WAVE RUNNERS GALORE[1]

John A. Weber

Anne Wolverton is the proprietor of Lakeside Recreation, a local retailer in Traverse City, MI. Her store specializes in selling and servicing personal watercraft, featuring the popular Wave Runner brand. Wave Runners are built for any water conditions and come in various sizes and power ratings.

It is already early July and the water sports season is well along. While her Wave Runner sales have been brisk, she is still carrying five expensive 3-seat Wave Runner models in inventory and is afraid she might get stuck holding them over the winter. In that case, with new models becoming available by next spring, she would have to heavily discount any stock she holds over the winter, not to mention paying finance charges on her stock over the winter! She is determined to sell these 3-seat units.

This was the first year she stocked the 3-seat Wave Runner. She was optimistic about being able to quickly sell these units, given the glowing sales story she had heard from the Wave Runner rep: "They are big, roomy and safer than the single and double seaters." So far she has sold only one of the six units she purchased! Common complaints from potential customers have been that 3-seaters are perceived as having very slow acceleration, getting poor gas mileage, and costing nearly twice as much as the more common one and two-seaters.

Alan Carbone is a very successful, 29-year-old software consultant who has just purchased a waterfront home on Elk Lake, just north of Traverse City. He is single and plans to entertain a large group of friends in his new place. He also plans to eventually have a family. Today he has ventured down to Traverse City and Anne's store in search of some "water toys" for his new place.

Alan is very friendly, outgoing and receptive when approached by Anne. He indicates he has never lived on the water before and really doesn't have a clue about what sort of personal watercraft might be most appropriate for his place. All he knows is that he wants a "jet ski" of some sort or other, because he has seen them cruising around the lake and they look "like a blast." Sensing this might be an opportunity to unload one of her 3-seaters, Anne takes control of the situation and is able to build Alan's vision of which Wave Runner model might be most appropriate for his place. She convinces him that the 3-seater Wave Runner will be more conducive to entertaining guests, as it is quite roomy. She also points out other features such as a larger storage area under the seat for life vests, flares, other safety equipment and a larger gas tank.

She purposefully does not tell him about the poor gas mileage or the relatively slow acceleration. Alan is apparently quite well-to-do, since he doesn't seem put off by the $9500 price tag. Anne's sales proposition begins to make sense to Alan. She gets him thinking about how well suited a 3-seater would be for his guests, and eventually,

---

[1]This case was prepared by Professor John A. Weber of Notre Dame (2003) and is to be used for classroom discussion rather than to illustrate either effective or ineffective handling of an administrative, ethical, or legal decision by individuals or management. Reprinted with permission.

for his family as well. She caps the story emphasizing Wave Runner's impeccable reputation for dependability.

Alan leaves the store with a $9500 Wave Runner and a $1500 trailer in tow. It's been a good afternoon for Anne.

1. Did Anne treat Alan ethically? Why or why not?
2. What responsibility does a salesperson have to point out the weaknesses of a product?

A RETAILER IN BRAZIL[1]

Miriam Jordan

SAO PAULO, Brazil—Maria Pereira visited a Casas Bahia store recently to pay a $38 monthly installment on a music system that she bought last year. On her way out, a set of five cooking pots on sale for $25 caught the housewife's attention, and she purchased it as well, in four installments. "I hadn't thought of buying anything, actually," says Mrs. Pereira, whose husband earns $167 a month as a security guard.

That is the secret of how Samuel Klein, a 78-year-old Holocaust survivor with four years of schooling, has unlocked the buying power of the poor in Latin America's biggest country and become Brazil's version of Sam Walton. By selling in installments, Mr. Klein makes products accessible to people like Mrs. Pereira. And by requiring customers to return to the store each month to pay, he induces two-thirds of them to make another purchase. About 90% of sales are on credit. Mr. Klein's closely held Casas Bahia chain is Brazil's biggest nonfood retailer, last year selling about $1.5 billion of furniture, household goods and appliances—including one-third of all new TV sets in Brazil.

While most mainstream Brazilian retailers shun the poor, the former peddler courts them assiduously. Mr. Klein's stripped-down stores are located in some of the most deprived neighborhoods of Sao Paulo and Rio de Janeiro. His clients include free-lance masons, hot-dog vendors and blue-collar workers whose average monthly income is $190, below the national average of $290. Surprisingly, their default rates are lower than the market average, too, and their loyalty intense—a combination that has turned Mr. Klein into a billionaire.

"The poorer the customer, the more punctual his payments," says Mr. Klein, who shuffles around company headquarters in plastic slippers. "The poor know they need to guard their reputations" or they jeopardize buying on credit, he adds.

His critics say retailers such as Casas Bahia are preying on the most vulnerable members of society, burying huge interest charges in the prices of the goods they sell. "Uneducated consumers only consider whether a monthly installment fits in their budget," says Donizete Piton, president of the national debtors' association, who adds that retailers should do a much better job of informing consumers of the cost of immediate gratification.

Filling a Need

Others regard Mr. Klein as a hero, keeping consumer spending alive at a time when the Brazilian economy is in the doldrums. As similar businesses crop up throughout the developing world, they fill a need for credit among the poor that risk-averse banks won't meet. Ultimately, consumer spending could smooth out economic bumps for poor countries in much the same way as debt-laden Americans have spent the U.S. out of its latest recession.

"Of course Klein isn't thinking about the economy. He's thinking about his business," says Miguel de Oliveira, economist at the National Association of Financing Executives. "But the economy is benefiting."

---

[1]Jordan, Miriam, "A Retailer in Brazil Has Become Rich By Courting Poor," *Wall Street Journal*, June 11, 2002. Reprinted with permission.

In a country where annual credit-card rates surpass 200% for the minority of Brazilians who qualify for plastic, Casas Bahia's policies aren't exceptional. The retailer used to charge monthly interest of between 3% and 5%, depending on the payment plan, roughly in line with the rates at other retailers, such as the Brazilian outlets of Wal-Mart Stores Inc. More recently, the company has begun promoting "interest-free" programs. But Mr. Klein still manages to squeeze money out of the deal by bumping up the prices he charges.

When Yolanda Moises, a 49-year-old maid in a Sao Paulo suburb, outfitted her home with a refrigerator, stove, VCR, stereo system, bed and closet from Casas Bahia over the past two years, she didn't know how much interest she was paying, but says the vendor told her it was "very small." It didn't matter, she says: Casas Bahia was the only store that would give her credit. Installments worked out to more than half of her $190 monthly salary. She says she didn't deprive her four children of any basic needs, but for months she wouldn't allow herself the luxury of replacing her disintegrating sandals. "I preferred to drag my feet in sandals with broken straps than delay my installment payment," she says.

Mr. Klein, a stout man with a rugged boxer's face, is aware of the sacrifice that his customers often make. "Some people live to eat and pay my bills," he says. But he argues that his terms are more generous than those of many competitors, considering that he lends to a poorer, and thus arguably riskier, clientele. What's more, higher-end retailers such as Wal-Mart demand something from Brazilian borrowers that Casas Bahia doesn't: proof of income. Wal-Mart declined to comment on its credit policy here.

"My talent is trusting the poor and giving the poor good service," says Mr. Klein. "Many poor have a better character than the rich. I was poor once."

Escape from Nazis

The third of nine children of a carpenter, Mr. Klein grew up near Lublin, Poland. In 1942, the Nazis sent the 19-year-old Mr. Klein and his father to the Maidanek labor camp. He escaped two years later during a forced march to flee advancing Red Army troops, taking advantage of a guard's momentary distraction to dart into the woods. But Mr. Klein's mother and five younger siblings died on a train bound for the Treblinka death camp.

After the war, Mr. Klein and his wife, Ana, eventually accepted an invitation from an aunt of Mr. Klein's to live with them in Brazil. Settling in the industrial Sao Paulo suburb of Sao Caetano do Sul in 1952, he bought a horse, a cart and a list of 100 clients from a fellow Jewish immigrant.

He hawked bed linen and towels in neighborhoods inhabited by migrant laborers arriving in droves to work at General Motors and other factories. When customers hesitated to buy a blanket, he'd urge them to "keep it until next month, in case you change your mind." By then, the chill of Sao Paulo would have caught the migrants from the tropical state of Bahia by surprise. When Mr. Klein returned, often they would thank him profusely, pay for the blanket and buy something else.

In 1958, Mr. Klein opened his first clothing and furniture store in Sao Caetano and named it Casa Bahia, or Bahia House, in honor of the home state of his original customers. Despite his broken Portuguese, Mr. Klein enticed shoppers with unorthodox installment schemes, which he calculated in his head on the spot. "He implicitly trusted people that others would doubt," says Gilda Sanchez, one of Mr. Klein's first employees.

Mr. Klein's empire expanded to a new level in 1994, after the government launched an economic program, the Real Plan, which eradicated hyperinflation that had eroded the purchasing power of the poor. This country of 170 million became the world's third-largest market for TV sets and fourth-largest for refrigerators. The Real Plan "made the poor less poor," says Mr. Klein. Meanwhile, "the Real Plan made me a billionaire," he says. Sales jumped 500% in six months, and the number of Casas Bahia stores doubled in six years.

Today, Mr. Klein presides over an empire of 310 stores and 16,800 employees that moves 18% of all electrical appliances sold in Brazil each year. Mr. Klein has added an average of 20 stores annually since 1991. In the first quarter of this year, Casas Bahia's sales were $410 million, 25% higher in local currency than the same period last year, despite a general retailing slump.

Casas Bahia's popularity was on display one recent morning as 1,000 people gathered for the opening of a store in a graffiti-covered street of Capao Redondo, a blue-collar district of Sao Paulo. A five-man band played popular tunes, until the store's metal shutters rose at 9 a.m. The crowd charged inside. Lacking desk space, some salesmen helped customers fill out credit applications on top of washing machines on display.

The company decided to build the store after a zip-code analysis indicated that many deliveries were made to the area. Francisca da Cunha, a hot-dog vendor whose income is about $150 a month, was thrilled. Her two-room shack nearby is a veritable Casas Bahia showroom, with a bed, bookcase, sofa and kitchen cupboard from the chain. To celebrate the new store, she is filling out a credit application to buy a stove.

The average monthly installment at Casas Bahia is about $14. Only a permanent mailing address is required to get credit approval, though about a 10th of applicants are rejected, usually because their names appear on a federal list of defaulters.

Faced with a slowing economy and electricity rationing that forced Brazilians to cut electricity use by 20% in mid-2001, Mr. Klein overhauled his pricing strategy to stimulate sales. He introduced so-called interest-free plans of as long as 15 months for furniture and 10 months for electrical appliances. Gathering 30 regional directors at headquarters for a pep talk, he urged them to push beds and sofas because "furniture doesn't go in sockets." By the end of the rationing in February, furniture accounted for one-third of Casas Bahia's sales, up from 10% before.

Many customers say they are aware they may pay more at Casas Bahia. But "here the terms are good for me," says Maria Nogueira, a building superintendent, after depositing a $13 installment on a $200 sofa. Plus, she notes, Casas Bahia gives a five-day grace period and marginally discounts early installment payments.

Mr. Klein doesn't apologize for his pricing strategy. "I'm not a low-baller," he declares. Mr. Klein's 51-year-old son, Michael, the chain's finance director, adds: "We speak a language that our clients understand—installments. And we are sparing them a trip to the bank for a loan."

Growing Sales

Even as Brazil's average salary has fallen 10% since 1998, deflating consumer demand, Casas Bahia's sales are growing. That's because Mr. Klein has combined shrewd business with homespun practices that boost the self-esteem of the povao, or masses. Casas Bahia's yellow preferred-client card is a status symbol that gives punctual payers automatic credit approval. As he stands in line to pay for a fan, Sebastiao Feitosa, a bricklayer, displays a form letter that he received from Mr. Klein "thanking you for paying on time." Indeed, the letter was intended to woo Mr. Feitosa into a store because computer records showed he hadn't bought anything for months. In 2000, Mr. Klein also pardoned debts of one million customers, a tax and marketing move that lured back clients blacklisted since 1997.

Casas Bahia makes much of its furniture and owns its fleet of 1,040 delivery trucks. Mr. Klein built Latin America's biggest warehouse to stock uncommonly large inventories and centralize distribution. In an empire spanning eight states, Mr. Klein keeps an iron-fisted control over spending: Only he, his wife and two sons can sign checks. He is adamant about not selling a stake to outside investors. "Partners boss you around," he says.

Mr. Klein's affinity for Brazil's povao is reflected in his headquarters, which he chose to keep in blue-collar Sao Caetano. In his spartan office, a commemorative miniature wooden cart sits on one shelf.

But Sao Paulo's infamous crime problem has forced Mr. Klein to accept one extravagance. Like many Sao Paulo executives, he travels to work in a helicopter to avoid unsafe, traffic-snarled streets, and uses bullet-proof cars whenever he drives. He is shadowed by three bodyguards. Once a fixture at every store opening, Mr. Klein no longer ventures out of Casas Bahia's well-protected headquarters, thanks to a kidnapping wave in Brazil. His sons, Michael and 48-year-old Saul, run day-to-day operations, and have been groomed to take over as the lifelong workaholic scales back.

"I miss visiting the stores," Mr. Klein says, glancing up from Mother's Day sales reports. "But since I am the mind of the company, I need to be in the office anyway."

1. Is Mr. Klein treating his customers ethically? Why or why not?
2. How much annual interest is he charging them? Is this right?

CHAPTER

4

Long Cases

KOFFUM FILTERS[1]

Anu Davgun

Background

Olivia Yeun was a real up-and-comer in advertising. Born in Singapore, she graduated from Brown University with a double major in psychology and English literature. Olivia had intended to return to Singapore after graduation, wanting to put her degree to use in her home country. This intent was prompted by the country experiencing an extraordinary growth due in large part to Western and domestic involvement. Her dream job was to open a creative ad agency, specifically an advertising boutique in Singapore, that would nurture local "creatives" and move away from the reliance of Western holding company ad agencies.

However, during her final semester at Brown, Olivia was heavily recruited by Veritaes Agency,[2] a trendy New Age advertising agency in New York City. Her background in psychology and English literature made her a natural fit for a position in account management. Promising herself that she would remain at the agency for only a few years and then return to Singapore, Olivia accepted the position. Veritaes told her that as a new recruit they would place her on a large account, allowing her to gain valuable experience, though never specifying which account it would be. Olivia desperately wanted to work on the LaVisage account because of her interest in the French cosmetics firm.

Veritaes Agency

After graduating from Brown University in May 1998, Olivia moved to New York City and began her employment at Veritaes. Her first client was Smoke & Mirrors Tobacco Company,[3] a Virginia-based firm that was enormously popular with young smokers.

---

[1]This case was prepared by Anu Davgun under the direction of Patrick E. Murphy for classroom discussion rather than to illustrate either effective or ineffective handling of an administrative, ethical, or legal decision by individuals or management.

[2]The name of this agency is fictitious. Any resemblance between this firm and any actual advertising agency is purely coincidental.

[3]The name of this tobacco company is fictitious. Any resemblance between this firm and any actual tobacco company is purely coincidental.

Smoke & Mirrors had recently come under criticism from many advocacy groups for its misleading and reckless advertising. It attempted to remedy its damaged brand identity by acquiring several consumer package group companies.

The tobacco industry was unfamiliar territory to Olivia; her knowledge of the industry was derived entirely from news clippings taken from the *Wall Street Journal* and CNN. However, she was commissioned by the client to design a campaign that would be provocative and attractive to Smoke & Mirrors' desired target market of 18- to 24-year-olds. Olivia's superior, Mike Estrada, was also her account director and mentor. He gave free reign regarding the account to Olivia, instructing her to follow her instincts in managing the account. Working with "creatives," Olivia created a campaign that "implied cool"—nothing overt that would appear to be very enticing to 18- to 24-year-olds yet hip and trendy enough to make it highly visible and attractive to the target market. She created a print ad campaign where several "hip" young-looking males and females were shown in a relaxed party setting. They were shown in conversation and most were holding a cigarette.

Olivia presented the campaign first to Mike, who approved of the ads, and then to the team from Smoke & Mirrors. The tobacco company was resistant at first, stating that the campaign was not aggressive enough. However, Olivia relied on her acumen in psychology and her growing knowledge of consumer behavior to point out that the appropriate strategy for the tobacco company was to be unintentionally cool. In the end, Smoke & Mirrors agreed to the campaign that she and her team had created.

The campaign proved to be a huge success. Sales for the target market increased by 3 percent during the running of the campaign, and Smoke & Mirrors turned to Olivia and her team to create follow-up campaigns. Olivia, however, did not want to continue working with the Smoke & Mirrors account. She did not feel comfortable knowing that her work was leading to tobacco addiction of young people. She expressed to Mike, who was well known for his informal and approachable style, her desire to transfer to another account. Mike advised her to stick with the account for another two years, and then she could move on to an account that was more in line with her interests.

Shortly after her meeting with Mike, Smoke & Mirrors came under attack for their advertising campaign yet again. Several advocacy groups alleged that the tobacco company was trying to encourage younger teens to smoke. These groups stated that the nature of the advertising campaign, because it pursued this tone of being unintentionally cool, was really trying to market itself for a younger—and illegal—target audience. Smoke & Mirrors was one of five companies that came under attack because of the nature of its advertising campaign.

Olivia was thoroughly shocked. She had been aware of the potential problem that the ad would be attractive to a younger audience, but she, as well as the creatives, had felt that the ad was successful in focusing on an older audience. However, because she did not have extensive knowledge about the laws governing tobacco advertising, Olivia devoted her time outside work to learning about the current legalities of cigarette advertising.

The climate surrounding tobacco advertising had changed dramatically during this time. Legislation provided strict guidelines to tobacco companies on how they could advertise and what was considered inappropriate for young audiences. Olivia and her team pulled the campaign for Smoke & Mirrors and created a fresh campaign that met the new guidelines. These new ads became wildly popular, in part because of the media attention that the recent legislation was generating. She continued to work with the Smoke & Mirrors account even though she wanted to move to LaVisage. The Smoke & Mirrors account became so valuable that Mike did not want to jeopardize the agency's relationship by changing account management personnel.

A New Job in Singapore

After devoting two more years than she had originally intended, Olivia finally formalized her resignation with the Veritaes Agency. She did this with the firm intention of finding work in Singapore more compatible with her personal values. However, finding a new job in Singapore did not go as smoothly as expected. After searching for months for a job that would have a positive social outcome, Olivia found that the only firms that were really interested in her knowledge, skills, and attributes were tobacco companies. In particular, Koffum Filters[4] was aggressively pursuing Olivia because of her familiarity with the tobacco industry.

Koffum Filters

Koffum Filters is a Singapore-based tobacco company that has followed the Phillip Morris–Kraft model and acquired a number of smaller consumer-packaged good companies in an effort to project the image that they were a wholesome company. Similar to many other Southeast Asian countries, Singapore had a strong antismoking policy by the early 1980s. Despite these laws, the country could only enforce laws that prohibited cigarette littering but not those dealing with cigarette smoking. However, Singapore did have control over advertising by tobacco companies, strictly prohibiting it from print and media advertising. Although the law was rigid, it was not perfect, as tobacco firms and their advertising agencies were about to find a number of loopholes. For instance, if the tobacco firms extended their brands so that they acquired businesses in other industries, they were able to legally pursue nontraditional advertising media such as sponsorships. Having recently acquired a number of unrelated companies, Koffum Filters used this loophole and sponsored several outdoor sporting events, including hockey and skateboarding tournaments, as well as landmarks like public libraries and parks. At the height of their sponsorship endeavors, Koffum Filters employed numerous scantily clad women (with the tobacco company's logo covering what little material that did exist in the uniforms) positioned in several high-impact city locations who offered free cigarettes to anyone who was interested—even children.

The free reign that companies like Koffum enjoyed with nontraditional advertising was greatly restricted when the government conducted a study that showed a dramatic increase in cigarette smoking among minors and young adults. Singapore adopted a stringent United Nations antismoking initiative and formulated it into a law, making it difficult for tobacco firms to advertise to the mass population. It is in this climate, with the new UN-inspired legislation taking effect, that Koffum Filters is

---

[4]The name of this tobacco company is fictitious. Any resemblance between this firm and any actual tobacco company is purely coincidental.

pursuing Olivia. The company has made it clear to Olivia that they intend to use their extended brand network to serve as a leveraging tool for forthcoming sponsorships. The newly adopted legislation still has a number of loopholes, especially in relation to sponsorships that attract younger audiences. Free sampling of cigarettes and event sponsorships by cigarette companies are prohibited in any situation where minors are present, but this pertains only to those tobacco companies where cigarettes generate more than half of all company sales. Koffum has responded to the new legislation by acquiring more consumer package group companies so that their cigarette units produce less than 50 percent of corporate sales.

Despite the new laws, Koffum believes that there still exists untapped profitability in the younger target audience and that this group can be reached legally. The firm wants to be "top-of-mind" with this age-group, as studies have shown 15- to 18-year-olds demonstrating great loyalty to the cigarette brand holding this position. The challenge for advertisers lies in creating "top-of-mind" recall to this group without actually promoting the cigarette products. This is the problem that Koffum is calling on Olivia to solve for them.

Olivia could not, in good conscience, accept such an offer. However, Oon Behrani, the vice president of marketing at Koffum, assures her that the company is not interested in selling cigarettes to illegal minors. Instead, the firm wants to focus heavily on advertising that would merely serve in making this population aware of the brand for further down the road. When they do become of age, they would select the Koffum brand for their tobacco needs. Ms. Behrani also states that she recognizes Olivia's interest in pursuing a more mainstream advertising career and offers the assurance that if she were to take the offer at Koffum, she would be able to work in any other division within the company after three years. In particular, Ms. Behrani mentions that Koffum Filters has recently acquired a smaller company that is developing a low-cost, nutritious snack that is being targeted to low-income families. Ms. Behrani guarantees Olivia that if she were to accept the current offer, she would be automatically placed in the position of her choice in the new snack division. Olivia must decide whether she will accept the offer. She determines that there are three courses of action available to her.

Option 1   Olivia could take the job offered by Koffum Filters. She would earn a great deal of money ($80,000), but it would be from doing work that she was not interested in. For three years she would work for the cigarette division and then move into the low-cost, nutritious snack division. The amount of good that she could do with the second division might more than offset the damage she would be doing in the cigarette division. Furthermore, the work she would be doing for the cigarette division would not be promoting smoking for minors but rather creating "top-of-mind" awareness in the cigarette category for the under-30 demographic.

Option 2   Negotiate with Ms. Behrani to work exclusively with the snack division. By using her background in psychology as leverage, she would be able to guide the new division on what types of foods to create and how to market its products to the target audience. The compensation in this position would not be nearly as large as in the cigarette division (approximately $50,000), but the work would be extremely rewarding. Also, there are indications that this market will be experiencing enormous growth in the next five years.

Option 3   Flatly refuse the offer. Koffum Filters obviously wants Olivia because of her skill in the cigarette industry. They are using the lure of moving to the snack division as a negotiation tool. Three years is a substantial amount of time, and the damage to minors is currently unknown but has a potential to be great.

1. Which option would you choose? Why?
2. What concepts in Chapter 1 relate to this case?

STARBUCKS COFFEE COMPANY: A FAIR TRADE?[1]

Anne Kozak, Peggy Cunningham, and Tim Jones

John Taylor, Senior Vice President of Social Responsibility at Starbucks Coffee Company, cringed as yet another negative headline caught his eye: *Starbucks' Struggle for Moral Ground: Program to aid poor coffee growers off to a slow start.* Although a relative newcomer to the Fair Trade coffee movement, John felt that Starbucks had moved forward quickly to satisfy consumer demand and the complaints of protesters, and, in doing so, had maintained the company's ethical image.

In November 2001, in collaboration with Conservation International, Starbucks launched its latest Corporate Social Responsibility (CSR) initiative, including the industry's first-ever *Coffee Purchasing Guidelines.* The eleven-page document was accompanied by a two-year implementation plan. "Two years is a realistic timeline," thought John, as he considered the numerous communication and control challenges of dealing with the coffee farmers, who are situated in under-developed countries.

Even before the *Guidelines* were released, Starbucks had been the main target for many environmental and human rights activists groups, namely the Organic Consumers Association (OCA), and Global Exchange (GE). Not long ago, OCA had executed a "Global Week of Action Against Starbucks," the ending of which coincided perfectly with Starbucks' annual meeting. OCA and GE felt that although Starbucks claimed to be an "ethical business," its actions proved otherwise.

"Is it a PR problem?" John wondered as he leafed through Starbucks' inaugural 2001 CSR annual report. "We are environmentally aware, involved in the community, practice Fair Trade, and avoid Genetically Modified (GM) materials in our products wherever possible." Since its inception in 1987, the Starbucks Coffee Company has taken pride in being a socially responsible corporate citizen. It seems, however, that no matter what the company does, the anti-Starbucks protests and campaigns never end.

"I just don't know what else we can do." John picked up the paper and began reading the article. With plans to more than double the number of Starbucks coffeehouses by the end of fiscal 2006, it was imperative that Starbucks' ethical image be restored. John was concerned that the more successful the company was, the more frequent would be the international protests. "Of course we want to make money, but not by compromising our values and integrity. How can we change our reputation? How can we convince people that we are not evil?"

Company History

In 1971, the first Starbucks Coffee & Tea opened in Seattle's Pike Place Market, named after Captain Starbuck in the classic novel, *Moby Dick.* Howard Schultz became the first director of retailing and marketing in 1982, with a mission to make the company

---

[1]This case was prepared by Anne Kozak under the supervision of Dr. Peggy Cunningham and Tim Jones for use in the Inter-Collegiate Business Competition and is not intended to illustrate either effective or ineffective handling of a management situation. While the case facts are based on real incidents documented in the public press, the case character (John Taylor) is fictitious. The thoughts and quotes attributed to Mr. Taylor are also supposition. The case may not be reproduced without the express written consent of the authors and Queen's School of Business. Copyright, Queen's University School of Business, 2002. Reprinted with permission.

"the most recognized and respected brand of coffee in the world."[2] While on vacation in Italy, Schultz noticed the distinct Italian focus on espresso and other fine coffees, and one year later, he opened a very successful trial "coffee bar" in Seattle. This experiment laid the foundation for his first independent shop in 1985, *Il Giornale*. Offering specialty coffees made from Starbucks' beans, *Il Giornale* became the prototype for today's Starbucks stores.

Coffee: A Global Commodity

Economically and politically, coffee is considered the second most precious global commodity, exceeded only by petroleum. In 2001, the estimated total market value was $11 billion USD.[3] The coffee industry employs over twenty million people worldwide, and is the chief export in over fifty developing countries.[4] Brazil and Colombia are the two largest producers, with approximately 700 local growers in Central and South America.[5]

Coffee is traded on the futures and commodity/cash markets, most notably in London, England and New York City. A buyer on the cash market pays the current market price per pound of coffee purchased. In the futures market, contracts are purchased in advance, guaranteeing the buyer and the seller a certain price and quantity in the future. The futures market is used to hedge against variable coffee prices.

Coffee Growers

Coffee growers, primarily in under-developed countries, face poor standards of living, low wages, and little opportunity for economic advancement (see Exhibit 4-1 for statistics on coffee-producing regions). Recently, this problem has been compounded as the price per pound dropped to an all-time low of less than $0.50 (see Exhibit 4-2).

Activists are strongly promoting Fair Trade, Organic, and Shade-Grown coffee to help support the coffee growers and their families. But setting environmental and production standards are not enough—supporters of Fair Trade have gone a step further by guaranteeing a minimum price of $1.26 USD/pound of coffee beans.

Coffee Plants

Flowers grow on the coffee plant, three to five years after it has been germinated. The cherries on the plant turn red in about 30–35 weeks, and the outer flesh of the cherries must be dried, using either the "wet" or "dry" method. Both techniques are used to extract two beans from each cherry. Once this process is finished, the beans are known as "green coffee" and are sent to the next stage, roasting.

Coffee Beans

There are two main species of coffee bean, *arabica* and *robusta*, members of the botanical family Rubiaceae. *Arabica* coffee makes up more than 70% of world production, and is grown in Latin America, Central and East Africa, and India. *Robusta* coffee has higher caffeine content, and is grown in West and Central Africa, Southeast Asia, and

---

[2]Starbucks Coffee Company, http://cbpa.louisville.edu/bruce/cases/starbucks/starbucks.htm.
[3]www.conservation.org.
[4]www.conservation.org.
[5]www.conservation.org.

EXHIBIT 4-1 Coffee-Producing Regions

Country
Harvesting Time
60-Kg Bags Harvested in 1999
60-Kg Bags Exported

Brazil
March–October
27,170,000
23,135,000

Colombia
October–February and April–June
9,300,000
9,995,000

Costa Rica
Atlantic coast: August–November
Pacific coast: September–December
2,467,000
2,196,000

Dominican Republic
August–June
1,058,000
161,000

Ecuador
June–October
1,533,000
988,000

Ethiopia
August–January
3,833,000
1,818,000

Guatemala
October–January
4,500,000
4,669,000

Haiti
October–November and
    February–March
385,000
161,000

Honduras
October–March
3,067,000
1,987,000

Indonesia
7,833,000
5,084,000

Jamaica
August–September
40,000
24,000

Kenya
October–December (main) and
    June–August
1,433,000
1,113,000

Malawi
December–February
61,000
54,000

Mexico
High altitudes: November–January
Low altitudes: August–November
6,193,000
4,358,000

EXHIBIT 4-1   Coffee-Producing Regions (*Continued*)

Nicaragua
South: November– January and
   August– September
North: December– March
1,304,000
983,000

Papua New Guinea
April– September
1,286,000
132,000

Tanzania
October– December
773,000
634,000

Uganda
September– December
4,000,000
3,841,000

Venezuela
September– March
1,073,000
452,000

Zambia
October– March
45,000
54,000

Zimbabwe
July– October
189,000
141,000

Source: © 2001. Coffee Research Institute (www.coffeeresearch.org/market/exportation.htm).

Brazil. *Liberica* and *excelsa* coffee beans are grown on a much smaller scale. It takes four thousand beans to produce one pound of roasted coffee beans, of which millions of pounds are sold to Starbucks annually.[6]

Climate

Environmental conditions vary depending on which type of coffee is being grown, but it is generally classified as a tropical plant that requires a considerable amount of annual rainfall. Coffee is cultivated in regions with temperatures ranging from 15–24 degrees Celsius for *arabica* beans, and from 24–30 degrees Celsius for *robusta* beans. Altitude, shade, wind and soil type are all important considerations for coffee production. Frost is one of the main enemies of coffee production, and is most hazardous in Brazil.

Sun vs. Shade-Grown Coffee

Coffee plants are small, shrub-like plants, and are traditionally grown in shaded areas. In recent years, however, sun-grown coffee is becoming increasingly popular.

[6]www.coffeenewlincoln.com/trivia.htm.

EXHIBIT 4-2 Historic Prices of Coffee (U.S. cents/pound)

Year/Month	Composite Price	Other Mild Arabicas			Robusta			Other Prices	
		New York	Bremen/Hamburg	Weighted Average	New York	Le Havre/Marseilles	Weighted Average	Colombian Milds	Brazilian Naturals
2000									
January	82.15	109.17	116.82	111.11	53.62	52.41	53.18	130.13	97.68
February	76.15	101.17	110.19	103.44	49.41	47.97	48.86	124.73	91.51
March	73.49	98.26	108.13	100.73	47.26	44.73	46.25	119.51	89.93
April	69.53	92.41	101.51	94.61	45.21	43.31	44.45	112.67	86.46
May	69.23	91.76	100.99	94.15	45.19	43.01	44.32	110.31	87.23
June	64.56	84.10	92.94	86.44	43.72	41.12	42.68	100.30	78.32
July	64.09	85.20	93.36	87.35	41.93	39.19	40.82	101.67	79.89
August	57.59	74.52	84.08	76.92	38.94	37.22	38.25	91.87	70.57
September	57.31	73.83	81.61	75.78	39.47	37.86	38.83	89.98	71.14
October	56.40	75.43	80.41	76.66	36.55	35.51	36.14	90.25	72.28
November	52.18	70.47	74.63	71.54	33.34	31.94	32.81	84.01	68.95
December	48.27	64.81	70.00	66.16	30.78	30.03	30.38	75.81	64.39
2001									
January	49.19	64.98	68.93	65.98	32.97	31.59	32.40	75.33	62.38
February	49.39	67.00	67.65	67.19	31.96	31.04	31.58	76.70	62.50
March	48.52	65.88	68.35	66.50	30.96	29.87	30.52	76.94	60.35

Source: Coffee Research Institute (www.coffeeresearch.org/market/pastip.htm).

Clear-cutting forestland allows farmers to grow larger crops, with the help of numerous pesticides and chemicals. Clear-cutting harms the environment by reducing the number of oxygen-producing trees, eliminating the homes of birds and jungle animals, and reducing the diversity of crops that farmers can maintain (to hedge against falling coffee prices). As consumers become more aware of this issue, they are demanding more and more shade-grown coffee to protect the environment.

Roasting

Roasting the beans is a three-step chemical process that alters the beans' flavour to certain specifications:

1. The green beans are heated and dried even further, until they are a yellowish colour.
2. The temperature is raised to approximately 205 degrees Celsius, expanding the bean to twice its original size, and changing the colour to light brown. Once this step is complete, the bean is 95% of its original weight.
3. The final stage heats the bean anywhere from 220–240 degrees Celsius (depending on the desired taste), resulting with a 13% weight loss. As the bean changes to a dark brown, its chemical composition changes, and carbon dioxide is released.

Coffee has three distinct dimensions along which the taste is classified: acidity, aroma, and bitterness. The length of roasting, the mineral composition and temperature of the water, and the blend determine the extent of each of these qualities.

Coffee Consumption

North Americans are currently the largest consumers of coffee in the world, with Seattle, Washington pegged as the "spiritual home of coffee." Not surprisingly, Seattle is also the home of Starbucks Coffee Company, the world's largest specialty coffee retailer. Specialty coffees are becoming increasingly popular, and consumer prices are rising, despite the all-time-low market price per pound of coffee (see Exhibit 4-2). It is estimated that 2.25 billion cups of coffee are consumed daily, with over four billion pounds of coffee beans purchased annually in the United States.[7]

Starbucks Coffee Company

In 1987, Howard Schultz purchased the Starbucks assets, and changed the name to Starbucks Corporation. Within one year, the number of outlets was doubled, and a mail order catalogue was designed to service all fifty states. The mail order catalogue offers gifts such as Starbucks mugs, whole and ground coffee beans, and other paraphernalia.

Within fifteen years, the product offerings in-store increased dramatically—in both quantity and in the diversity of specialty coffees such as expresso drinks and a growing number of cold coffee-flavored beverages. Pastries, coffee-related accessories and equipment, ice cream, CDs, and whole bean coffee are all part of the Starbuck's line.

The name changed once again to Starbucks Coffee Company, and in 2001, the corporation consisted of 4709 stores with about 1,000 of them in 28 markets (e.g., Australia,

---

[7]www.conservation.org, www.ico.org.

EXHIBIT 4-3 Increasing Specialty Coffee Consumption in the United States

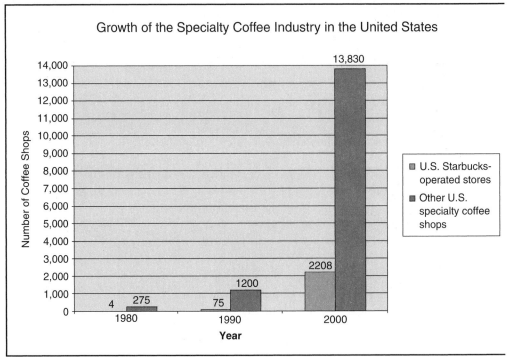

Growth of the Specialty Coffee Industry in the United States

Source: Starbucks Fiscal 2001 Corporate Social Responsibility Annual Report, p. 15.

Germany, and Singapore) outside North America (see Exhibit 4-3).[8] The international expansion can be largely attributed to Mr. Schultz. In 2000, Orin Smith became the second President and CEO of Starbucks, and found himself in charge of a company that currently dominates the American university/college coffee market, and has exclusive agreements with many large hotel chains (such as Host Marriott International, Starwood Hotels), retail outlets, airlines (e.g., American Airlines), and airports (e.g., Toronto's Lester B. Pearson International). Howard Schultz took on the new roles of Chairman and Chief Global Strategist, and remains an active member of the company.

Starbucks also owns a number of roasting facilities, and sells its coffee beans instore, online, through a mail-order catalogue, in supermarkets, and through specialty sales groups. Additionally, the Frappucino® line of cold beverages is bottled and sold in conglomeration with Pepsi Co., and a line of Starbucks® Ice Cream and Ice Cream Bars is co-produced with Dreyer's Grand Ice Cream.

Mission Statements

Starbucks' corporate and environmental mission statements reflect the company's goals: to be the leader in the specialty coffee industry, to be an excellent workplace for

[8]Timeline & History, www.starbucks.com.

its employees, and to be a socially responsible corporation. Starbucks is committed to offering only the best coffee beans and coffee-related products to all of its customers. On top of the two mission statements, Starbucks has established six guiding principles.

Corporate Mission Statement: Establish Starbucks as the premier purveyor of the finest coffee in the world while maintaining our uncompromising principles while we grow.

The following six guiding principles will help us measure the appropriateness of our decisions:

1. Provide a great work environment and treat each other with respect and dignity;
2. Embrace diversity as an essential component in the way we do business;
3. Apply the highest standards of excellence to the purchasing, roasting and fresh delivery of our coffee;
4. Develop enthusiastically satisfied customers all of the time;
5. Contribute positively to our communities and our environment; and
6. Recognize that profitability is essential to our future success.

Environmental Mission Statement: Starbucks is committed to a role of environmental leadership in all facets of our business.

We fulfill this mission by a commitment to:

- Understanding of environmental issues and sharing information with our partners;
- Developing innovative and flexible solutions to bring about change;
- Striving to buy, sell and use environmentally friendly products;
- Recognizing that fiscal responsibility is essential to our environmental future;
- Instilling environmental responsibility as a corporate value;
- Measuring and monitoring our progress for each project; and
- Encouraging all partners to share in our mission.[9]

Employees

Employees, referred to as "partners," are recognized as one of the key components in the company's success:

At all levels of the company, Starbucks partners strive to be good neighbors and active contributors in the communities where they live and work. It's part of the Starbucks culture.[10]

Starbucks is one of the few US companies to offer stock options, medical, dental and vision benefits to all "partners," even those who work part-time. Starbucks was named one of the best employers by Fortune in 2001, with a total of 59,541 employees

---

[9]Mission Statements, www.starbucks.com.
[10]Starbucks Partners (employees) Give Back, www.starbucks.com.

on its international payroll. Twenty-six percent of these employees represented visible minority groups, and 60% were female.[11]

Corporate Social Responsibility (CSR)

Starbucks has committed to being socially responsible, practicing ethical business, and improving the environment at all levels. Partners volunteer in a number of programs to help local communities and the company worldwide. Affiliations with other organizations (e.g., Conservation International, TransFair USA) have also helped Starbucks realize its mission of being a socially responsible and ethical corporation.

John knew that studies prove there is more than just profit to be gained from being socially responsible. "It's not just all about the money. The whole company participates and believes in being socially responsible. Employee morale and motivation increases, customer loyalty improves, and community support is greater" (see Exhibit 4-4 for a comprehensive list of all CSR initiatives).

John felt that Starbucks' environmental and educational programs seemed to be wholly ignored by activists: "They always want to pick on us about something, but there is never any praise for the good things we do. Sometimes I wonder, why bother? I feel like for every step forward, we take two steps back. Our '*Commitment to Origins*' programs are continually under fire. Protest groups simply don't understand that change takes time. We are committed to each and every one of these programs, and have donated over $3 million to various causes, but they will not be successful overnight."

Commitment to Origins

John believes that through the following initiatives, Starbucks has proven its commitment "to addressing social and environmental issues in order to help sustain the people and places that produce Starbucks coffees."[12]

Organic Coffee: This class of coffee beans is grown without fertilizer, pesticides, or any other chemicals that harm the environment. By purchasing and selling certified organic coffees, Starbucks helps keep the environment and the water clean and healthy. Many of Starbucks' farmers produce "passive organic coffee." In this case, the beans are grown organically, but are not officially certified. Although Starbucks' purchase of these beans may be deemed responsible practice, the absence of the official organic seal may result in consumers being unaware of Starbucks' actions. As an industry leader, the company remains a target for activist groups.

Shade-Grown Coffee: Coffee grown in its traditional habitat—protected by a canopy of trees—is known as shade-grown coffee. The plants are shielded from the tropical sun, and the forests are home to many other species of plants, animals and insects. Supporting shade-grown coffee discourages clear-cutting of the tropical forests, and allows the coffee farmers to produce a number of different crops (to hedge against the extremely volatile coffee prices).

In collaboration with Conservation International (CI), Starbucks offers a *Limited Edition Shade-Grown Mexico Coffee,* grown in Chiapas, Mexico. Over the next three years, Starbucks has pledged to donate $600,000 USD to CI (on top of the

---

[11]Fortune 100 Best Companies to Work for, 2001, www.fortune.com/list/bestcompanies/snap_1267.html.
[12]Commitment to Origins, www.starbucks.com.

EXHIBIT 4-4   Starbucks' CSR Initiatives

Building Community

Starbucks proudly boasts a corporate culture that encourages employee participation in community events:

Make Your Mark: Since the program's inception in January 2000, employee teams have been encouraged to volunteer in their communities. In turn, Starbucks will reward every volunteer hour with a cash donation to local not-for-profit organizations.

Community Leadership Program: Many boards across the US have members from Starbucks' executive team, including the American Red Cross, AIDS awareness groups, YWCA, and Alliance for Education.

Caring Unites Partners: A partner assistance program, CUP is funded by employees themselves, and all donations are matched by Starbucks. The money goes toward helping partners suffering from medical problems, natural disasters, and other extenuating circumstances.

Choose to Give! This annual campaign is facilitated through each Starbucks coffee shop. Partners can donate through salary deductions, or a one-time contribution. Starbucks matches all donations, up to $1000 per partner. In 2000, over $500,000 was raised through this fund.

The Starbucks Foundation

In 1997, Howard Schultz established the Starbucks Foundation to promote literacy by helping less fortunate children learn to read and write.The primary focus of the Foundation is supporting local reading programs, and encouraging partners to get involved.

Literacy Grants: Also called "Opportunity Grants," the Foundation funds a number of local literacy organizations, many of which Starbucks partners are actively involved in.

Jumpstart: This national non-profit organization is devoted to preparing preschool children (especially those from low-income families) to learn how to read and write. Highly trained post-secondary students are partnered with preschool kids, and participate in one-on-one tutoring. Starbucks has promised $1 million USD over the next four years to help Jumpstart reach its goal of promoting literacy among children.

Language of Hope: Starbucks is also committed to supporting young, aspiring writers.

Environmental Affairs

In 1992, Starbucks initiated its environmental mission statement, outlining the company's commitment to environmental leadership. To fulfill this mandate, Starbucks has adopted a number of environmentally friendly business practices.

Organic Products: Beginning in 2001, Starbucks became the target of many activist groups. The company was accused of selling products (specifically dairy products) containing genetically modified materials (GM) or produced using Bovine Growth Hormones (rBGH). These hormones induce cows into producing more milk than what one would normally yield. To combat these accusations, Starbucks reexamined all suppliers and the entire product line.

EXHIBIT 4-4 Starbucks' CSR Initiatives (*Continued*)

Currently, the United States does not have any food guidelines regulating the labeling of GM materials, so Starbucks adopted the most stringent international standards from the Australia/New Zealand Food Authority. A thorough review of all milk products was conducted, to determine the amount of rBGH milk used. As an alternative to cow's milk, Starbucks has started offering organic milk, organic yogurt, and soymilk.

Composting, Waste Reduction, Energy Conservation: Starbucks purchases as many environmentally friendly products, and recycles as much of the waste from stores, as is possible. Waste reduction, in terms of administrative paperwork, energy, and packaging, is another key concern at Starbucks. The company encourages composting, conducts energy audits, and reduces energy consumption wherever possible.

The Green Team: A voluntary employee group, the Green Team is a valuable part of the company. The Green Team promotes the use of reusable cups, ensures blue boxes are prominent in all stores, and organizes community events. The group was created in the early 1990s, and has advised the Starbucks executive team since then.

Source: www.starbucks.com, 2002.

$750,000 already donated), and has hopes to expand the Chiapas program. Results of the Chiapas project have been outstanding (see Exhibit 4-5). Five new shade-growing sites are planned in Latin America, Asia, and Africa.

Orin Smith commented:

> We are very pleased with the early results for the farmers, their communities and the surrounding environment in the Chiapas program. By working with Conservation International, Starbucks can bring a quality coffee to our customers and provide positive social and environmental benefits in coffee-growing regions. We are excited to take this model to other parts of the world with CI.[13]

Coffee Purchasing Guidelines: In order to ensure minimum price and quality, Starbucks introduced the first coffee purchasing guidelines in history. These regulations were developed in partnership with The Center for Environmental Leadership, a division of CI, and are currently in their pilot year of 2002–2003. It is a point-based system, where coffee suppliers who support sustainable coffee are rewarded (up to $0.10/pound) based on their performance against a number of criteria (see Exhibit 4-6).

---

[13]Conservation International—A Growing Partnership, www.starbucks.com.

EXHIBIT 4-5   Starbucks and Conservation International: Chiapas Project

Growing on Success in Chiapas

Starbucks formed the initial partnership in 1998 with Conservation International (CI) to support growers of shade coffee and to promote the cultivation of coffee in a way that protects biodiversity, encourages the use of environmentally sustainable agricultural practices and improves the livelihood of coffee farmers. Until now the partnership has focused on CI's flagship Conservation Coffee™ project site in the El Triunfo Biosphere Reserve in the Sierra Madre de Chiapas, an area that CI's conservation experts consider one of the world's most important biodiversity "hotspots." (See CI's website for more information on the hotspots campaign.) Through its Conservation Coffee™ program, CI assists small farmers who grow coffee in the buffer zone of the reserve under the shade of the forest canopy, thereby protecting the reserve's forests, streams and wildlife.

So Far, the Chiapas Project Has Produced Substantial Results

- $200,000 in harvest loans to farmers' cooperatives

- 40% average increase in participating coffee farmers earnings
- 100% growth in the cooperatives' international coffee sales
- 30% increase in the number of farmers participating in the Chiapas project

The new partnership increases the amount Starbucks will contribute to Conservation International projects to $200,000 a year for three years and will focus on four key elements:

1. Expand our work with farmers to promote conservation and improve livelihoods in a wider range of global biodiversity hotspots.
2. Support the introduction of a year-round product line that reflects Starbucks' commitment to alternative environmental agriculture and socio-economic improvement in certain coffee growing regions.
3. Develop coffee sourcing guidelines that incorporate sound environmental management practices and provide fair livelihoods to farmers.
4. Seek to engage other leaders in the coffee business in a collaborative effort to articulate industry-wide guidelines for environmental and social quality.

Source: www.starbucks.com, 2002.

CARE: Starbucks has supported this international relief organization since 1991, and has since helped raise and donate over $1.5 million USD. The money has been used to improve the standard of living of coffee farmers and their families through job training, community building, financial aid and education.

Fair Trade Coffee: In April 2000, Starbucks formed an alliance with TransFair USA. With coffee beans trading at an all-time low price per pound, the Fair Trade movement has become increasingly visible. Beginning in October 2000, Starbucks has

EXHIBIT 4-6 Coffee Purchasing Guidelines

Starbucks Green Coffee Purchasing Guidelines

Quality Criteria: Prerequisite

Every coffee offered must meet Starbucks quality standards in order to be considered for purchase. High quality is an integral component of sustainability at all levels of the coffee supply chain.

Qualifying varieties	Only arabica varieties of coffee will be purchased.
Flavor characteristics	Starbucks cup quality standards are based on specific descriptions for each coffee purchased. Every coffee is expected to represent the flavor character unique to the country or region of origin. All coffees are expected to provide a prefectly clean cup, with medium to heavy body, and excellent aroma. All washed coffees must be of Good Hardbean or better density and have good acidity.
Defect-free beans	Starbucks requires zero defects in grade, good even color, and consistent bean size.

Environmental Impacts: 50 points

Coffee growing and processing systems should contribute to conservation of soil, water and biological diversity; employ efficient and renewable energy technologies; minimize or eliminate agrochemical inputs; and manage waste materials consistent with the principles of reduction, reuse and recycling.

Soil management	Farm management practices should effectively control erosion and enhance soil structure and fertility, relying as much as possible on means such as organic fertilizers, cover crops, mulch and compost.	5 points
Water reduction	Coffee should be processed using methods that reduce water consumption.	5 points
Clean water	Coffee should be processed using methods that prevent pollution of surface water and ground water	5 points
Water buffer zone	Vegetative buffer zone should be in place adjacent to all water sources. No alteration should be made to the courses or hydrology of streams or other surface water bodies.	5 points
Forest and biodiversity conservation	Coffee production systems should maintain and enhance biological diversity on farms and surrounding areas without disturbance of natural forests.	5 points
Use of shade	Existing coffee farms in forest regions should maintain or enhance shade canopy cover with diverse tree species that conserve local and endemic biodiversity.	5 points
Energy use	Coffee growing, processing and drying should use energy efficiently, employ renewable sources wherever possible, and not rely on firewood obtained from forest clearing. For example, patio drying should be used as much as practical and solar coffee drying technology employed where feasible.	5 points

EXHIBIT 4-6   Coffee Purchasing Guidelines (*Continued*)

Pest management	Integrated pest management systems are employed, limiting pesticide application to extreme cases when necessary to avert severe crop loss and substantial economic failure.	5 points

Accepted agrochemical	Coffee production systems should minimize and wherever possible eliminate inputs of agrochemicals such as chemical pesticides and synthetic fertilizers.
	    Farms are certified organic, use organic management techniques or are otherwise demonstrating significant reductions in the quantity of synthetic agrochemicals being applied.
	    No agrochemicals that are banned for agricultural use in their country of use, country of origin or by international agreement are stored or used on the farm.
		5 points

Waste management	Waste and coffee by-products are managed to minimize environmental impacts by applying the principles of reduction, reuse and recycling; for example, composting or recycling of coffee pulp and parchment.	5 points

Social Conditions: 30 points

Coffee production systems should ensure protection from workplace hazards and conform to local laws, as well as to applicable international conventions related to employee wages and benefits, occupational health and safety, and labor and human rights.

Wages and benefits	Coffee farms that employ workers should conform to local laws and applicable international conventions related to workers' rights and benefits and are in a process of continual improvement over time. Wages and benefits should meet or exceed the minimum required under local and national laws. Workers' rights to organize and negotiate freely with their employers are guaranteed in accordance with local laws and international obligations.	10 points
Health and safety	Working conditions should meet or exceed applicable laws and regulations related to health and safety of workers. Effective measures should be taken to ensure the health and safety of farm workers who may handle or be exposed to agrochemicals.	10 points
Living conditions	Workers and their families, including seasonal workers, are provided with access to potable water, sanitary facilities, adequate housing, education and training, transportation, and health services.	10 points

Economic Issues: 20 points

Coffee production systems and commercialization should benefit rural communities by boosting producer incomes, expanding employment and educational opportunities, and

EXHIBIT 4-6   Coffee Purchasing Guidelines (*Continued*)

	enhancing local infrastructure and public services. In order for coffee production to be sustainable, it must be economically viable at all levels of the supply chain, from seed to cup.	
Long-term relationships	Starbucks seeks to develop long-term trading relationships with preferred suppliers.	
Incentives	Through its purchasing and pricing policies, Starbucks seeks to provide incentives and support for sustainable coffee production, processing and shipping methods.	
Economic transparency	In order to ensure that the entire supply chain—farmer, miller, exporter, and importer—benefit from the Starbucks preferred supplier program, vendors are expected to provide reliable documentation regarding prices paid to their suppliers.	20 points

Source: Starbucks Green Coffee Purchasing Program Pilot Program for Preferred Suppliers, November 2001, www.celb.org/pressreleasesPreferred%20Supplier.pdf.

sold certified Fair Trade coffee in every café in the US, with plans to make this an international initiative. The Fair Trade coffee beans are currently sold in take-home packages priced at $11.45/lb; however, these beans are not used for brewed in-store coffees.[14]

TransFair USA

TransFair USA, the American division of TransFair International, is the only organization in the US that can certify Fair Trade consumer products. Founded in 1996, TransFair USA became active in 1998. Initially, the organization focused on certifying coffee importers, but later the emphasis shifted to roasters, and now currently targets and promotes Fair Trade to different geographic regions in the US. The TransFair symbol clearly identifies Fair Trade products, and can be found on tea, bananas and coffee.

TransFair USA has two main goals:

1. To increase the availability of Fair Trade Certified products throughout the country by creating partnerships with industry, and
2. To increase consumer awareness about the importance of Fair Trade, thereby building consumer demand for Fair Trade Certified Products.[15]

Partnerships with international companies like Starbucks will continue to help TransFair USA accomplish its mission by raising consumer interest and awareness of Fair Trade goods. Roasters, importers and retailers are the three primary groups targeted by TransFair USA. These outlets are focusing their efforts on the rapidly growing specialty coffee market, as the "café culture" continues to expand. A recent survey has concluded that 49% of respondents would buy Fair Trade coffee, and 78% of adults surveyed would pay a premium price for a socially responsible product.[16]

---

[14]www.starbucks.com/shop/category.asp?category%Fname=Coffee.
[15]About Us, www.transfairusa.org.
[16]About Us, www.transfairusa.org.

The Fair Trade Movement

In the late 1950s, Alternative Trading Organizations (ATOs) began to emerge in Europe and the US. ATOs believed in trade without the middleman, and purchases were made directly from Third World countries. A fair price was paid, and, at that time, handicrafts were the most popular commodity. Producers of these goods realized higher incomes, and they no longer had to rely on the corporate intermediaries. The original ATOs expanded into an organization of approximately 3000 shops in Europe, and 100 in the USA, altogether forming the Fair Trade Federation.[17]

Max Havelaar

Max Havelaar was the first Fair Trade certification initiative, originating in Holland in 1988. A Fair Trade seal (see Exhibit 4-7a) was for sale to all coffee roasters. Unlike today, in order to qualify for certification, coffee roasters were required to have only a minute portion of their total output traded in accordance with Fair Trade guidelines. As the seal became more prominent and recognizable through supermarket distribution, European consumers quickly became more aware of the benefits of Fair Trade, and more farmers realized the gains from participating.

Other European countries quickly followed suit, and TransFair International was born, and became the first international body to govern Fair Trade. There are currently 17 member nations, all of which import and sell Fair Trade coffee bearing the TransFair certification seal[18] (see Exhibit 4-7b).

EXHIBIT 4-7   Fair Trade Certification Seals

(a) Max Havelaar

(b) TransFair International

Source: www.maxhavelaar.no.   *Source:* www.transfairusa.org/why/index.html.

---

[17]The History of Fair Trade, www.globalexchange.org/economy/coffee.
[18]The History of Fair Trade, www.globalexchange.org/economy/coffee.

Fair Trade Labeling Organization International (FLO)

The seventeen member nations of TransFair International started the FLO in 1997. The group's goal was to create a standardized set of criteria that can be applied internationally to all coffee roasters, importers, and producers (see Exhibit 4-8). The criteria can be applied to all products currently traded under the Fair Trade system, including tea, cocoa, bananas, sugar, honey and orange juice. The FLO maintains and oversees the certification systems in each country. Coffee producers are inspected annually by FLO members, and the organization is funded by the member nations.

Unlike other Fair Trade goods, coffee is typically produced on small, family-owned plantations. As such, the Fair Trade movement does not address the wage inequities and questionable working conditions at the larger plantations. However, most small farmers do not have the finances to clear-cut land, nor to purchase expensive chemicals to treat their crops. As a result, these small farmers tend to produce shade-grown, organic coffee. Coffee beans that are certified as Fair Trade, shade-grown, and organic, all help to improve the natural environment, the standard of living for the farmers, and promote the sustainability of coffee.

Starbucks' Fair Trade Plans

Last October, Starbucks announced plans to expand its Fair Trade initiative, with a commitment to buy one million pounds of Fair Trade beans over the next 12–18 months. These beans will be sold in all stores, on university and college campuses, and hopefully extended to the international markets by the end of 2002.

In response to consumer demand, Starbucks will start offering brewed Fair Trade coffee as the "Coffee of the Day" in May 2002. Once a month, all North American consumers will be able to taste the brewed beans, and Starbucks also plans to continue to work closely with the International Fair Trade Labeling Organization (FLO) to begin worldwide distribution of Fair Trade coffee.

The Protests

Most recently activists have challenged Starbucks' Fair Trade coffee programs. OCA and GE have both staged "leaflet" campaigns, demanding that Starbucks "really promote" Fair Trade coffee, and offer brewed coffee made from Fair Trade beans in-store (see Exhibits 4-9 and 4-10). OCA has designed a derogatory logo to promote their cause, and consumers are encouraged to send a pre-written fax to Orin Smith (see Exhibit 4-11), and to boycott Starbucks products. Petitions are continually being circulated, and protesters have even targeted Starbucks stores.

Headlines such as *"Protesters demand Starbucks pay fair prices for beans," "Starbucks braces for another round with eco-protests,"* and *"Activist takes up the fight for fair-trade coffee"* are slowly having the desired impact. People are becoming increasingly aware of the Fair Trade movement, and politicians are even beginning to use Fair Trade as a campaigning tool.

Despite Starbucks' promises to purchase one million pounds of Fair Trade beans, and to begin brewing Fair Trade Coffee in-store, protesters maintain that this is not enough. The OCA believes that one beverage on the menu, offered one day per month (refer to Exhibit 4-3), does not make Starbucks a socially responsible corporate citizen, nor does it really help improve the coffee grower's lives.

EXHIBIT 4-8   Fair Trade Labeling Organization Criteria

Roasters

Any coffee roaster that complies with the following conditions can apply for the right to use of one of the Fair Trade Labels of FLO-International.

1. The purchasing price must have been fixed in accordance with the conditions established for this effect by FLO-International:
   - Guaranteed floor price of $1.26 per pound for washed arabica.
   - For arabicas the New York "C" market shall be the basis of calculation. The price shall be established in US$-cents per pound, plus or minus the prevailing differential for the relevant quality, basis F.O.B. origin, net shipped weight. Over the established prices, there shall be a fixed premium of 5 US$-cents per pound.
   - For certified organic or biological coffee with officially recognized certification, that will be sold as such, an additional premium of 15 US$-cents per pound green coffee will be due, on top of the FLO-International price.
2. The roaster/buyer is obliged to facilitate the coffee producers' access to credit facilities at the beginning of the harvest season, up to 60% of the value of the contracted coffee at Fair Trade conditions, at regular international interest rates. The credit will be cancelled upon shipment of the coffee.
3. Producers and roasters/buyers depend on reliability and continuity. For that reason, relations between both should be based on long-term contracts (1 to 10 years).

Producers

1. The majority of the members of the organization are small scale producers of coffee. By small producers are understood those that are not structurally dependent on hired labor, managing their farm mainly with their own and their family's labor-force;
2. The organization is independent and democratically controlled by its members. This means that the members of the organizations participate in the decision-making process which determines the general strategy of their organization, including decisions related to the destiny of the additional resources which result from operations in the framework of this agreement;
3. Administrative transparency and effective control by the members and its Board over the management is secured, minimizing the risk of fraud and offering members the necessary instruments to be able to act adequately in case of fraud;
4. The philosophy motivating the organization is based on the concept and practice of solidarity;
5. No form of political, racial, religious or sexual discrimination is practiced;
6. The organization is statutorily open to new members;
7. The organization is politically independent, and there are sufficient guarantees that the organization will not become the instrument of any political party or interest;

EXHIBIT 4-8   Fair Trade Labeling Organization Criteria (*Continued*)

8. The organization shares with the FLO-International and with the other organizations inscribed in the Producers' Register the following principles and general objectives:
   - integral economic development, concentrating on improvement of production techniques and diversification of the production, in order to diminish dependency on one single product as a cash crop;
   - integral organizational development, improving the managerial and administrative capacity of the actual and future leadership of the organization and ensuring full participation of the members in the definition of strategies and the use of extra income resulting from fair trade;
   - integral social development, for instance through health care and educational programs, improvement of housing and water supply, thus creating better living conditions for the members and their families and the communities they live in;
   - sustainable development strategies, applying production techniques which respect the specific ecosystems and contribute to the conservation and a sustainable use of natural resources, in order to avoid as much as possible—or even totally—the use of chemical inputs;
   - integral human participation, offering especially women the opportunity to play a more active role in the development process and in the decision-making process and management of the organization;
   - improvement of the quality of the products as a strategic requirement for the small producers to defend themselves on both the Fair Trade market and the regular market.

Source: Coffee Production and Labor, www.organicconsumers.org/Starbucks/coffeelabor.htm.

Mr. Kelly, director of the OCA's American branch, argues that Starbucks' pledge to purchase one million pounds of Fair Trade beans is ridiculous. The beans will comprise only 1% of the company's total annual spending on coffee, and such a small step will do little to protect and improve the livelihood of third world farmers. With Starbucks grossing over $2.6 billion dollars in 2001 (see Exhibit 4-12), protestors argue that there is money to spare.

The new CSR annual report has also been scrutinized, as it was not subject to external verification. Mr. Kelly recently commented on Starbucks' first CSR annual report: "Why should people take such statements at face value? To prove what it says it's doing, Starbucks should submit to third-party verification, available only via the Fair Trade movement, which guarantees growers a premium wage."[19]

The same activist groups claim that it is possible to sell more Fair Trade coffee and still turn a profit. A common example is Equal Exchange. This company has been

[19]Alison Maitland, "Coffee: Bitter Taste of Success," *Financial Times,* March 11, 2002.

EXHIBIT 4-9 OCA Leaflet

CONSUMER WARNING

DO YOU WANT
your coffee beverages and food to be free of genetically engineered ingredients and dangerous hormones?

DO YOU WANT
To support fair wages and living conditions for coffee farmers and plantation workers?

IF SO HERE ARE SOME THINGS YOU SHOULD KNOW ABOUT

STARBUCKS

Despite rising consumer concerns, most Starbucks outlets are still using milk from dairies where cows are injected with Monsanto's controversial Bovine Growth hormone (rBGH), a hormone often associated with higher risks for cancer. rBGH is a powerful drug which cruelly damages the health of dairy cows, forcing them to give more milk. Milk from rBGH-injected cows is also likely to contain more pus, antibiotic residues, and bacteria. *rBGH is banned in every industrialized country in the world — except for the US.*

Starbucks refuses to guarantee that the milk, chocolate, ice cream, bottled Frappuccino drinks, and baked goods they are selling are free of rBGH (also known as rBST) and other genetically engineered ingredients.

Although Starbucks now offers non-rBGH organic milk and soy milk as an option in its US cafes, most customers are unaware of this. *In addition, they are charging an extra 40¢ per cup for these safer, non-genetically engineered alternatives.*

Although Starbucks has bowed to consumer pressure and begun selling certified Fair Trade or organic coffee in bulk, they are still refusing to brew it on a weekly basis. Many of Starbucks competitors, however, are already brewing Fair Trade and organic coffee daily. Starbucks boasts that in 2002 they will buy one million pounds of Fair Trade coffee and brew it once a month. *This is a nominal amount — less than 1% of the company's total coffee purchases*

In 1995, Starbucks promised to pay a living wage to small farmers and impoverished workers on the coffee plantations of its suppliers. *Seven years later, Starbucks has done little or nothing to meet this pledge.* They claim to pay "top dollar" for their coffee, at least $1.25 per pound, yet most of this money goes to middlemen, not the farmers or workers. Buying significant amounts of certified Fair Trade coffee would guarantee farmers a living wage.

Turn this leaflet over to see what you can do to pressure Starbucks to change its policies...

STARBUCKS OR FRANKENBUCK$?
TAKE ACTION NOW!

Go into a Starbucks coffee shop and talk to the manager or person in charge. Show them this leaflet and ask for written assurance that they will remove rBGH and other genetically engineered (GE) ingredients from their coffee beverages and their foods; that they will start brewing Fair Trade coffee as their "coffee of the day" at least one day a week; and that they will fulfill their pledge to pay a living wage to small farmers and coffee plantation workers.

Ask Starbucks to show you what brand of milk they are using in your coffee or bottled Frappuccino and take note of whether it is labeled as rBGH-free. If you are ordering organic milk or soy milk with your coffee, tell them you think the 40¢ surcharge is outrageous. Ask if their baked goods are organic or free from GE soy, soy derivatives, corn sweeteners, and cooking oils.

If you order a coffee from Starbucks, ask them to brew your coffee with Fair Trade or organic coffee beans. If they won't, take your business elsewhere.

Ask Starbucks for written assurance that they will cooperate with international human rights monitors and organic and Fair Trade certifiers to guarantee that they are paying a living wage to the small farmers and coffee plantation workers who supply their coffee.

Patronize local, socially responsible businesses and products. If local coffee shops are brewing organic and Fair Trade coffee and avoiding GE ingredients, give your business to them instead of Starbucks.

Join the Organic Consumers Association and the growing Fair Trade Movement across the world. Talk to the person who handed you this leaflet to get involved locally. Keep informed on this campaign by visiting our web site at *www.organicconsumers.org*

Call, write, fax or email Starbucks. Since we began this campaign last year, Starbucks has sworn off the use of GE coffee beans and has begun to address a number of other issues. But they still have a long way to go. *Keep up the pressure.*

STARBUCKS CONTACT INFORMATION:

Call: 800-235-2883
Fax: 206-447-3432
email: osmith@starbucks.com
Write: Mr. Orin Smith, CEO
Starbucks Coffee Company
P.O. Box 34067
Seattle, WA 98124-1067

For more information or to get further involved

Organic Consumers Association
6101 Cliff Estate Road
Little Marais, MN 55614
Telephone: 218-226-4164
Fax: 218-226-4157
campaign@organicconsumers.org
www.organicconsumers.org

Source: www.organicconsumers.org.

EXHIBIT 4-10   Global Exchange Leaflet

Fair Trade Coffee Campaign

STARBUCKS PROFITS AS FARMERS STARVE
STARBUCKS: BREW FAIR TRADE!!

Starbucks, the largest specialty coffee chain in the world, offers Fair Trade coffee at all its US stores as a result of grassroots pressure to demand a living wage for farmers. Now, we need to increase that volume. If Starbucks were to offer BREWED Fair Trade as Coffee of the Day in all its stores, it would represent about 37,500 pounds (one container of coffee) a day. And while world coffee prices plummet from an average of $1/pound to LESS THAN 50 cents, last quarter Starbucks increased its profits by 34% to $46.8 million!

type of trade	market price per pound	price to farmer, container a week for one year
Fair Trade	$1.26	$2,047,500
current crisis	$.50 (farmers get only half of this)	$292,500
Revenues for Starbucks on same volume:		$78,000,000

(estimate based on $1 per cup, 40 cups/pound)

Farmers are losing their land and facing starvation.

Outraged?!!
What YOU
can DO:

* Write Starbucks with your concerns:
    Orin Smith, CEO, Starbucks Coffee Company
    P.O. Box 34067, Seattle, WA 98124-1067
    fax: 206.447.3432   email: OSmith@Starbucks.com
* If you are a Starbucks customer, always buy Fair Trade!
* Tell the Starbucks workers and customers about your commitment to buy only Fair Trade.
* Keep asking for Fair Trade brewed coffee.
* Join the Organic Consumers Association (www.purefood.org) ···· ···· ··· ·· ····· ···· ·· · ···· ·· ···· ·· ·· ···· ·· · ···· · · · ···· · ·· · ···· · ···· ··

GLOBAL [●] EXCHANGE

2017 Mission St., Rm. 303, San Francisco, CA 94110   (415) 255-7296   FAX (415)255-7498
fairtrade@globalexchange.org · www.globalexchange.org/economy/coffee

Source: www.globalexhange.org/economy/coffee.

EXHIBIT 4-11 OCA's Fax Campaign to Orin Smith

Send a Fax to Starbucks CEO

HELP PRESSURE STARBUCKS TO REMOVE GENETICALLY
ENGINEERED INGREDIENTS FROM THEIR FOOD AND DAIRY
PRODUCTS ON A WORLDWIDE BASIS, IMPROVE WORKING
CONDITIONS FOR COFFEE PLANTATION WORKERS,
AND BREW AND SERIOUSLY PROMOTE FAIR TRADE COFFEE IN
ALL OF THEIR CAFES.

Dear Orin Smith,

As a health conscious, socially and environmentally-concerned consumer I am upset
about the current policies and practices of Starbucks. I am upset about the
introduction of untested, unlabeled, and potentially hazardous genetically
engineered ingredients—without my knowledge—into the foods that I consume and
serve to my family. I am dismayed to learn that Starbucks allows recombinant
Bovine Growth Hormone (rBGH) and other genetically engineered ingredients (soy
and soy derivatives, corn sweeteners, etc.) in your coffee beverages, ice cream,
chocolate, and baked goods.

I am also upset that Starbucks is refusing to brew and serve Fair Trade, shade-grown
coffee in its cafes (as opposed to just selling the beans in bulk); and that you are not
following through completely and transparently on a previous agreement to improve
the wages and working conditions for the thousands of workers on coffee
plantations that supply you with coffee in Guatemala and other nations. As you
know, shade-grown Fair Trade coffee (most of which is organic) is much better for
the environment, helping to preserve biodiversity and the precious habitat of
migratory birds and other creatures, as well as being safer for coffee workers. As you
also know, wages and working conditions for small coffee producers and plantation
workers who supply your company with its primary product are abysmal.

I have reviewed the current information on genetically engineered foods and crops
and I'm gravely concerned about the effects they could have on human health and
the environment. Since these foods have been rushed to market, there has been no
time to conduct long-term human health studies. Numerous scientists have warned
that genetic engineering could likely introduce allergens and novel toxins into food,
could lower its nutritional value, and in the case of milk produced with genetically
engineered bovine growth hormone (rBGH), possibly increase the risk of cancer. I
would like to see Starbucks publicly state that you are removing all genetically
engineered ingredients from your brand-name products and that you will label your
bottled coffee beverages and ice cream as certified rBGH free (or organic).

EXHIBIT 4-11 OCA's Fax Campaign to Orin Smith (*Continued*)

If you cannot guarantee me in writing that you are moving to banish untested, unlabeled rBGH and other genetically engineered food ingredients from your brand-name products, brewing and promoting Fair Trade coffee in all your cafes, and following through completely and transparently on your previous pledge to improve the wages and working conditions of the plantation workers who supply you with your coffee—you leave me no choice but to boycott your products, and to tell everyone else I know to do the same thing. I look forward to receiving a response from you in writing.

Source: www.organicconsumers.org/Starbucks/Starbucks.htm/#fax.

one of the pioneers of the Fair Trade movement since 1986. Trading directly with 17 partners in 10 developing countries, protesters congratulate Equal Exchange, while Starbucks is criticized for not offering 100% Fair Trade products.

The Dilemma

Mr. Taylor recalled a recent confrontation with Mr. Kelly. The OCA director had publicly acknowledged that "the coffee chain (Starbucks) has gone some way to meet activists' demands."[20] But he still criticized the company's efforts as inadequate.

"We have promised that next year our CSR report will be externally audited, are planning to sell Fair Trade internationally, and have always been environmentally and socially aware. As I told Mr. Kelly, doing well and doing good are not opposites, they're companions. I firmly believe that—and it is just one more reason I chose to accept this position at Starbucks. The company as a whole has really made an effort to make a positive difference in the world."

John Taylor sat down at his desk with a resigned sigh. He was tired of all the criticism. After all, wasn't Starbucks doing more than most other firms in the same industry? On the other hand, he had to ask, "Maybe the folks at OCA and GE are right. Perhaps we need to reexamine our motives. Our research has shown that consumers are willing to pay extra to 'do the right thing.' The question will be, however, how to publicly justify the higher prices, especially if our competitors don't take similar actions and can undersell us."

The big question in his mind was whether or not Starbucks should to try to take the lead on this issue or whether it should respond to the activists' pressure tactics in a more limited way. If we work to be more proactive, John thought, questions remain about what we should do and how can we make people understand and appreciate our efforts. Tied to this is the issue of what we should spend both on the initiative and on the promotion of the effort. On the other hand, John wondered, should we just "weather the storm." We do follow ethical business practices, John believed, and they have always been ingrained into our culture.

---

[20]Maitland, "Coffee."

EXHIBIT 4-12 Financial Data (all figures are in thousands, except earnings per share and store data)

As of and for the fiscal year ended (1)	Sept. 30, 2001 (52 Wks)	Oct. 1, 2000 (52 Wks)	Oct. 3, 1999 (53 Wks)	Sept. 27, 1998 (52 Wks)	Sept. 28, 1997 (52 Wks)
RESULTS OF OPERATIONS DATA					
Net Revenues					
Retail	$2,229,594	$1,823,607	$1,423,389	$1,102,574	$836,291
Specialty	$419,386	$354,007	$263,439	$206,128	$139,098
Total net revenues	$2,648,980	$2,177,614	$1,686,828	$1,308,702	$975,389
Merger expenses (2)	—	—	—	$8,930	—
Operating income	$281,094	$212,252	$156,711	$109,216	$86,199
Internet-related investment losses	$2,940	$58,792	—	—	—
Net earnings	$181,210	$94,564	$101,693	$68,372	$55,211
Net earnings per common share—diluted	$0.46	$0.24	$0.27	$0.19	$0.17
Cash dividends per share	—	—	—	—	—
BALANCE SHEET DATA					
Working capital	$148,661	$146,568	$135,303	$157,805	$172,079
Total assets	$1,851,039	$1,491,546	$1,252,514	$992,755	$857,152
Long-term debt (including current portion)	$6,483	$7,168	$7,691	$1,803	$168,832
Shareholders' equity	$1,375,927	$961,013	$961,013	$794,297	$533,710
STORE OPERATING DATA					
Percentage change in comparable store sales (3)	5%	9%	6%	5%	5%
Stores open at year end					
Continental North America Company-operated stores	2971	2446	2038	1622	1270
Company-operated stores	809	530	179	133	94
Licensed stores					
International Company-operated stores	295	173	97	66	31
Company-operated stores	634	352	184	65	17
Licensed stores					
Total stores	4709	3501	2498	1886	1412

(1) The Company's fiscal year ends on the Sunday closest to September 30. All fiscal years presented include 52 weeks, except fiscal 1999, which includes 53 weeks.
(2) Merger expenses relate to the business combination with Seattle Coffee Holdings Limited.
(3) Includes only Company-operated stores open 13 months or longer.
Source: Starbucks Coffee, Fiscal 2001 Annual Report, p. 20.

John was perplexed. There seemed to be risks associated with either option. Furthermore, he wondered if he was viewing the issue from the "right" perspective. Was the firm being more proactive on this issue because it's the right thing to do, or because it will help protect or improve the bottom line? In fact, he wondered, were there other principles and criteria that should influence his decision other than the long-term well-being of his stockholders? With these questions whirling through his mind, John picked up the phone and called Orin Smith. He made an appointment for the following morning to discuss the issues at hand. "No matter what route we take, the whole senior executive team needs to be involved," he thought. "Our reputation and future direction seem to be hanging in the balance."

BASTA PASTA FOOD COMPANY INC.[1]

John E. Bargetto and Patrick E. Murphy

Introduction

It is early December 2000, and Georgia Daniels is sitting in her office in Pleasanton, California, which is located in the San Francisco Bay Area. Georgia works for (fictitious) BuyMore, a California grocery chain store. The chain consists of 46 stores from Sausalito in the north to Santa Cruz in the south.

BuyMore focuses on bigger-volume grocery purchases in warehouse-style retail outlets. The 1999 sales revenue for the chain was $980 million. All items for the stores are purchased centrally and shipped from the main warehouse. There are 19 different buyers for the various grocery items, from pimentos to frozen turkeys. Georgia served as the wine buyer for four years and enjoyed the work, having been responsible for purchasing various wines from all around the world: from French Bordeaux to California Chardonnays. Even though Georgia liked her job, she knew that in order to be considered for promotion, she would need to get experience in additional departments. That is why, when her boss came to her office to offer her a promotion to a premium deli food buyer, she jumped at the chance.

A New Practice for Georgia: Slotting Fees

Sitting by her computer, Georgia contemplated the last meeting with her new boss Victor Bergamino, a 35-year veteran food buyer. Bergamino worked for Safeway for 30 years prior to moving to BuyMore. The point of the meeting was to discuss the slotting fee figures for the year to come. The slotting allowance practice was something new to Georgia but something she had to become aware of in the food industry. At this point, she knew only that in the grocery retail business, slotting fees correspond to payments made by manufacturers for a slot on retailers' shelves.

To learn more about it, she started doing research on the Internet. To begin, she found a summary of the various forms of slotting fees with their descriptions (see Exhibit 4A): free goods, ongoing charge for shelf space, advertising paid for by suppliers, in-store demos, and so on. Slotting fees may take the form of money, merchandise, or promotional supports, but the aim is always to get suppliers' products into the retail stores and keep them in place. Above all, the product has to be prominent. It must catch the consumer's eyes, not on the bottom shelf where you have to be on all fours to find something.

Commenting on her research to her boss the next day, she said, "It's amazing, there seems to be a unique jargon associated with these slotting allowances!" "It's not just jargon, but also a very important practice with some rules you have to understand," replied Bergamino.

At this point, she started to realize that BuyMore, a leading chain like Safeway and Albertson's, wields tremendous economic power and can force suppliers to pay slotting allowances. She read in the magazine *Milling and Baking News*[2] that more

---

[1]This disguised case was prepared by John Bargetto and Patrick E. Murphy for classroom discussion rather than to illustrate either effective or ineffective handling of an administrative, ethical, or legal decision by individuals or management. The authors want to thank Coralie Ratte for her assistance.

[2]"Slotting Fees Raise Irksome Issues for Bakers and Others," *Milling and Baking News,* January 13, 1998.

EXHIBIT 4A Slotting Allowances and Fees

Type of Fee	Description
Presentation fees or Hello Money	Fees paid by a manufacturer to a retailer for the privilege of making a sales presentation.
"Slotting" fees	Up-front payments of cash, promotional dollars, or merchandise given by a manufacturer to a retailer to obtain shelf space for a product. Also known as slotting allowance.
Display fees	Fees paid for special merchandising and display of products.
Pay-to-stay fees	Fees paid by a manufacturer to a retailer to continue stocking and displaying a product.
Failure fees	Fees paid by a manufacturer to a retailer when a product does not meet expected goals and is being dropped from the retailer's inventory.
Success fees	Fees paid after a new product achieves success.
End cap	A massive merchandise display at the end of an aisle, often for high margin, impulse items. These prime selling locations, also known as ends or end display, command among the highest fees.
Street money	Cash offered to retailers by suppliers or middlemen for reaching specific performance goals, meeting conditions, or making purchases.
Push money	A manufacturer's incentive to wholesaler to actively market their products. Usually payments are based on the number of cases sold. Also called promotion money or a spiff.
Listing allowance	Money that a manufacturer or wholesaler gives a retailer to advertise a product.
Table allowance	A manufacturer's payment to a retailer to display or highlight a product on supplemental tables. Also called a Table Display Allowance (TDA).

than 8 out of 10 manufacturers in the food, health and beauty care, and general merchandise/nonfood categories reported paying a slotting allowance for their most recent new product introductions, and the incidence is even higher among smaller companies (see Exhibits 4B and 4C). She also read that according to an AC Nielsen's annual trade promotion survey, 90 percent of food retailers were reported to charge these fees.[3]

Georgia knew it was not just a matter of figures but a harsh reality for small suppliers. She couldn't stop thinking about this issue during the weekend while visiting San Jose to help out on a new store opening. She picked up a local paper and read how

---

[3]Robin Fields and Melinda Fulmer, "Markets' Shelf Fees Put Squeeze on Small Firms," *Los Angeles Times,* January 29, 2000.

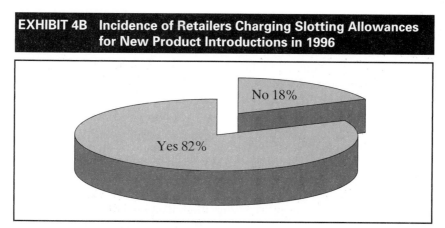

Source: "Slotting Fees Raise Irksome Issues for Bakers and Others," *Milling and Baking News*, January 13, 1998.

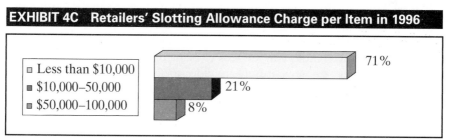

Source: "Slotting Fees Raise Irksome Issues for Bakers and Others," *Milling and Baking News*, January 13, 1998.

a small firm nearly went bankrupt because of slotting fees. "These practices can easily be associated with the unfair abuse of power by large retailers," Georgia thought to herself. "How can smaller companies avoid being squeezed out because they cannot afford to pay this cost in addition to their already existing distribution costs?"

Thinking about the consequences such fees could have, she already knew one major impact is a decrease in choice for consumers since there are fewer competing products on the shelves. She also wondered whether the consumer gets a lower-quality product as a result of slotting allowances because smaller quality producers cannot compete with larger firms that can afford slotting fees. Georgia already knew that producers were simply increasing their prices to pay for the practice because she remembered meeting a sales representative for a spice company. She asked him how they could afford slotting allowances: "Oh, we just add them to our price," he answered. Thinking about this practice further, Georgia knew it is obviously much easier to support an introduction for larger companies such as Kraft than for smaller ones. But she wondered if it means that a Kraft product is of better quality than one from a smaller manufacturer or if it is just a question of financial means.

Georgia was amazed by the information she found while looking on the Internet. There is even some discrimination among suppliers. She was really shocked by the fact that strong brands like Tide, Kellogg's, and Coke don't have to pay slotting fees because they have clout. Even if they make such payments, they are powerful enough to dictate terms and conditions to retailers. An article she downloaded titled "High Price of Shelf Space"[4] stated that manufacturers are generally reluctant to discuss slotting fees for fear of alienating retailers and jeopardizing their sales. Some manufacturers, like Procter & Gamble (P&G), don't pay them at all. For instance, Cincinnati-based P&G refuses to pay cash for shelf space. Instead they pay directly for in-store promotions or special price deals.[5] They promise and provide advertising that spurs strong demand for their products.

Three company examples were given in the article. Frito-Lay pays $100,000 to chains to carry new products. Truzzolino Pizza Roll was charged $25,000 by one chain to carry its products, and Lee's Ice Cream, a Baltimore company, was asked to pay $25,000 for each flavor it wanted stores to carry. So, in many cases the amounts are arbitrary and secret. In fact, retailers and manufacturers often referred to slotting fees as the grocery industry's "dirty little secret."[6] Some grocery retailers require a flat fee of $5,000 per product for an introduction, whereas others have a graduated fee schedule linked to the shelf space location: an eye-level slot will cost more than a knee- or ground-level slot. Some retailers even require a "kill fee" to be paid when a product does not sell.

It seemed many fees are often made in cash and are nonuniform. As a result, there is an atmosphere of mistrust on the market. Georgia said to herself, "Quantity discounts are one thing, but this outright payola is another. In the wine industry, these payoffs never happened."

Georgia found out that the U.S. Senate Small Business Committee staffers interviewed 79 small-business owners in late September 1999 in order to prepare for a hearing on slotting fees. Nearly all refused to tell their story publicly for fear of having their products blacklisted. The three witnesses who testified agreed to do so only with their names withheld and their voices electronically altered. The outcome of this hearing was reported widely, and Georgia found accounts in the print[7,8] and electronic media (www.senate.gov/~sbc/hearings/internet.html).

Contrast to Wine Division

Georgia is quite startled by the pervasiveness of slotting allowances. As a wine buyer, she knew for a fact that slotting allowances were strictly prohibited. The advertising of wine was paid for by the store and would not be paid for by any supplier. Georgia was well aware that by law, "nothing of value" could be given to the retailer by a supplier. In her food division, Georgia oversees all aspects of slotting allowances plus in-store demos, which the suppliers support. If a product fails, the supplier purchases back in-store stock

---

[4]Sean Somerville, "High Price of Shelf Space," *The Sun*, June 1, 1997, 1D.
[5]Fields and Fulmer.
[6]Robert J. Aalberts and Marianne M. Jennings, "The Ethics of Slotting: Is This Bribery, Facilitation Marketing or Just Plain Competition," *Journal of Business Ethics* 20, no. 3 (1999): 207.
[7]Jim Barlow, "Grocery Practices May Harm Stores," *Houston Chronicle*, September 26, 1999.
[8]Roger K. Lowe, "Stores Demanding Pay to Display Products on Shelves, Panel Told," *Columbus Dispatch*, September 15, 1999.

and covers the cost to ship it back to the supplier. This is certainly a form of consignment sales, strictly forbidden in the wine division as well as in the whole wine industry.

Amazed by the lack of laws in the food industry, she decided to call a family friend who is a California state senator, the Honorable Mr. William Blackfield, chairman of the California Senate Committee on Trade Practices (in Sacramento). He certainly would be able to shed light on these practices for her. She picked up her phone and called him. After talking about their respective families and Georgia's new position, she explained the reason for the call: "I'm very surprised. There are these laws in the wine industry but nothing in the food sector. Right?"

Mr. Blackfield responded, "As far as I know, the reason for such a difference is historical. Actually, it is the postprohibition laws that gave rise to laws controlling the alcohol beverage industry. But I know I have the Federal Alcohol Administration [FAA] Act somewhere, so I can look for it and fax you a copy. Anyway, I can explain in a few words the aim of this act which is the basis of the slotting fees prohibition."

The FAA Act was enacted in 1935 to regulate the alcohol beverage distribution after the repeal of Prohibition. It represents congressional determination to combat what was perceived at the time to be "an unusually dangerous menace" and because of "many factors not common to other industries," the antitrust laws were deemed "insufficient to accomplish the objective."[9]

Blackfield continued, "That menace came from their prevailing practices, which tended to produce monopolistic control of retail outlets, such as arrangements for exclusive outlets, creation of tied houses, commercial bribery and sales on consignment or with the privilege of return. Such promotional arrangements were considered to increase the consumption of alcohol and therefore were prohibited."

Georgia listened carefully to this explanation, taking some notes in order to do her own research later. Then they discussed the more recent 1995 amendment by the Bureau of Alcohol, Tobacco and Firearms (BATF). It amended those trade practice regulations to totally ban slotting fees and their practices in the retail sale of alcoholic beverages (see Exhibit 4D). [Note: The complete act can be consulted in the *Federal Register* 60, no. 80, April 26, 1995, p. 2042.] The definition of slotting allowance practices was also revised as "the act by an industry member of purchasing or renting display, shelf, storage or warehouse space."[10]

Although slotting fees have been attacked in private suits several times, this 1995 amendment is the only significant public policy action taken toward the practice to date. No court has yet restricted their use and regulated their amount. But this could rapidly change. For instance, in 1998, a complaint has been filed accusing Sara Lee International Baking Corp. of unfair competition. According to the complaint, slotting fees deprive customers of being exposed to certain brands and possible new products, in addition to larger manufacturers being given the edge over smaller firms in the introduction of new varieties of existing products.[11]

---

[9]*National Distributing Company Inc. v. BATF*, 1980, pp. 1005 and 1008, citing House Report No. 1542, 74th Congress, 1st session, 1935, pp. 5–6.

[10]Federal Register, *Rules and Regulations*, Vol. 60, No. 80, April 26, 1995, 20424.

[11]"Slotting Fees Called Unfair in California Sara Lee Suit," *Supermarket News* 48, no. 37 (September 14, 1998): 1.

**EXHIBIT 4D   Manufacturers' Costs of Slotting Allowances for 1996
National Product Introductions**

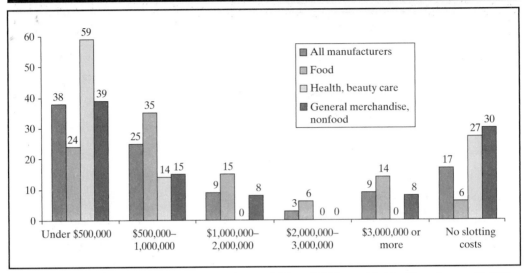

Source: "Slotting Fees Raise Irksome Issues for Bakers and Others," *Milling and Baking News*, January 13, 1998.

More recently, the spice giant McCormick & Co. has been the subject of a Federal Trade Commission investigation based around allegations that the company violated the Robinson-Patman Act by paying selective discounts to food retailers.[12] This investigation will take several years to be completed, but it could result in legitimizing the practice of slotting fees.

Slotting Allowances: Pros and Cons

After she hung up, Georgia tried to find some more information on the topic and especially some figures to give herself a precise idea of the amount slotting allowances represent. She found that sometimes it costs up to $40,000 to introduce a frozen food product (see Exhibit 4E), and now slotting fees are demanded not only in the canned and dry goods sections but also in fresh produce sections. Even in the software, music, and bookseller industries, slotting fees are becoming a usual practice, costing a very large amount to suppliers. For instance, in the retail book industry, particularly the large chains now demand fees from publishers to give books a prominent space. And in the computer software industry, the display of programs in electronic stores is also subject to a fee. Georgia felt very uncomfortable with the lack of fairness and the pervasiveness of these practices.

To get her mind off this issue, she decided to go down to the cafeteria. While drinking her coffee, she bumped into a colleague, John Wilson, the health and beauty

---

[12]Kalpana Srinivasan, "Staff of FTC Ready to Urge Lawsuit," *The Wire*, December 7, 1999.

EXHIBIT 4E   Manufacturers' Incidence of Slotting Allowance for Most Recent National Product Introduction

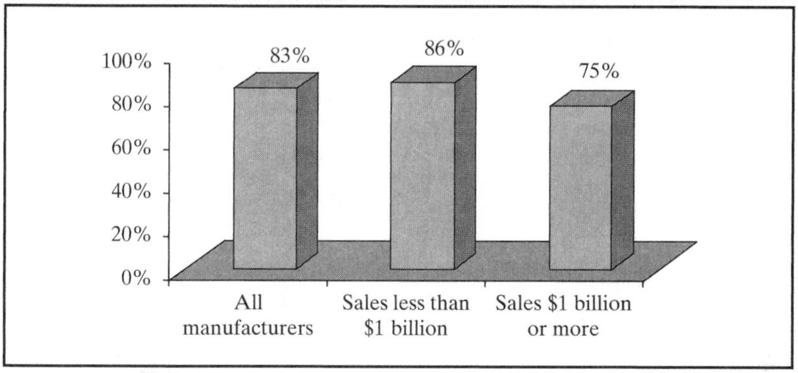

Source: "Slotting Fees Raise Irksome Issues for Bakers and Others," *Milling and Baking News*, January 13, 1998.

buyer. She couldn't resist talking to him about her impressions. He started laughing, "Hey, Georgia, all BuyMore buyers—from me to the bulk food purchasers—are expected to procure maximum slotting fees from manufacturers. You know, we all have a revenue goal for our department and if we expect to get our year end bonus, we have to secure slotting fees. And even worse than losing a bonus, if you don't get enough, you won't stay long in the position. That is part of the job!" Georgia knew what he was saying was true because she had two financial goals that determine her bonus, one for sales and one for slotting allowances.

Then John got up to leave. "Oh, Georgia, I almost forgot to tell you the best one. You know, I used to work in the spices and I got $15,000 per year, per store, for their 20-foot-wide spice racks. And guess what! They provided the racks!" After this unsettling discussion, Georgia went back to her office. "This coffee break was not very relaxing. Slotting fees are everywhere!" she thought.

She decided to spend another hour on the Internet doing research on the subject before going back to her current files. She found even more examples of slotting fees in various fields, such as some toiletries companies providing six cases of free goods per store when the product is introduced, plus it is expected to run advertisements every other month in the supermarket To-Home-Mailer.

Wondering about the official purposes of the slotting allowance practice, Georgia found that the retailers' principal argument is really their need to assume risk of allocating shelf space to a new product that might not sell at a level sufficient to provide even a narrow margin. When grocers agree to put a new product on their shelves, they are uncertain of its success. Yet they have to absorb the cost of warehousing the product, bar coding, accounting for inventory, stocking the shelves with it, and so on. These are the basic costs that cannot be reduced. But there is also the cost of advertising the

EXHIBIT 4F   Summary of the Treasury Decision

DEPARTMENT OF THE TREASURY
Bureau of Alcohol, Tobacco and Firearms
27 CFR Parts 6, 8, 10 and 11
[T.D.ATF-364, Re: Notice No. 794 and Notice No. 796]
RIN 1512-AB10
Unfair Trade Practices Under the Federal Alcohol Administration Act (93F-003P)
AGENCY: Bureau of Alcohol, Tobacco and Firearms (ATF), Treasury.

ACTION: Final Rule, Treasury Decision.

SUMMARY: The Bureau of Alcohol, Tobacco and Firearms (ATF) is amending trade practice regulations under the Federal Alcohol Administration (FAA) Act on tied-house, exclusive outlets, commercial bribery, and consignment sales by adding standards for enforcing the "exclusion" element where appropriate.

Under the FAA Act, "exclusion, in whole or in part, of distilled spirits, wine or malt beverages, sold or offered for sale by other persons" is a necessary element of a violation of the tied-house, exclusive outlets or commercial bribery provisions. In this final rule, ATF promulgates a framework for establishing "exclusion," identifies promotional practices which result in control of a retailer or in exclusion under the Act, identifies factors which will apply in evaluating exclusion, and identifies those practices for which there is no likelihood that exclusion will result and for which the Bureau will not take action (safe harbors). Other regulatory amendments are also made as a result of an ATF review of the regulations and an industry petition submitted in 1992.

EFFECTIVE DATE: May 26, 1995.

Source: FAA Act as amended in 1995 by the Bureau of Alcohol, Tobacco and Firearms, *Federal Register* 60, no. 80, April 26, 1995, p. 2042.

new product when the manufacturer is a small company. In that case, insufficient advertising might undermine the innovation because of a tight budget. Therefore, the retailer has to stimulate trial by offering in-store coupons, for instance, if costs are to be covered. (Additional positive aspects of slotting fees are discussed in Exhibit 4F.)

In a way, by requiring slotting fees, retailers evaluate the product. New product failures often are due to a lack of market research and testing or not enough promotional support. So, by asking for substantial slotting fees, a retailer is suggesting to the manufacturer to do more market research on his product to avoid a failure.

Slotting fees are also a way of protecting stores that have tiny profit margins compared to manufacturers. Between 1970 and 1991, the average share of sales of grocery and meat retailers was 1.5 percent (before tax profit) compared to 5.7 percent for food manufacturers.[13] The most recent figures indicate that the profit margins for food retailers have shrunk 22 percent.[14]

Georgia found an article from the *Dallas Morning News*[15] stating that according to industry sources, in a typical slotting fee scenario, a grocery store would charge a supplier $500 per linear foot of shelf space per store to get a new product on the shelves. In the case of a 100-store chain offering two feet of shelf space in each store, that's a payment of $100,000. It is not a one-time payment either, especially if a competing food supplier comes in later and makes a higher offer for the same coveted shelf space. Since huge amounts were involved, some small companies have to focus their attention on foreign markets (such as Mexico). They cannot afford to play the slotting game in the United States.

A Small Manufacturer's Position

A few weeks later, after Georgia gained greater understanding of the food department, Bergamino allowed her to begin meeting alone with some of the smaller suppliers. One of the first meetings was with a local food company.

Ernest Di Luca, owner of Basta Pasta Food Inc., presented a new item for Georgia's consideration, a line of family-size premium pasta items: ravioli, spaghetti, and lasagna. These pastas are very good quality and also very easy to cook for the working families who don't want to eat fast food despite a lack of time. Georgia liked the concept and the product. The price is very affordable. He explained to her that his line scored very well in a blind taste test and would be happy to show her the results. "That won't be necessary, Ernie. You know I like your product, but we'll need support in the form of slotting fees from Basta Pasta to introduce this product line. First, we would need a modest cash payment of $5,000, and then we could make an agreement on six free cases of each item per store, plus some free demos."

Up to now, Ernie had been selling items to small independent grocers and did not have much experience with the chains. He was aware of the slotting allowance practice since he heard several other small manufacturers complaining about how hard it was to deal with large chains. But this was the first time Ernie had to face the problem, and he had little idea of the amounts that retailers were demanding for slotting.

"Hey, wait a minute!" exclaimed Ernie. "Could you be more precise? I want to know how much it's going to cost us!" After some rapid calculations, they figured out that the total cost for the Basta Pasta Company would be $34,000 for the first year. "You have got to be kidding, that is downright extortion! I can't believe it!" said Ernie in a shocked voice. "Now I understand what the others meant by 'abuse of power' when they were talking about it. You are going to kill us with such practices and kill the promise of the 'American Dream'! Don't forget that the American economic system is supposed to be based on the belief that small businesses can grow and flourish with fair competition. It is people like you who are killing these ideals."

---

[13]Paul R. Messinger and Chakravarthi Narasimhan, "Has Power Shifted in the Grocery Channel?," *Marketing Science* 14 (1995): 189–223.
[14]Lowe, "Stores Demanding Pay to Display Products on Shelves, Panel Told."
[15]Martin Zimmerman, "Struggle for Shelves," *Dallas Morning News,* June 18, 1996, 1D.

Georgia felt very uncomfortable because, in a way, she agreed with Ernie, but she felt helpless. This extortion, as Ernie called it, was part of her new job. She tried to explain arguments that retailers use to defend their position on slotting fees. She rattled off the usual points such as carrying costs and shelf allotment. She talked about the stimulation of awareness, the means to signal product quality, and the risk shared among manufacturers and retailers. She concluded by saying, "You know, Ernie, this amount of $34,000 is far less than your big competitors who we would charge between $200,000 and $270,000 for fees. You have to keep in mind that BuyMore's customers buy more because the suppliers pay more." Ernie's Italian blood began to boil. "It's incredible; it's impossible to afford this extortion, and even if I could afford it, I wouldn't pay." Ernie grabbed his catalog and his briefcase and stomped out of the room.

After Di Luca left, Georgia reviewed the heated conversation, especially the word "extortion," and wondered if slotting allowances are really a form of bribery. She recalled how the day before when she was talking to one of the other buyers, he explained to her how a food broker had offered him $6,000 cash instead of an $8,000 check. The buyer had not accepted the cash, but with all these payments being extracted, Georgia did wonder if the temptation to accept money on the side had gotten too strong for some of her colleagues. The opportunity for bribery seemed so obvious, she thought. She also read in an article[16] that the former chief executive officer of Harvest Foods, a food retailer in the South, "has been indicted on charges of bribery and other related offenses for the alleged receipt of hundreds of thousands of dollars in cash for slotting fees."

A Challenge to Georgia's Conscience

Georgia talked to her boss, Bergamino. As they both sat in his office, she questioned him about the ethics of slotting fees and about the development of such practices. "As far as I know, slotting allowances started very slowly, after World War II, and the fees were low at first. You have to keep in mind that before then, there were not too many independent grocers, at least in northern California. There were just a few chains like Safeway or Lucky. I don't think too many people knew about what they were doing. But, in the late 1940s, several independent supermarket businesses started to open stores. To help independents celebrate grand openings, some suppliers started to provide a few free goods. So this concept of extortion, as you call it, was not present at all. After the 1970s, the independents started to mushroom, and they even became stronger than the chains. I guess that was the starting point for slotting fees; it became a widespread practice."

"Now, I know what you think about it, extortion, payola. But you have to keep in mind that above all, slotting fees are a form of insurance that the chains need in order to be compensated for the risk of introducing new products." He pointed this out, pulling up some tables on his computer. "Back in 1975 there were approximately 2,000 new products; in 1990 the number was up to 12,000. Today, 20,000 new products per year are displayed on most chains' shelves, and the typical supermarket carries about 30,000 items (see Exhibit 4G). Slotting allowances are a way of dealing with all the new

---

[16]Aalberts and Jennings, "The Ethics of Slotting."

EXHIBIT 4G	Average Slotting Allowances per Item Nationally			
	1982	1987	1992	1997
Refrigerated/ frozen foods	$1000	$10,000	$20,000	$40,000
Candy/snacks	$300	$3,800	$6,000	$7,000
Overall range	$300–1,500	$1,000–10,000	$2,000–20,000	$3,000–40,000

Source: "More Facts and Figures on Slotting," *Supermarket Business*, 52, no. 7 (1997).

products, keeping in mind that the failure rate for new food products is about 85 percent through the first year." Georgia noted the significant difference between wine and groceries. She explained to him, "In the alcoholic beverage industry, there are fewer introductions each year than in the grocery industry, and the failure rate is lower. For instance, from 1982 to 1992, only 87 major malt beverages were introduced with 78 still on the market in 1992.[17] So in the wine sector, chains do not necessarily need such failure insurance as in the grocery retail sale sector."

And the fact that chains charge slotting fees for each new product can also lead to abuses, thought Georgia. "It is true that the practice has its roots in the proliferation of new products, but how can we ensure that chains are not taking advantage of this proliferation? If they are regularly rotating brands, then they can usually get some slotting allowances!" She did not articulate this point because she didn't want to tell her boss that she thought there is a bias at BuyMore to rotate new products in order to secure greater slotting fees. Yet, for Georgia, if the risk of new product failure was the principal reason to charge suppliers, it would be more fairer to set up a failure fee system rather than a slotting fee paid regardless of the outcome. That way, the fees are tied to actual costs.

Georgia and Bergamino also talked about the difference in profit margins between the two businesses: wine and food industries. Retailers make generally 24 percent on wine and only 1.5 percent on food items. These low food margins might be one explanation for such a difference in slotting fee practices. Bergamino said that such margins do not enable food retailers to absorb the costs and risks of new product introductions. That is why they are charging back these costs to manufacturers in the form of slotting fees. Georgia wondered if this was just. "These arguments could at least explain the difference of practice between the two sectors," thought Georgia. Finally, they talked about the rising costs of warehousing, stocking (see Exhibit 4H), and promoting products.

"Slotting fees allow us to bring in new and different products, and then it is a consumer's prerogative to decide which products they want!" added Bergamino. "Imagine what prices the stores would have to charge if they did not have the slotting allowances

---

[17]Gregory T. Gundlach and Paul N. Bloom, "Slotting Allowances and the Retail Sale of Alcohol Beverages," *Journal of Public Policy and Marketing* 17, no. 2 (Fall 1998): 173–184.

EXHIBIT 4-H   Additional Positive Aspects of Slotting Fees

The answer . . . is "slotting fees." What began as a way to compensate the store owner for the cost of making room in his system for a new product has evolved into a "pay-to-stay" fee that, depending on the product, can amount to millions of dollars a year. Supermarkets earn only the narrowest mark-up on the goods themselves, so slotting fees can represent 20% to 40% of the profits of some chains. . . .

A manufacturer paying for shelf space has every incentive to use that space efficiently. Logically, the highest bidder will be the one who can generate the biggest sales. Nor does this keep small producers off the shelves: They can win space if they're willing to put their money where their mouth is.

Not the least of the benefits, slotting fees discourage excessive "line extension" by which manufacturers create meaningless variations on a single product in order to crowd competitors off the shelves. That doesn't wash when you're paying top dollar for the space.

Putting a nefarious spin on these developments, some argue that consumer choice is being reduced, when the truth is that costs are being lowered. But you can always find a mom-and-pop producer to claim slotting fees kept them off the shelf. Italy is using the issue to drub Coca-Cola, a popular pastime in

Europe. In this country, the Justice Department spent eons investigating Frito-Lay. The enforcers are obviously confused by the changes rushing through the economy. . . .

Supermarket folks have been using the word "deflation" for a decade, and slotting fees grow out of a competitive environment. Procter & Gamble and Campbell's soup can still get away with refusing to pay slotting fees because they pour billions into direct advertising to keep their goods jumping off the shelves. But even they have started to question whether this spending is efficient.

Surveys by Nielsen and Cannondale Associates show money has been shifting out of advertising budgets to bulk up "trade promotion" budgets. Network TV is losing viewers, yet ad rates keep going up. Why should consumers go on footing the bill for large advertising budgets that have an uncertain effect on buying habits? Unadvertised store brands are now the most serious competitors to the famous names.

Folks have been predicting the death of brands for years, and brands are still around. But there is no question that the ad agencies and their TV network pals are getting pushed out of the loop. As technology takes the mass out of mass marketing, slotting fees are just one of the strategies stepping into the breach.

Source: "We Love Slotting Fees," *Wall Street Journal*, September 22, 1999.

as another source of revenue. Anyway, if all the chains do it, BuyMore needs to follow industry practice just to stay competitive. But don't think that the practice is just a way for retailers to secure monies from suppliers. In fact, to avoid the perception of this activity as unethical, in January 1996, grocery retailers formed an ethics committee for the first time in the organization's history.[18] The aim was to review their industry practices. Even, if up to now, nothing concrete has been done, this was a big step in the right direction!"

Trade Show Payments

Three weeks later, Georgia attended her first trade show in San Jose, hosted by California Foods, a large food wholesaler with a national network. Department buyers evaluate new products and are given incentives to purchase items during this two-day event. She is exposed to "Fast Bucks," whereby all suppliers who take part in the show by demonstrating their products through individual booths provide cash incentives to various retail buyers. On orders taken during the two-day event, buyers are induced by the various suppliers and given play money based on the size of individual orders they place. The buyers then take money and exchange it for real cash at the "bank" set up on-site at the trade show. This money goes either to the individual buyer personally or to the retail corporate customer. She knew of one buyer walking away from the show with $75,000.

Georgia was informed that in another trade show, each buyer is given "Bonus Points" for purchases made at the trade show. These points are then redeemed for merchandise: cars, appliances, and vacations. She wondered if she should share her experience and concerns about these dubious practices with Bergamino.

Georgia's Dilemma

Georgia is torn. If she "stirs the pot," she might even lose her job. The head buyer, Bergamino, is set to retire in only two years. Georgia would have a shot at his job. However, if she does nothing, she thinks she is participating in a process that is perhaps unethical or worse. That would make her part of the problem. She wonders how change will ever come. The grocery chains are not going to curb slotting practices. The food brokers and suppliers, for fear of being blackballed, won't raise a voice.

Georgia is sitting at her desk very early one morning. The next day she is supposed to give a report to Bergamino on all the slotting allowances contemplated for the coming year. Looking through her computer telephone directory, she sees the names "Blackfield" and "Bergamino."

1. Who should she call? Senator Blackfield or her boss, Mr. Bergamino?
2. What advice should she seek?

---

[18]Aalberts and Jennings, "The Ethics of Slotting."

ETHICS IN RETAILING: WHERE DOES ONE DRAW THE LINE?[1]

Amanda Hilger and Gene R. Laczniak

Jessica was pleased to be enjoying a sunny spring afternoon shopping with her younger sister Emily. Jessica, known has Jessi to her friends, had just finished final exams at Boston College and felt satisfied now that her sophomore year was drawing to a close and summer was on its way.

Jessi is much like her college classmates. She appreciates time spent with friends and family, enjoys planning social get-togethers, and boldly tackles any project. You can always count on Jessi for making the most of every opportunity and enjoying her time at college.

Today, Jessi and Emily are shopping for new summer fashions in anticipation of the fast approaching warm weather. As they stroll through the mall, they come to Abercrombie & Fitch (A&F). Jessi and Emily have a great time trying on the store's new arrivals of tank tops and skirts. They enjoy shopping at A&F because they know they will be able to find trendy styles in great colors for the upcoming season. As Jessi comes out of the fitting room sporting a burgundy corset cami and a striking denim mini, she is approached by the store manager.

"Well, hello—how are you doing today? My name is Craig Johnson! So, has anyone from Abercrombie & Fitch ever approached you about a job in our store?"

Jessi started to smile as she caught a glance from her sister. Emily was rolling her eyes and muttering under her breath "Not again. This happens every time I come here shopping with you."

Company Background

Jessi decides that she wants to learn more about A&F before taking a position in their stores. She is flattered that they would want her to work for them, and after being approached by several store managers at multiple locations, she is thinking that this might be the answer for a summer job. She begins with a Web search on A&F and is surprised by what she finds.

A&F is a leading specialty retailer encompassing three concepts: A&F, abercrombie, and Hollister Co. The company focuses on providing high-quality merchandise that complements the casual, classic American lifestyle. The merchandise is sold in retail stores throughout the United States as well as through catalogs. The company also operates an e-commerce Web site at www.abercrombie.com and one geared to kids at www.abercrombiekids.com and publishes a magalog called the *A&F Quarterly*.

A&F, which targets ages 18 through college, went public in October 1996 and spun off from The Limited in May 1998; abercrombie kids (ages 7–14) was introduced in 1997. The latest concept, Hollister Co., was introduced in July 2000 and targets 14- to 18-year-olds.[2]

---

[1]This case was prepared by Amanda Hilger under the direction of Gene R. Laczniak for classroom discussion rather than to illustrate either effective or ineffective handling of an administrative, ethical, or legal decision by individuals or management.

[2]Abercrombie & Fitch, Corporate Overview, www.corporate-ir.net/ireye/ir_site.zhtml?ticker=ANF&script=2100%27 (accessed July 31, 2003).

Exhibit 4I shows that A&F has been undeniably successful over the past five years in comparison to the retail industry as a whole ("ANF" in the exhibit, the top line).

It can be seen that in 2001, A&F was able to distance themselves from their competition. Some contribute the stock's success to the clothing retailer being a fashion favorite among college students with the company's trendy product lines, while others contribute A&F's success to their "buzz marketing" tactics.

Media Scrutiny

A&F has found themselves in the media spotlight on multiple occasions throughout the past few years. Both A&F and the abercrombie kids store have been criticized for questionable product lines. The company has been accused of racial bias in their hiring practices at their A&F stores, and the *A&F Quarterly* has been described as more of a soft-core porn magazine than a mail-order catalog.

Buzz Marketing

Industry insiders have accused A&F of creating fake controversies as a form of buzz marketing. What A&F is said to be doing is creating controversy around its brand name, apologizing for the offense, then sitting back and watching the curious shoppers traveling to their company's stores to see what the buzz is all about. Marketing in this form has its drawbacks; there is always the risk of backlash and damage to the company's brand loyalty.[3]

EXHIBIT 4-I   Sales Percent Change from October 1998 to October 2003

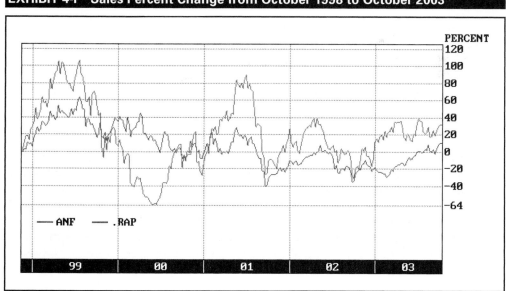

Source: www.businessweek.com

---

[3]C. Stewart, "In Buzz Marketing, Any Trick Is a Fair Game," *Potentials* 35, no. 10 (October 2002): 8–9, ProQuest database (accessed July 31, 2003).

One of the product lines that caused controversy was introduced in April 2002, when A&F started selling T-shirts with racist sayings regarding and referencing Asians. One of the shirts showed two slanted-eyed men and the slogan "Wong Brothers Laundry Service: Two Wongs Can Make It White."

After about a week of protests outside stores and thousands of phone calls and e-mails, A&F pulled the shirts from the selling floor. The following day, executives apologized for the offense, but interestingly enough, in the midst of the buzz, the company's stock hit a 52-week high.[4]

Just a month later, A&F introduced child-size thong underwear into its abercrombie kids stores. The underwear was targeted to 10- to 16-year-old girls with sayings such as "eye candy" or "wink wink" printed on the front. A&F defended themselves by stating that the underwear were "cute, fun and sweet." Hampton Carney, a spokesperson for the company, went on to say that the thongs were designed for girls to enjoy and that he could list 100 reasons why a young girl would want thong underwear, with the need to hide panty lines being one of them.[5]

Executives pulled the product within a month, once more apologizing for the misunderstanding. Once again, the campaign could be considered a success, as A&F received repeated media exposure, because it induced people to talk about the edginess of their company.

During the past several years, the company has also been in the media spotlight for its publication of its *A&F Quarterly* magalog. A 1998 issue contained a controversial piece titled "Drinking 101," which included drink recipes and a cutout quick guide for cocktails. With a target market of 18 to college age, most of which is under the legal drinking age, this was considered inappropriate and received a great deal of backlash from activist groups such as Mothers Against Drunk Driving.[6]

Recently, A&F has produced catalogs with college-age and younger models kissing and fondling each other, often in the nude. The company has taken the necessary measures in an attempt to limit the distribution of its catalog to underage persons by requiring buyers to be 18 years of age or older. The catalogs continue to be produced, and controversy continues to follow each issue. Protestors question what A&F is selling: clothing or sex appeal? All the commotion results in more press coverage and further enhancement of A&F's image as a rebellious retailer looking to challenge the status quo.

For years, brands such as Victoria's Secret and Calvin Klein have made a reputation for themselves by pushing the envelope in their advertising campaigns.[7] Likewise, one must remember that just a few years ago, the public was ridiculing the Italian clothier Benetton for its infamous "death-row" ad campaign. Featured ad images included dying AIDS patients, a nun and priest kissing, and a black woman nursing a white baby.[8] Buzz marketing has been used by other retailers and will continue to be

---

[4]Stewart, "In Buzz Marketing, Any Trick Is a Fair Game."
[5]V. Oritz, "Parents Say Kid's Thong Is Just Plain Wrong," *Milwaukee Journal Sentinel,* May 17, 2002, www.jsonline.com/news/gen/may02/43941.asp?format=print (accessed July 31, 2003).
[6]K. Lee, "Pimped by Abercrombie & Fitch," *Asian Pacific American Issues News Magazine,* www.hardboiled.org/5.5/55-08-af.html (accessed July 31, 2003).
[7]*Wall Street Journal,* "Abercrombie & Sex," April 25, 2002, ProQuest database (accessed July 31, 2003).
[8]Oritz, "Parents Say Kid's Thong Is Just Plain Wrong."

used as a way to push the promotional envelope. Again, it must be noted that a company is free to market itself as it pleases and that the public is equally free to shop and spend money where it pleases.[9]

Hiring Practices

A&F has also made media headlines in regard to their hiring practices, and multiple lawsuits have been filed against the company for discrimination in A&F stores. On June 16, 2003, a group of former and prospective employees filed a racial discrimination lawsuit against A&F accusing the retailer of denying them job opportunities based on their race, color, and/or national origin.[10] The nine plaintiffs accused the company of "denying employment, desirable job assignments, job transfers, allocation of weekly hours, compensation, and other terms and conditions of employment to minorities in A&F stores."[11]

Tom Lennox, A&F's communications director, emphatically denied job bias but acknowledged that the company liked hiring sales assistants, known as brand representatives, who "look great." Mr. Lennox went on to say that "brand representatives are ambassadors to the brand. We want to hire brand representatives who will represent the Abercrombie & Fitch brand with natural, classic American style, look great while exhibiting individuality, project the brand and themselves with energy and enthusiasm, and make the store a warm, inviting place that provides a social experience for the customer."[12]

A former A&F assistant manager, Antonio Serrano, stated that it is policy to offer jobs to beautiful-looking people. "If someone came in with a pretty face, we were told to approach them and ask them if they wanted a job," Serrano said. "They thought if we had the best-looking college kids working in our store, everyone will want to shop there."

Serrano, who quit working for A&F when he was told that he would be promoted only if he accepted a transfer, went on to say, "We were supposed to approach someone in the mall who we think will look attractive in our store. If the person said 'I never worked in retailing before,' we said, 'Who cares? We'll hire you.' But if someone came in who had lots of retail experience and not a pretty face, we were told not to hire them at all."[13]

It has been argued certain industries have been said to hire their employees on the basis of good looks—cocktail waitresses, flight attendants, even salespersons. But recently, more companies are said to have taken a "sophisticated approach" in hiring workers that helps project a certain image for their company. The Hooters restaurant chain is an example of a company that hires based on an image that they are attempting to portray. Their Web site states that "there is no set requirement in order to be a nearly World Famous Hooters Girl! We look for the All-American Cheerleader/Surfer-Girl-Next-Door image to fill our restaurants. In other words, very bubbly, outgoing personalities!" Companies like Hooters have danced around a fine line where hiring attractive

[9]*Wall Street Journal,* "Abercrombie & Sex."
[10]S. Branch and M. Tkacik, "Lawsuit Accuses Abercrombie Chain of Racial Bias," *Wall Street Journal,* June 18, 2003, ProQuest database (accessed July 31, 2003).
[11]Branch and Tkacik, "Lawsuit Accuses Abercrombie Chain of Racial Bias."
[12]S. Greenhouse, "Wanted: Pretty People," *New York Times,* www.jsonline.com/lifestyle/people/jul03/154723.asp (accessed July 23, 2003).
[13]Greenhouse, "Wanted."

people is not considered discriminatory but where hiring on the basis of age, sex, or ethnicity is considered discrimination. This gray area is where the matter becomes complicated, and as a result an increase in the number of lawsuits has occurred.[14]

The Decision

Store managers have approached Jessi no fewer than five times over the past two years when she shops at A&F stores. Is this just a coincidence, or is it because she is a five-foot eight-inch, beautiful, blond-haired, blue-eyed college student who looks as if she just walked off the pages of an A&F magalog?

Mr. Johnson, the store manager, explained to Jessi that she was hired if she wanted the job. No interview, application, or references were necessary. She was told that these were all things that could be taken care of on her first day of work. "We have an image to sell," he told Jessi, "and you have the A&F look that we want to project." These words replay in Jessi's memory as she remembers that just a few short weeks ago her college friend, Lauren, was turned down after her first interview for a summer job at A&F. Lauren is a great student, is very responsible, and seemed to be very qualified for the job. Why would she have been turned down when store managers seem so anxious to hire?

Her mind was swimming as she began to evaluate the results of her Web search. Jessi learned that A&F had been in the media a lot over the past few years for marketing tactics that various critics have considered racy and excessively sexual. In addition, the company recently made newspaper headlines for potential discrimination in their hiring practices. Jessi is also aware that A&F has been in the public spotlight for product lines that some considered unethical. A business student, Jessi recognizes the importance of taking risks from time to time as a necessary element in contributing to a retailer's success.

Are these reasons enough not to take the job? Jessi is interested in doing some summer work, and as a student she could use the extra income. While the hourly pay is rather basic, the employee discount on clothing is very enticing. Jessi likes many clothing items in the A&F product line, part of the reason she has returned to the store so many times.

Through her Web search, Jessi has learned much about A&F and now must take this information into consideration when weighing the pros and cons of whether to take the job. She promised the store manager that she would come back tomorrow and give him her decision.

1. Should Jessica take the job? Why or why not? What role should ethics play in her decision?
2. Has A&F gone too far with their buzz marketing?
3. Who is a company most responsible in answering to? Customers? Stockholders? Employees? The media? The public?
4. Do you think that A&F's hiring practices are discriminatory?
5. Would you consider buying stock in A&F? Why or why not?

---

[14]Greenhouse, "Wanted."

ATHLETE'S FOOT[1]

Lance Kidder

John Park was one of the youngest franchise owners in the international Athlete's Foot chain at 23 years old. The son of a Korean American, Mr. Park was operating his store on the corner of 63rd and Halsted on the South Side of Chicago. This violent neighborhood was not typical of the suburban mall locations favored by most Athlete's Foot executives.

Four years later Eric Lymore walked into Mr. Park's shoe store looking for a job. Mr. Lymore held the details of his background to himself as he pleaded to Mr. Park for a job. He wanted just one week to prove that he could outsell any other salesperson in the store.

There was good reason for Mr. Lymore to be vague about his past. The then 19-year-old was a member of the Gangster Disciples, an infamous urban gang; he had stolen clothes while working at Sears, sold drugs, and stuck up a Burger King. Most recently, he had just been released from Cook County Jail.

Mr. Lymore's salesmanship came through, and Mr. Park took a chance on him. A week later some of the other employees began complaining that Mr. Lymore was causing trouble by stealing customers as they entered the store. Mr. Park's advice: "Cause trouble. I like it."

Mr. Lymore quickly became Mr. Park's premier salesman. Mr. Park reinforced an insight through the hiring of Mr. Lymore and developed a strategic plan based on that insight. He would bring a national chain shoe store with a professional attitude to the urban cities. Mr. Park understood that urban kids were not comfortable shopping in malls. All too often security guards would follow them, they would attract stares, or they may get accused of stealing. By offering a professional shopping experience in their neighborhoods, Mr. Park's customers would receive service and quality products. And Mr. Lymore helped him realize that the best people to give them this service were people from the same streets. Four years after Mr. Park hired Mr. Lymore, his stores were manned by former and in some cases current, thugs, drug dealers, and gang members. At that time Mr. Park estimated that 90 percent of his sales staff had criminal records.

Athlete's Foot executives say they don't know all the details of Mr. Park's operations, and they might feel somewhat uneasy if they did. Mr. Park began running his first Athlete's Foot store in 1992 with the support of his father, who had owned two independent shoe stores. In the beginning Mr. Park hired more "professional" employees. These were clean kids who did not get involved in the temptations of street life. Mr. Park now realizes these kids were not aggressive enough for his stores' clientele. His early employees believed they were too good to work at a shoe store, and many of them didn't last long. Now Mr. Park looks for loud, vocal, aggressive salesmen similar to Mr. Lymore. At times he hires right out of prison. These hires have exactly what Mr. Park is looking for—street credit.

---

[1]This case was prepared by Lance Kidder under the direction of Patrick E. Murphy classroom discussion rather than to illustrate either effective or ineffective handling of an administrative, ethical, or legal decision by individuals or management.

Mr. Park's retail operations and management practices are not typical of similar businesses. He does not ask too many questions about his employee's life outside their working hours. He pays his employees minimum wage or slightly above. Mr. Park also offers a check cashing service for his employees so employees can receive their pay in cash, net of tax withholdings.

None of the salesmen are allowed to work the cash register. Money is only handled by Korean American managers. In the event of an emergency, Mr. Park is available with bail money or short-term loans that he eventually deducts from wages. He will also get involved with police if one of his workers is questioned. Mr. Park believes that he hires mostly good guys who sometimes get hassled for the wrong reasons.

Success in the athletic shoe business is largely about predicting fashion trends. Like other retailers, Mr. Park must buy his shoes six months in advance, but styles can come and go in a matter of three or four weeks. Inventories depend on the neighborhood of the store and the gang allegiances within those neighborhoods. So a few times a week, Mr. Park will work his sales floors, talking with customers to see what they want now and what they will want next season. He is considered to have some of the best fashion instincts in the country. Designers will fly into Chicago from New York to work with Mr. Park on new designs for upcoming seasons.

Mr. Park's success allowed him to keep expanding. One particular store Mr. Park was very nervous to open was a store in an urban mall. This was a stretch of his philosophy of selling shoes on tough streets. A project this important called for the help of Mr. Park's ace salesman, Mr. Lymore, who had been coming to the store since it opened. At $8.25 an hour with no benefits, working six days a week, commuting an hour each way across Chicago, Mr. Lymore was stretching his days to 12 hours door to door. Mr. Lymore's girlfriend was not happy with the new arrangement and was trying to get him to either quit or ask for a raise. The problem was that Mr. Lymore felt stuck. He was convinced that his boss was taking advantage of the fact that few other people would hire ex-cons. He didn't have much leverage to make any demands. He would continue to make the commute and work long hours.

At closing time, all the salesmen walk back to the stockroom to retrieve their coats before lining up at the sales counter for the end-of-the-day pat-down. Each in turn, they hand their jackets to their boss, who squeezes and bunches each one looking for stolen shoes. This ritual even applies to Mr. Lymore. Mr. Park believes every employee needs to be treated equally.

Mr. Lymore usually takes the pat-downs in stride, but one particular day, after a series of 12-hour days, the pat-down does not sit well with Mr. Lymore. It is a mood Mr. Lymore carries with him into the next day. His scheduled time for work came at 10 A.M., but Mr. Lymore did not show up. The idea of calling Mr. Park crosses Mr. Lymore's mind, but imagining Mr. Park's reaction is satisfying, as is the passing notion of what it might be like not to go back at all.

Mr. Park anxiously awaits Mr. Lymore's attendance in the mall store. He has heard from another worker that Mr. Lymore is upset. Unsure if Mr. Lymore will ever show up for work again, Mr. Park is sure that everything is wrong.

Another day passes and still no word. Mr. Lymore has no phone, so Mr. Park can't call him. Mr. Park never saw it coming because Mr. Lymore never complained to him. Mr. Lymore was usually very happy at work. Now, Mr. Park's mall store was losing a lot of sales as a result of his absence.

The following day Mr. Park again opens the store without the help of Mr. Lymore. At this point concern has turned into agitation. Mr. Park is angry that his employee portrays that he cares about the store but could disregard his responsibilities so carelessly.

An hour passes, and Mr. Lymore slips into the store. For a while the two men do not speak to one another. Eventually they meet in the back room to discuss Mr. Lymore's absence. Immediately a sense of a more compliant attitude in Mr. Park shows through in the discussion, although it is clear that exceptions will not be made for Mr. Lymore. Breaking the tension, Mr. Lymore asks his boss if he is happy this stunt wasn't pulled over a busy weekend. Both men find themselves laughing.

A schedule is worked out so that Mr. Lymore can work in his neighborhood at the 63rd Street store four days of the week. He will work the mall store only on the weekends. It is little for Mr. Park to give since the majority of the mall business is done on the weekends. Although he did not get the raise he wished, Mr. Lymore's victory comes in the elimination of a daily commute. He considers this a modest victory and display of his value to the organization.

That November, Mr. Park became anxious about the new mall store. Sales for November were between $150,000 and $200,000, making it the number two grossing Athlete's Foot franchise store in the nation that month, but sales were down 20 to 25 percent. Park then moved John Kim, an impressive new manager, to the mall store to help revive it.

Mr. Park is very accommodating to Mr. Kim by giving him as much support as he needs. Mr. Kim wanted only one thing—Mr. Lymore. Mr. Park, still upset at Mr. Lymore's three-day hiatus, believes that Mr. Lymore is likely to "screw up." Through a little persuading, Mr. Kim is able to convince Mr. Park that if Mr. Lymore is given responsibility for all the salesmen at the mall store, he will understand the disruption caused by someone blowing off a shift. Although skeptical, Mr. Park is willing to try anything.

The next day, Mr. Lymore gets a new position as assistant manager at the mall store. He still is not able to handle cash, nor does he get benefits. His pay is up to $375 a week in cash after taxes. He can now hire and fire workers and has official authority to oversee displays and direct sales. His pay is still modest, but the responsibility is enough to persuade Mr. Lymore to resume daily commutes to the mall store.

1. How would you evaluate John Park's hiring strategy from an ethical viewpoint?
2. What is your view of John Park's decision not to allow his employees to use the cash register?
3. Comment on how the two subcultures at focus in this case (Korean American businessman and urban youth) create synergy and conflict regarding the success of Athlete's Foot franchises.
4. Someone from the news media informs Athlete's Foot headquarters that some franchisees are systematically hiring "unsavory" retail clerks. How should the headquarters respond?

ANDORRA ELECTRONICS, LTD.[1]

Raymond Keyes

At 28 years old, Michael Olivier had reached the first plateau in his strategy for launching a career in international business. Two months ago, he had been transferred to the European International Headquarters of U.S. Electronics Enterprises, Inc. (USEE), to assume responsibilities as a sales representative working out of the company's international sales offices in Paris. Having been raised in Villejuif and educated in Paris, this assignment was a welcome return "home" for Michael after five years in the United States, first as an MBA student in a leading American business school and then as a trainee and sales representative in the New York sales division of USEE. Michael's decision to work for USEE was based on his perception that this billion-dollar, multinational company would offer challenging opportunities for him to gain experience and earn advancement in the field of international business.

USEE is a major worldwide supplier of electronics components for industrial applications. USEE conducts its business through its own subsidiaries and through its highly developed network of exclusive distributorships in nonsubsidiary regional markets. Although this system of regional distributors did not provide as much control over business operations as did the company-owned subsidiaries, the distributors provided a practical alternative in areas where the business short- and midterm potential did not warrant costly subsidiary coverage. In each of the assigned regions, the independent distributor acted as the exclusive representative of USEE for all its electronics products. Distributors were not required to make heavy investments in electronics inventories and business facilities, but they were expected to maintain close working relationships with industrial users of electronic components. As the regional representative, the distributor was also expected to be well versed regarding local business regulations, practices, and political realities. It was not unusual to have a distributor who was "well established" in relation to both business and government contacts.

In his new position as the regional sales representative for the Barcelona-Zaragoza-Toulouse region, Michael was responsible to the distributors for developing and maintaining the electronics components business with approximately 70 industrial accounts in the region encompassing southern France and southern Spain. Michael worked through the local distributors in the area to promote USEE business with the local manufacturers of electronics products. Included in the region was the tiny self-governing country of Andorra, one of the smallest countries in the world. In spite of its small size, Andorra was developing a thriving manufacturing business in electronic products (radios, televisions, VCRs, music systems, and so on) for the European consumer markets. Shortly after assuming his new responsibilities, Michael decided to make an initial tour of his new sales territory to introduce himself to his industrial customers and to his distributor partners. It was in Andorra that Michael was confronted with a situation that caused him to reexamine his company's policies and his own

---

[1]This case was prepared by Professors Raymond Keyes (deceased) and Joseph Gannon, Carroll School of Management, Boston College, as a basis for class discussion. The situation in the case is based on an actual business experience. However, the situation, names, and facts have been disguised.

personal position in relation to the complex and controversial issue concerning the use of commissions—"gratuities" or dubious payments—in international business situations.

On arrival in Andorra, Michael was met by the local distributor, George Bianci. George had represented USEE in Andorra for over 20 years, and Michael was pleased to note that during that period, USEE's business had grown steadily from virtually nothing to its current level of significant sales revenue. George was quick to point out that this success was due in part to his own excellent working relationship with Michael's predecessor in the job, Jean Pierre Dumont. According to George, Jean Pierre was an experienced, attractive gentleman who understood the realities and nuances of doing business in a close-knit society where "business is not always conducted in the most sophisticated manner." George went on to observe how unfortunate it was for everyone that Jean Pierre was stricken with a serious heart problem at such an early age. "One day he was here, healthy and vibrant. Two weeks later, we hear that he has been hospitalized and confined with little chance that he will be back with us again. Ah, what a tragedy! What a nice man!"

From the outset, Michael was impressed with George in terms of his sincerity and his congeniality. Not only was he a conscientious host, but he gave evidence of being an astute businessman. Early in their discussions, George pointed out that his success was also the result of the Andorran government's commitment to develop an industrial base for the country, which historically had been a farming and sheepherding economy. One of the major industries receiving government support was electronics products manufacturing, and foremost among the several companies in this business was Andorra Electronics, Ltd, one of USEE's major customers in the area. George pointed out that Andorra Electronics had purchased more than $500,000 worth of electronics components from USEE during the previous business year. In view of the importance of this account to USEE and to his own distributorship, George suggested a dinner meeting with Carlo Ducci, the director of purchasing at Andorra Electronics. George pointed out that, as far as USEE was concerned, Carlo was the key man at Andorra Electronics. Jean Pierre had developed a close personal relationship with Carlo over the years. George pointed out that, as a member of one of the leading families in Andorra, Carlo participated actively in the social and political activities of his small country. His brother, Ramon, was an elected member of the Andorran Council, the 24-member council that governed this small republic. George had planned the Wednesday dinner meeting so that Michael and Carlo could get to know one another in a relaxed social setting prior to their business meeting on the following day. Michael was quite conscious of the Thursday meeting at which they would be discussing Andorra Electronics' requirements for next year and the renewal of their contract. This would be Michael's first major negotiation in his new position, and he was keenly aware of the importance of the Andorra Electronics business.

At the dinner meeting on Wednesday, Michael was impressed with the cordial reception he received from Carlo. On being introduced to Michael, Carlo was quick to express his appreciation of USEE and Jean Pierre for the excellent support that they had provided over the years and also for the enjoyable "USEE Customer Appreciation Weekends" in Paris, Rome, and Madrid that had provided much-needed relaxation for Carlo and his small family. In his subsequent conversation, it was clear that Carlo was a person of warmth and culture.

During dinner, both Carlo and George discussed with pride the strides that their small country was making in emerging from a simple farming society to a more industrialized economy. Carlo observed, however, that progress has its price: "Although we Andorrans are happy with our economic progress, we are also concerned with maintaining our ancient customs."

As they were enjoying their after-dinner brandies, Michael commented on the fine meal and the excellent wine. Carlo's response caused Michael to deliberate: "Ah, Michael, it must be good for you to be back home after your five years in America—back to where people truly know how to prepare and enjoy delicious cuisine. Now, I have nothing against Americans—except that they know nothing about good food and fine wine. They are more interested in the quantity of food that they are served at a meal rather than the flavor. They know little about the careful preparation of food and the skillful blending of the ingredients. It is the seasoning that is important. Good food as well as good business requires discreet seasoning, appropriately applied."

While Michael was pondering the reference to "discreet seasoning" as it related to "good business," Carlo continued in a more explicit way: "Has George discussed with you the arrangement that we have had over the years, Jean Pierre and myself? Yes, yes, Jean Pierre appreciated the significant business that we were able to give to him—and to USEE. He was generous in his 'seasoning'—ah, I believe he called it 'our commission.' He said, 'One half per cent is a small commission to pay to such a loyal friend.' I am assuming that you will wish to continue this arrangement, Michael." As Michael hesitated in responding, Carlo turned to George and said, "That was the way we worked wasn't it, George? Jean Pierre would give me my envelope with the one-half percent cash payment for each previous order. Unfortunately, he was not able to give me the payment for our last order, but we will forget that. If you wish to continue this arrangement, we will work out the details of the order at our meeting tomorrow, and you may pay me my commission on your next visit. That is the way the arrangement works, isn't it, George?"

"That was really between you and Jean Pierre," George responded. "Of course, you know that we value you as a key customer, and we want to keep you as a customer."

Noticing Michael's surprise and uncertainty, Carlo stood up and extended his hand: "Perhaps you would like to think about this overnight, Michael. We can confirm it at our meeting tomorrow. Merci, Michael and George for a most pleasant evening."

When Carlo had left, Michael turned to George: "What the hell is going on here, George? What that man is asking for is bribery. You know that it is strict company policy not to pay any form of bribery. It's hard for me to believe that Jean Pierre would go along with such an arrangement."

"Relax, Michael. You are not in New York now. You are in Andorra—and this is the way business is done in Andorra. This is nothing more than an extension of your company's 'Customer Appreciation' program."

"I am sorry to disagree with you, George, but this is bribery—and bribery is illegal everywhere that I know of."

"Yes, Michael, this type of 'commission' bribery is regarded with some concern in the United States, but in other parts of the world it is a long-standing way of doing business. If you do not wish to continue the arrangement, someone else most certainly will be more flexible in order to get the Andorra Electronics' business. Please, Michael, we have a lot at stake here. USEE wants this business. They will not be happy to lose a customer who gives them over a half million dollars worth of business a year. I also need this business. Andorra Electronics is my largest customer. I do not think I will be able to survive without them. And you, my young friend—you are just starting in your career. How will it look if you lose this most valued account? And how will it affect your sales commissions? In situations like this, the best rule to follow is 'When in Rome, do as the Romans do.'"

"George, you know and I know that it is against company policy to pay bribes in order to get business. This was really stressed in our company training program; in fact, we had a separate session on this subject, and the vice president of sales came to our session to state the company's position in person. He emphasized that bribery was not only bad business but also illegal under the Foreign Corrupt Practices Act of 1977."

"Michael, even the Corrupt Practices Laws allow for some exemptions in situations where companies would be put at a severe competitive disadvantage. The reasoning is, I believe, that if commissions to company or government officials, though illegal in some countries, are customary practice, then sellers should be allowed to compete on an even basis."

"That may be so, George, but our company does not allow the practice, and they are clear about warning us that it could cost us our jobs. The company believes that we should make excellent products and sell them at competitive prices. There is no room for payoffs."

"Michael, I am distressed that you see it this way. Jean Pierre understood that this was the way to do business here. He worked out a fair arrangement with Carlo. It was no big deal. I suggest that you consider the consequences of changing this arrangement. Perhaps a good night's sleep will help you to put things into perspective. We can meet tomorrow morning to discuss this before our meeting with Carlo."

On returning to his hotel room, Michael was unable to go to sleep. He had a serious problem and an important decision to make before the meeting. Bribery, even under the disguise of a "commission," was repugnant to him both personally and professionally. And the company position on this was quite clear. Yet Jean Pierre had been an honorable and respected USEE employee, and Jean felt that it was a necessary accommodation. Michael was genuinely impressed with George Bianci as a person and as a businessman, and George sincerely believed that the payment was appropriate in this situation.

Michael also realized that he could not ignore the impact of the lost business on his commission earnings. When he took over the territory, he was told that Jean Pierre had averaged between $75,000 and $100,000 (American) in commissions annually. Although the sales commission varied on different products, the average commission to the sales rep was 2 percent. The sales quota for the territory was $4,000,000. If Michael could sustain the 2 percent commission rate and also retain the business with his 67 assigned accounts, he could look forward to an income of $80,000 in his first year, which was a healthy increase over his income for the previous year in the New York territory. Not all his accounts were the size of Andorra Electronics, however. Although there were three other sizable accounts in the territory, most of the customers were much smaller. The accounts ranged in size from $25,000 per year to $600,000, with the majority being under $100,000. As he considered the makeup of his territory, Michael was again reminded of the importance of the Andorra Electronics account. He wondered if he could realistically turn his back on one of his top accounts and the $10,000 commission income generated from that account.

Michael realized that he must reach a decision before his meeting with George in the morning. He also realized that he had neither the time nor the opportunity to consult with his sales manager in the Paris office. As he sat thinking about his problem, he remembered his naive reaction to the discussion of bribery in the ethics session in the training program and in his previous MBA classes. It all seemed so clear and simple then. However, no one told him that he would be called on to make these decisions under such great pressure and in situations where it was not at all clear what the appropriate business decision should be. He realized that the textbooks couldn't really prepare a person for the kind of situation that he now found himself in—one that involved a costly decision, no time to get advice, and significant financial consequences to his company, to his distributor partner, and to himself. And he was reminded that he was not dealing with sleazy people but with good, cultured businesspeople for whom this was a way of life. The meetings with George and Carlo tomorrow should be quite challenging.

1. Should Michael refuse to follow his predecessor's "customs" and run the risk of losing a large client?
2. Should Michael inform USEE of his decision if he chooses to follow past agreements?

Index